WINNING ACROSS

GLOBAL

MARKETS

WINNING ACROSS
GLOBAL
MARKETS

HOW
NOKIA
CREATES **STRATEGIC ADVANTAGE**
IN A FAST-CHANGING WORLD

DAN STEINBOCK

JOSSEY-BASS
A Wiley Imprint
www.josseybass.com

Published by Jossey-Bass
A Wiley Imprint
989 Market Street, San Francisco, CA 94103-1741—www.josseybass.com

Readers should be aware that Internet Web sites offered as citations and/or sources for further
information may have changed or disappeared between the time this was written and when it is
read.

Limit of Liability/Disclaimer of Warranty: While the publisher and author have used their best
efforts in preparing this book, they make no representations or warranties with respect to the
accuracy or completeness of the contents of this book and specifically disclaim any implied
warranties of merchantability or fitness for a particular purpose. No warranty may be created or
extended by sales representatives or written sales materials. The advice and strategies contained
herein may not be suitable for your situation. You should consult with a professional where
appropriate. Neither the publisher nor author shall be liable for any loss of profit or any other
commercial damages, including but not limited to special, incidental, consequential, or other
damages.

Jossey-Bass books and products are available through most bookstores. To contact Jossey-Bass
directly call our Customer Care Department within the U.S. at 800-956-7739, outside the U.S. at
317-572-3986, or fax 317-572-4002.

Jossey-Bass also publishes its books in a variety of electronic formats. Some content that appears
in print may not be available in electronic books.

Library of Congress Cataloging-in-Publication Data

Steinbock, Dan.
  Winning across global markets: how Nokia creates strategic advantage in a fast-changing
world/Dan Steinbock. — 1st ed.
      p. cm.
  Includes bibliographical references and index.
  ISBN 978-0-470-33966-4 (cloth)
  1. Nokia (Firm)—Management. 2. Cellular telephone equipment industry—Finland—
Management. 3. Cellular telephone systems. 4. Telecommunication—Management. I. Title.
  HD9697.T454N6574 2010
  338.7'62138456—dc22

                                        2009051933

Printed in the United States of America
FIRST EDITION
HB Printing 10 9 8 7 6 5 4 3 2 1

CONTENTS

WINNING ACROSS
GLOBAL
MARKETS

INTRODUCTION

"Our industry is undergoing one of the biggest transformations in its history, which has been accelerated by the economic crisis," reported Nokia's CEO Olli-Pekka Kallasvuo in early fall 2009. The Internet, PCs, and mobile communications were converging faster than had been anticipated. At the same time, consumers were no longer interested in just mobile devices but also in solutions. "There is no turning back," Kallasvuo warned.

Winning Across Global Markets is the first book to tell the story of how Nokia prepared for this great transformation. It is the first book on Nokia's strategy, organization, and values that is based on interviews with all of Nokia's leading senior executives in the past two decades. No other independent author has gained such privileged access. The book tells the story of how Nokia creates strategic advantage in a fast-changing world—with the goal of showing how companies operating in technology-intensive or marketing-intensive industries, or both, can compete in order to win in a global marketplace.

A Brief History of Nokia's (and Finland's) Challenges

In the 1990s, Nokia's senior executives found themselves ahead of both the United States and Japan in the mobile communications industry. The Finnish company seemed to emerge from nowhere as an industry leader; *Newsweek* once called it "an overnight success." The reality, however, is more complex. Nokia's worldwide clout is barely a decade old, but the company itself was created almost 150 years ago, in 1865.

Nokia was founded during the early industrialization of Finland, a small Nordic country that has been ruled for centuries by its neighbors, Sweden and Russia. Over the past century and a half, Nokia has been created, re-created, and restructured again and again. It was born amid Finland's national awakening and has endured Russian oppression, a struggle for independence, the Bolshevik Revolution in Russia, a devastating civil war, the rise of nationalism and protectionism in Europe, a worldwide depression, two wars against the Soviet Union and one against Germany, devastation and heavy reparations to Moscow, the loss of eastern territories and integration of more than 400,000 refugees, postwar reconstruction, the Cold War and insulation from the West, national industrialization, decades of rapid growth, years of leftist radicalism, cyclical recessions, Moscow's *perestroika* (reforms) and *glasnost* (openness), the suicide of its charismatic executive and the death of his right-hand man, the collapse of the Soviet Union and the Finnish-Soviet trade, Finland's most severe recession since the 1930s, participation in the European integration and monetary union, rejuvenation of growth and Nokia's boom years, the stagnation of the technology sector, outsourcing and offshoring, the rise of China and India, and, most recently, the global economic recession.

During these upheavals, Nokia has persevered and often led the country, overcoming one adversity after another and demonstrating remarkable resilience. Its global success, however, is the result of developments during the past two decades or so. Under the leadership of the legendary CEO Kari Kairamo, Nokia grew very fast and ambitiously already in the 1970s and 1980s. It initiated the transformation from the old industries of forestry, rubber, and cable and moved toward electronics. In the process, it began to seek growth in nontraditional areas and grew into a diversified technology conglomerate. It had great aspirations but lacked adequate capabilities.

Betting on the Future

In 1992, Nokia bet its future on a vision of digital mobile communications, under the leadership of its then-new CEO, Jorma Ollila, and the CFO, Olli-Pekka Kallasvuo (who became the company's CEO after Ollila retired in 2006). Along with the extraordinary group executive team, Nokia's leaders focused the company on mobile communications and divested all noncore properties. Unlike most of its rivals, Nokia was not content with the notion that the cell phone would remain just an executive tool or a yuppie toy. It believed that mobile devices should belong to everybody—not just those living in advanced economies but also to those in emerging economies and in the least developed countries as well.

Amid this massive transformation, Nokia helped transform the way people live, work, and play in every corner of the world. The numbers tell the story:

- At the beginning of the 1990s, there were only 17 million mobile subscribers in the world; in 2008, this figure exceeded 4 billion users. By 2013, it is projected to hit 5.9 billion, driven by China, India, and Africa.

- In 2001, there were 42 million mobile Internet users worldwide; in 2008, more than 400 million. By 2013, it is projected to exceed 700 million.

- 2009 saw a total of 1.2 billion mobile devices shipped. Shipments of these devices will nearly double in 2014 to a total of 2.25 billion. At the same time, application downloads are expected to reach 5 billion, from 2.3 billion in 2009.

As the world's largest device maker and with a market share of almost 40 percent, Nokia can take much of the credit for this enormous growth.

Staying Close to the Productivity Frontier

The communications transformation is not over; it is now entering a new stage. Technologically, mobile devices are turning into "converged mobile devices." Traditional cell phones are gaining greater intelligence and turning into "smartphones"; computers are growing smaller and gaining mobile communication capabilities; at the same time, both are converging and colliding. Geographically, communications used to be driven by advanced economies in the West; in the future, communications will be increasingly driven by large emerging economies in the East. More than any other company in the world, Nokia has seized these technological and geographic opportunities.

Unlike many of its rivals, Nokia is not known for complacency. When one source of growth has been exhausted, it has moved to another through competitiveness, innovation, and perseverance. During the past two decades, value has migrated from mobile infrastructure to devices;

now it is moving to software and services, especially solutions (shorthand for mobile devices plus services). In each case, Nokia has been close to the frontier in productivity. Through years of hope and glory, doom and gloom, it has stood the test of time and, unlike most of its rivals, has been unafraid to embrace change.

"What happened to us was that we were not expected to succeed. That's our story," says Jorma Ollila, Nokia's chief executive from 1992 to 2006 and currently chairman of Shell. "This is too personal," he adds quietly. "But the most important cultural element that I have helped to develop in this company is that you can come back.... It takes a lot of effort, sleepless nights, twenty-four hours a day, seven days a week, but *you can come back....*"

The question is, *how?* How has Nokia achieved its success? How does Nokia create strategic advantage in a fast-changing world? How has it been able to win across increasingly global markets? How does it innovate? What are its other strategic capabilities? How does it develop strategic advantage? How does it create and execute strategy? How does its organizational structure support and contribute to that strategy? What kind of values, culture, and people make that organization possible? Is Nokia's triumph sustainable? And what are its lessons to other companies operating in fast-changing environments across the world, in both advanced and emerging economies?

This book addresses all these questions.

Underestimating Nokia's Strengths . . .

"Nokia is history."
"Excuse me?"
"It's a nice story, underdog and all that. But let's be real, it's D.O.A. Dead on arrival."
"Why would you think that way?"
"Microsoft will kill Nokia."

The interviewer was a senior journalist at one of America's greatest business weeklies, in an interview with the author that took place in June 2001. Like Bill Gates at that time, this interviewer thought that Nokia was in the business of "manufacturing boxes," whereas Microsoft dominated software and operating systems. Since the value in the business was moving toward software and services, Microsoft would win and Nokia would lose. At least that's how the argument went. Like Gates, the journalist thought that Nokia would happily go to its grave making boxes.

True, Microsoft dominates operating systems and software in PCs, but it was a latecomer in mobile communications, which Nokia dominated. Besides, times change. In the past, Nokia and Microsoft were the toughest rivals. Today, they collaborate in a global alliance. More important, the Nokians had been building capabilities in operating systems and software already for half a decade. In the increasingly complex and global technology sector, no single company, not even a single nation (including the United States, which has ruled over the technology sector), can any longer dominate the entire ecosystem.

Coming from a tiny country, Nokia had little arrogance; it took nothing for granted and had a humble view of globalization. Global integration is not a pretext to command and control markets, but a new foundation to sense and respond to markets. Still, this humility has often been misinterpreted as a sign of weakness. For example, consider this conversation, which took place only two years after the previous interview:

"Nokia doesn't have a chance in hell."
"Why would you think that way?"
"Today it is the underdog, but tomorrow it will be buried by new challengers in Asia."

This analyst represented a leading investment bank (which got into serious trouble during the global financial crisis). The high-end challenge was not Nokia's only concern. With the burst of the technology bubble and increasing outsourcing and offshoring in the early 2000s, many analysts, observers, and practitioners were absolutely convinced that low-end challengers would condemn Nokia to extinction.

The argument was not entirely without basis. For example, in the 1990s, Chinese equipment manufacturers had no market share in China's nascent mobile marketplace; by 2003, their share had soared to 55 percent. But that was not the end of the story. Soon thereafter, foreign multinationals mounted their counterattack. After the dust settled, Nokia emerged as the winner not only in China but also in India, the two most critical marketplaces of the twenty-first century, whereas many of its traditional Western rivals began a slow but sure decline.

So why did the analyst quoted above misjudge Nokia? He took it for granted that because the company had initially built its manufacturing capabilities in high-cost Western Europe, the capacity would remain in Western Europe. In reality, Nokia began to move to China and India already in the mid-1990s. A decade later, Nokia could not be easily written off in the low-end marketplace because it enjoyed the kind of cost-efficiencies that were as great as, if not greater than, those of the most competitive Chinese players.

. . . And Overestimating Nokia's Vulnerabilities

Still, Nokia's track record has in no way discouraged the prognosticators. Consider this exchange, which occurred in summer 2009:

> "As you know, at this point in time most investors consider Nokia a doomed company."
> "But why would they think that way?"
> "The thinking is that Nokia will not be able to transform its business model and working practices to compete with Apple. iPhone will kill Nokia."

This industry analyst represents still another leading investment bank (one that also got into trouble but is doing better after government subsidies). Here the notion is that Apple is the driver of the future in communications. The assumption is, again, that Nokia will happily go to its grave making boxes while superior rivals like iPhone will deliver the future.

True, even if Nokia developed the first mobile multimedia devices, Apple was the first to come up with a highly attractive smartphone solution in the United States. Yet iPhone is not the only alternative in the marketplace, and, as critical as America remains in the broad technology sector, it no longer dominates the ecosystem of mobile communications.

The numbers may not tell the future, but they do illustrate the present:

- In 2008, the projected global market volume of mobile devices amounted to 1.2 billion units, whereas the sales of Apple's iPhone units soared to about 12 million. That means that in relative terms iPhone's growth has been explosive, but in absolute terms iPhone sales were less than 1 percent of the total.

- In stark contrast to iPhone's sales of 12 million units, Nokia shipped 468 million mobile devices in 2008—including some 61 million "converged devices"—that is, mobile computers and smartphones. Clearly, Apple's success in the United States and in some other countries is impressive, but it's not enough.

- Winning across increasingly global markets requires just that: winning across *global* markets.

Conversely, Nokia must speed up its transformation to cope with rivals, such as iPhone and BlackBerry, in America and elsewhere or it will risk its success in the future. After all, today one of the central challenges is to attract, grow, and retain developers for the new generation of mobile devices and solutions. It is not enough to have the capabilities to win the future; in order to truly benefit from the network effects, you must be *perceived* as the winner of the future.

Since the 1990s Nokia has served as a Rorschach test for many observers and analysts. The track record is that many tend to underestimate Nokia's strengths and overestimate its vulnerabilities. The question is, *why?*

Nokia Excels in Quality and Cost and Innovation

For an entire generation, American managers have been taught to choose between quality or cost advantage. That is the very basis of the most popular theories of competitive advantage in strategic management. Yet Nokia has demonstrated that you can (and increasingly must) excel in both quality and cost-efficiencies while also excelling in innovation.

A decade ago, Microsoft was seen as the "future winner" in mobile communications. Currently iPhone carries that mantle. In both cases the assumption is that the story of Nokia is over. Perhaps it could excel in quality; maybe it could thrive in cost-efficiencies. But innovation is seen as Silicon Valley's birthright and as American as apple pie. In fact, perceptions have fallen behind realities. In an era of global integration, innovation is bound to be increasingly global and dispersed. In the past, what was good for GE may have been good for America; today, what is good for Nokia may be good not just for America but the world at large.

And there is still more to the story. Both innovation and cost-efficiencies are necessary, but achieving one without the other is insufficient for success in global markets. Today companies must be able to sense and respond in all critical markets—in advanced economies but especially in emerging markets. During the past two decades or so, the rise of the large emerging economies and the accompanying collapse of traditional cost structures across industries have dramatically accelerated the forces for cost-efficiencies, quality, and innovation worldwide.

But even more is needed for sustained global leadership. As Nokia has demonstrated, it is the combination of strategy, organization, and values that is vital in the dynamic, increasingly global, and rapidly changing environment.

Throughout its recent history, Nokia has operated in an industry in which the forces for worldwide innovation are particularly intense. Since the 1990s companies have been forced to seek high volume—that is, economies of scale through worldwide R&D, production, distribution, and marketing and sales—in order to amortize, as quickly as possible, the heavy investments they've had to make because of rising R&D expenditures, new technologies, and ever shorter product life cycles.

Concurrently, the convergence of consumer preferences worldwide and the ever-faster diffusion of technology have contributed to the acceleration of change and fragmentation of innovation. In the postwar era, American companies still enjoyed the most sophisticated business environment. In contrast, today new consumer trends or market needs can emerge not only in New York, London, and Tokyo, or even Helsinki,

Seoul, and Hong Kong—but also in Shanghai and Mumbai, Rio de Janeiro and Dubai.

In the past, a U.S.-centered strategic mindset was the key to success. Even today it remains necessary because America dominates the technology sector. Still, it is no longer sufficient. Today, a global mindset is a must.

How to Succeed Without a (Large) Home Market

"Our situation is so difficult, if not hopeless," said a leading business journalist in Taipei. "We have great engineers and electronics companies, but our population is barely 23 million, whereas even South Korea has more than 48 million. That's no home market."

"Nokia comes from Finland, whose population is about 5.3 million and whose capital city Helsinki is located at 60 degrees north latitude, like Anchorage, Alaska," I replied. "Size is a great asset, when it is used strategically. But so is smallness, when it comes with speed and flexibility."

The story of Nokia is important across industries and heralds the future to many multinationals across the world. The reason is in its extraordinary positioning, in terms of the competitive environment and the marketplace. Most major multinationals operate in a marketing-intensive or a technology-intensive environment. Unlike these companies, Nokia operates in a technology- and marketing-intensive environment. Like Intel and Microsoft, it seeks to stay at the cutting edge of the latest technologies worldwide; like Coca-Cola and Procter & Gamble, it also monitors closely the latest fashions and trends in the increasingly global markets.

Nokia, however, is different from Intel, Microsoft, Coca-Cola, and Procter & Gamble in a crucial way. It was not born in a huge and prosperous home market. Today, Finland belongs to the prosperous elite of the world nations, but that legacy is fairly recent. Through much of their history, the Finns have struggled for survival, as witnessed by the national hymn: "Our land is poor, it has no hold / On those who lust for gain . . . / Yet this poor land of ours would still / Our hearts with longing fill."

Unlike large and wealthy nations, Finland, along with other Nordic countries, is dramatically dependent on international markets, foreign trade, and investment. As a result—and in contrast to most of its rivals—even Nokia's geographic distribution is much more even:

- Over a third of its net sales originate from Europe and almost as many from Asia.

- The other sales come from the Americas, the Middle East, and Africa.

- Its home market (Finland) accounts for less than 1 percent of net sales.

That makes Nokia, along with a few other multinationals, unique. When it comes to globalization, Nokia is in a category of its own. Unlike Coca-Cola, Procter & Gamble, Intel, and Microsoft, it is a multinational company that possesses virtually no home market of its own, from a commercial standpoint.

Despite the diversity of large-country multinationals, most come from advanced economies (United States, Western Europe, Japan) or large emerging economies (especially the so-called BRIC economies, that is, Brazil, Russia, India, and China). Because these multinationals originate from a great home base, their large home market is almost an inherited birthright. Due to its distinctive legacy as a small-country multinational with a tiny home market, Nokia must be flexible and very responsive locally. On the one hand, because of its peculiar global strategy, it sees the world as a single global village, emphasizing uniformity in customer needs, distribution channels, offerings, markets, and regulatory requirements. On the other hand, its legacy as a small-country multinational supports local responsiveness, pressuring the company to consider variations in customer needs, distribution, adaptations, market structure, and regulatory demands. This humility is a recipe for winning across global markets.

To large-country multinationals, foreign markets mean ancillary revenue sources. To small-country multinationals, foreign markets *are* their revenue sources. Large-country multinationals have most of their critical activities—from headquarters to R&D—in their home base. In contrast, small-country multinationals have many of their critical activities dispersed worldwide. To the extent that globalization will continue and the future of the world is multipolar, globalization will be driven by multiple power centers worldwide. Nokia is the bellwether of multinationals in an increasingly multipolar world and hence it is of interest to all of us and worthy of study.

Necessity is the mother of invention, and it is the inherent constraints of Nokia's landscape—a miniscule home market and a highly technology-intensive, marketing-intensive environment—that have forced this company to develop the distinctive strategy, organization, and values that have led to its success. In turn, they may offer strategic inspiration for success to many other companies in various industries and environments.

What This Book Reveals About Nokia

This book is not the first attempt to decipher the reasons for Nokia's success. However, it is the first independent effort based on free access to and dozens of interviews with all of Nokia's leading executives, including the CEO, chairman, board of directors, members of its famous group executive team, chiefs of functions, chiefs of key country markets, and former Nokians who have contributed critically to Nokia's success since the 1990s. It is also based on interviews with an extensive group of Nokia's managers, employees, rivals, partners, and suppliers, as well as public policy authorities and academic researchers in the Americas, Europe, Asia, Africa, and the Middle East. The underlying research and interviews have been carried out since 2004 (for more details, see the Acknowledgments section).

Unlike its rivals, Nokia has had to struggle for much that most multinational companies take for granted. Indeed, it is the tremendous perseverance of the Nokians, both individually and in teams, that has motivated the company to win against all odds.

Chapter One describes Nokia's success through legacy and globalization. Nokia has evolved through several eras and reincarnations, from a forestry company to a diversified conglomerate to a European technology concern to the globally focused mobile communications giant it is today. It is Nokia's ability to build on its legacy and take advantage of globalization that accounts for its success since the early 1990s.

Chapter Two focuses on Nokia's strategy and its executive team. Because Nokia is a small-country multinational without a large home market and operates in a technology- and marketing-intensive environment, it is a global company that seeks to be externally oriented and internally collaborative, as Olli-Pekka Kallasvuo, Nokia's CEO, puts it. It is the executive team that serves as Nokia's collective mind.

Chapter Three takes a closer look at Nokia's values, culture, and people. Initially driven by Finnish perseverance, Nokia today is characterized by increasing diversity around the world. It is building a shared purpose through values. Indeed, Nokia's values are the glue that keeps the whole together while providing guidelines for global human resource management.

Chapter Four describes Nokia's unique structure—its globally networked matrix. In order to cope with rapid environmental change, Nokia's executives have paid special attention to building organizational capabilities for changing markets. The company has moved from an area structure to a worldwide product structure. It is the flat, team-driven, and networked organization that accounts for Nokia's agility and flexibility worldwide.

Chapter Five explores Nokia's global innovation via R&D networks. Innovation, understood broadly, is Nokia's most critical capability. This is reflected by the rapid expansion of the Nokia Research Center, which engages in long-term research; the company's unit-based R&D, which focuses on short-term development; and its globally networked university cooperation, open innovation, and venture funds.

Chapter Six describes Nokia's other strategic capabilities. Nokia's competitive strategies in mobile devices and services, solutions, and infrastructure rest on the foundation of its strategic capabilities. In addition to innovation, these include scale, demand and supply network, distribution, a powerful brand, and strategic marketing and global consumer insight. Nokia seeks to share its strategic capabilities among its business areas.

Chapter Seven focuses on Nokia's business areas. Nokia is the world's number one manufacturer of mobile devices by market share and a leader in the converging Internet and communications industries. It comprises devices, services, solutions, and markets, augmented by infrastructure (Nokia Siemens Networks). This chapter illustrates Nokia's transformation in the converging mobile and Internet arena, and its transition toward solutions.

Chapter Eight describes Nokia's global markets, particularly its success in large emerging economies. Nokia's mission, "Connecting People," is not intended to include some people some of the time, but all people all of the time. Until recently, advanced economies—the United States, Western Europe, and Japan—drove global growth. Today, it is the large emerging economies—particularly China and India—that are driving growth worldwide. Nokia is taking advantage of this change while accelerating and contributing to the growth of developing economies.

Finally, Chapter Nine explores how Nokia seeks to maintain the drivers of its strategic advantages. The chapter focuses on the sustainability of Nokia's leadership (see Figure I.1). In the past, most accounts of Nokia's success have concentrated on a single driver of success. At best, these efforts highlighted one or another aspect of Nokia's success but not the layers and sources of Nokia's strategic advantages and capabilities. This chapter also takes a look at different scenarios for the future and the preconditions of success in the world of mobile computers and smartphones.

Today, Nokia accounts for twenty-five percent of the Helsinki stock exchange's capitalization and one third of the national R&D spending. In the early 1990s, technologists despaired to find any job at Nokia, which led Finland out of a severe recession and contributed to the tiny country's dramatic growth. In the beginning of 2010, Finnish technologists were striking for better contracts, even as Finland's economy shrank by 7.6 percent, its worst performance in over fifty years.

The future looked bleak; to many Finns, even bleaker than in the early 1990s. Few things are assured in Nokia's fast-changing world. What is certain, however, is that the lessons to be gained from this small-country multinational will be studied for years to come because they herald the future of all multinationals in increasingly global markets that are technology-intensive or marketing-intensive, or both. Nokia's story is relevant to multinationals originating from large countries and small countries and to those evolving in advanced economies and emerging economies. In this way, Nokia is the bellwether of the future. To see how, let's begin by looking at how Nokia grew from a forestry-based business in 1865 to the technological and marketing powerhouse it is today.

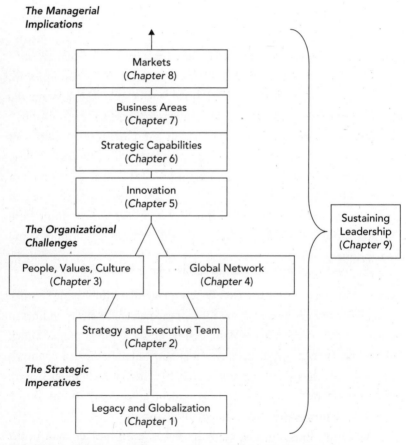

FIGURE I.1   Overview of the Organization of the Book

1

SUCCESS THROUGH LEGACY AND GLOBALIZATION

In the late 1990s, Nokia's success seemed to come out of the blue in the worldwide markets. In reality, the company is a decade or two older than many leading multinationals, including General Electric (founded in 1876) and Coca-Cola (1886), and almost a century older than such technology giants as Intel (1968) and Microsoft (1975). Nokia's legacy has evolved through several eras and reincarnations from a forestry company to a diversified conglomerate to a European technology concern and, ultimately, to the globally focused mobile and Internet giant it is today.

It is Nokia's ability to embrace change and adapt to the future that accounts for its global success since the early 1990s. But Nokia's organization is shaped by its past, as well as by the external environment. Like other multinational companies, it has been influenced by the path by which it has evolved: its organizational history. This chapter takes a closer look at the company's fascinating history and evolution, particularly the key forces, legacy, and globalization that have enabled it to embrace change and contributed to its enormous growth and success.

Origins of Nokia

Since Nokia's history is so embedded in Finland, a small Nordic country, some historical context is vital to understanding the company's growth and transformations.

15

A Forestry Foundation

From the late nineteenth century to the twentieth century, forestry was the industrial backbone of Finland's economy. In this era, most Finnish firms competed primarily on the basis of price in forestry-based or forestry-related industries that required little technology. At the same time, the Finnish economy remained sensitive to world economic cycles and exchange rates. Nokia grew along with the national ambitions of the small country that had been ruled for centuries by neighboring Sweden and Russia. Following the Crimean War (1853–1856), Finland was joined to Russia and made an autonomous state, a grand duchy.

The creation of Nokia, as a small forestry enterprise, coincided with the tremendous boom in the Finnish lumber industry, which put the country on the road to industrialization. But Finland was still a part of Russia.

Fredrik Idestam, Nokia's founder, came of age in this era of optimism, entrepreneurialism, and new technological opportunities. Born in 1838 to a religious and educated family, the young engineer graduated from Helsinki University in 1863 and traveled to Germany, where Wilhelm Ludwig Lüders had created a new and innovative process to manufacture pulp. In Mägdesprung, Idestam visited the famous factory, only to be thrown out by Lüders for what the German deemed industrial espionage.

But Idestam had seen enough. In May 1865, he received authorization to build his mill in Nokia, a small town about ten miles to the west of Tampere, Finland's then-industrial center. Over time, the Nokia factory attracted a large workforce and the town grew around it. That became the name and the foundation for the future Nokia Corporation, which is now located in Espoo, a garden city just a fifteen-minute drive from the center of Helsinki and close to the famed university and technology center.[1]

While studying in Helsinki, Fredrik Idestam had met Leo Mechelin, who later became Finland's first parliamentarian and played a crucial role in the struggle for independence. Nokia's two founding fathers—Idestam, the businessman, and Mechelin, the politician—were among the leading young Turks of a new Finnish generation. Their vision was an innovative company and an independent economy, deeply intertwined with the world economy. Finnish forestry leaders leveraged their dominance at home into foreign markets. In contrast, Nokia built its foothold first in foreign markets, which allowed it later to build a position in the domestic market. As a result, it developed a more international mindset.

Diversification into Electrical Power and Other Industries

In 1917, when Russia was swept by the turmoil of the Bolshevik Revolution, the Finnish parliament approved the declaration of independence. After Lenin's Bolsheviks recognized the independence of their small neighbor, the Finns drifted into a bitter and devastating civil war between the nationalists and the socialists.[2] These tumultuous years crushed many Finnish companies. Due to its increasing diversification and internationalization, Nokia was not as vulnerable as most forestry firms. By the 1920s, its paper and pulp mill, the Finnish Cable Works, and the Finnish Rubber Works sought leadership in their respective industries. Meanwhile, Nokia's corporate name became the joint foundation of all three companies. Indeed, it was only in 1966 that Nokia Ab, Finnish Rubber Works, and Finnish Cable Works were formally merged to create Nokia Corporation (however, Nokia had already been listed in 1915).

As Nokia transitioned from a family business to a public company, much of the correspondence was conducted in German, the business language of the era. Products were exported first to Russia and then to Great Britain and France. In the 1930s, China also became an important trading partner.

During the Second World War, Finland fought against the Soviet Union and, eventually, Nazi Germany.[3] Unlike the tiny Baltic states, Finland managed to retain its independence, but with a heavy price. After the devastation (86,000 dead; 57,000 permanently disabled; 24,000 war widows; 50,000 orphans; 400,000 refugees from the ceded Karelia in the East and 100,000 from Lapland in the North; 70,000 children evacuated; and the loss of eastern territories), nothing would remain the same, not even at Nokia.

The devastation reinforced the Finns' legendary perseverance, but Nokia's vision had to change. It had to adapt to a new and very different future.

The Rise of the Industrial Conglomerate

After the Peace Treaty of Paris in 1948, Finland assumed a policy of neutrality and nonalignment, dictated by its geopolitical location next to the mighty Soviet Union. Over time, the new *realpolitik* became known as the "Paasikivi-Kekkonen line," after the two prominent postwar presidents, Juho K. Paasikivi (who governed from 1946 to 1956) and Urho K. Kekkonen (from 1956 to 1981). For decades, every Finnish schoolchild would learn President Paasikivi's words: "Acknowledging the facts is the beginning of wisdom." The subtle maxim highlighted the constraints of the small country in the geopolitics between the West and the East.

The new era began in 1948, when the Finns signed the Treaty of Friendship, Cooperation and Mutual Assistance with the Soviet Union, while agreeing to pay the estimated $300 million war reparations to the Soviet Union. Although Finland preserved its independence, it grew insulated internationally. Fortunately, Nokia thrived in spite (and because) of the country's overall insularity. As Moscow's court supplier, Nokia's cable business became the cash cow of the three-firm concern (i.e., cable, rubber, and paper and pulp). Technology transfer was a different story because technology partnerships were seen as political alliances and thus eyed with suspicion at the Kremlin.

Opening Finland to Western Markets

Starting in the late 1950s, Finland opened its economy to Western Europe, that is, the European Economic Community (EEC) and the European Free Trade Association (EFTA). Whereas the Marshall Plan contributed to Germany's postwar economic miracle and the Korean War set the stage for the rejuvenation of the Japanese economy,[4] the Finns missed both the Marshall Plan and the Organization for European Economic Co-operation (later OECD), due to Soviet opposition. As the foundations for bilateral Finno-Soviet trade were laid down, a substantial proportion of

18

the Finnish economy adjusted to Moscow's command economy. Because of the delicate politico-economic balancing act with the Soviet Union, the first science and technology agreements with the United States were not signed until the late 1980s.

After the years of reparations and reconstruction, Finland's President Kekkonen called for an extraordinarily high national savings rate and rapid accumulation of capital to speed up industrialization. After 1960, Finnish commercial ties with the Soviet Union and the other members of the Council for Mutual Economic Assistance (Comecon) also deepened. Concurrently, Nokia's business with Moscow was thriving. Björn Westerlund had been in charge of its cable business since 1956; as Nokia's CEO, he grew skeptical of Nokia's ability to sustain growth based solely on these markets. When Soviet revenues amounted to 20 percent of Nokia's total cable business, Westerlund warned the senior management: "We must be cautious and not allow the proportion of Soviet business to grow too much . . . If one day they'll say *nyet* in Kremlin, we'll lose our business overnight."

When Westerlund left his job in 1977, half of Nokia's exports were to the Soviet Union and half to the West. His successor retained this balance, thus saving the company from a catastrophe when the Soviet Union collapsed. At the time, only 10 percent of Nokia's total revenues came across Finland's eastern border.

Diversification into Electronics

Primarily between 1945 and 1980, Nokia consolidated several critical state-controlled and privately owned units of Finnish electronics, radio phones, and TV. It was not a purposeful strategy, but a complicated series of piecemeal moves in an effort to invest in innovation and growth.

Televa   Starting in 1945, the State Electric Works—which had been launched in 1925 as a research laboratory of the Finnish Defense Forces—served as an industry catalyst. In 1981, Televa Oy was taken over by Nokia. This purchase was the final step in Nokia's consolidation of the nascent electronic and mobile communications industries in Finland.

Mobira In the early 1960s, Salora Oy, a veteran radio and TV set producer, diversified into radio phone manufacturing. Nokia's marketing activities with Salora resulted in increasing cooperation, which led to a joint venture, Mobira Oy (as in *mobile radio*), in 1979.

Nokia's Electronics In 1960, the Finnish Cable Works diversified into electronics. Concurrently, Nokia began importing computer systems by Elliot in the United Kingdom and Siemens in Germany.[5] The revenue base was tiny. To survive, Nokia had to internationalize.

Nokia's consolidation of these various different firms was really a "sum of a great many chances."[6] At the same time, Nordic cooperation contributed to the expansion of nascent mobile communications.

In 1967, the corporation took its current form as the Nokia Corporation.[7] The new industrial conglomerate operated in forestry, rubber, and cable, and it was entering electronics. As Finns saw it, the name of the new company, Oy Nokia Ab, came from wood processing, the management from the cable factory, and the money from the rubber industry. Yet in only a quarter of a century, all of these segments would be divested. It was the most insignificant business of all—electronics—that would position Nokia for the future. This meant a U-turn for a company that in the 1960s was still best known for its rubber boots, winter tires, and toilet paper.

At the same time, the parliamentary elections of 1966 marked a major turning point in Finnish politics. The socialist parties gained their first absolute majority in half a century. With a series of center-left governments until the late 1980s, more than 80 percent of Finland's total workforce was organized into unions.

Motivated by the fear of American multinationals and faith in socialist planning, a generation of "new radicals" began to promote the idea of a state-owned electronics giant, Valco. While Silicon Valley was emerging as the entrepreneurial hotbed in California, the Finns were moving in a diametrically opposite direction. Still, the plan, which required the socialization of Nokia, was in trouble from the beginning. It was driven by political posturing, not market opportunities. As the notion of a high-tech national champion failed, Nokia took over the ruins of Valco as well.[8]

Expansion into a European Technology Concern

In 1977 Kari H. Kairamo took charge of Nokia. Soon change and flexibility became the new catchwords. Born into a wealthy family, Kairamo was energetic, charismatic, hardworking, persistent, independent, entrepreneurial, innovative, and rebellious. For all practical purposes he *was* Nokia through the 1980s. He renewed and internationalized Nokia's vision. In the early 1970s, exports and foreign activities accounted for only 20 percent of total sales; by 1980, their proportion increased to more than 50 percent of total sales, while revenues quadrupled.

"Kari Kairamo was an extraordinary visionary, energetic and energizing, but he could be challenging to the organization," describes Sari Baldauf, one of Nokia's leading executives in the 1990s boom era. "At times, we had to cope with substantial uncertainty. Still, Kairamo's era meant bold risk-taking and a clear long-term perspective. Kari was very committed to the devices, joint ventures, and telecom technologies overall."

Growth Through Bold Mergers and Acquisitions

By the mid-1980s, Nokia had been transformed from a diversified industrial conglomerate into an electronics concern. CEO Kairamo's prime objective was to transform Nokia into a European technology concern. "European industry, as well as the cost structure of products, has become increasingly knowledge-based," he said. "To us, internationalization is not an alternative to something else. Finland has only two resources: the people and the trees." In the past, Finland had been about natural resources and comparative advantage. In the future, it would have to be about human capital and competitive advantage. Export success, however, was predicated on Nokia's sustained ability to internationalize. "That is the greatest risk facing the Finns," Kairamo stated; "the small amount of international business experience."[9]

If the Finns did not yet know much about the world, the world certainly knew little about the Finns. "Wherever you went during those days," recalls Baldauf, "you always had to spell the name of Nokia: N-O-K-I-A. *Nokia*. Not *Nokaia*, not Japanese. We were not internationally relevant yet, except for certain limited market areas."

At the time, Nokia had few alternatives. Western countries were still dominated by national telecom monopolies. The only opportunities were in Asia and northern Africa. "There was no global strategy yet," says Matti Alahuhta, who later became Nokia's executive vice president and president of the infrastructure and mobile device businesses, respectively.

To compete with the European national champions, Kairamo began a frantic wave of merger and acquisition (M&A) activities, and despite doubts, Nokia also pushed into consumer electronics in the 1980s. After Salora, the largest Finnish TV producer, it acquired Luxor AB, Sweden's faltering state-owned electronics and computer concern, which was followed by the purchase of Oceanic.[10] In 1988, Nokia also created the largest IT group in Scandinavia, Nokia Data, by purchasing Ericsson Group's Data Division.

By the late 1980s, Nokia was Europe's third-largest player in TV manufacturing, its market value had tripled, and it was the largest company in Finland.

A Balancing Act Between Western and Eastern Markets

At the same time, the company faced a delicate balancing act vis-à-vis the Soviet Union. Nokia's Soviet trade still amounted to 39 percent of the total in the early 1980s, but investments were moving into technology, and that meant the West. Kairamo could not easily distance Nokia from Moscow, nor could he approach Washington.

During the 1960s and 1970s, "Finlandization" became a cautionary catchword in the West. In the Soviet embassy, every major Finnish politician of significant standing had a "close friend" in the KGB with whom they kept in touch (a *kotiryssä*, or a "home Russian," as the Finns put it). Nokia's CEO was no exception; Viktor Vladimirov, a KGB general, deemed Kairamo one of the most important Finnish industrialists with whom he kept in regular contact.[11]

After the Soviet invasion of Afghanistan in 1980, the Reagan administration boycotted the Moscow Olympics and prohibited technology exports to the Soviet Union. At the time, Finland, spearheaded by Nokia, served as one of Moscow's key suppliers of Western technology. NATO suspected that the Finns were leaking technology to the East. The future of Finnish electronics depended on Silicon Valley and close contact with the U.S. technology sector, so Kairamo had to convince Washington and its allies that critical technology products were not being given to the Kremlin.[12]

That began Kairamo's quest for a third way, that is, European integration—and this was a decade or two before it became ideologically faddish and politically safe in Finland. In 1987, when the conservatives returned to the government after a quarter of a century, Kairamo led the talks of the nonsocialist parties. And in the spring of 1987, he triggered a national debate by insisting that Finland should join the European Council.

Kairamo was no longer part of the old Red capitalist guard, the corporate elite closely connected with Finland's President Kekkonen and the Soviet interests. Nor was he part of the boomer generation with its professional managers. "Kairamo was dynamic, charismatic, and more emotional as a leader," says one influential Nokia insider. "He was still close to the old Finnish patron generation of corporate chiefs." And, he adds with a gentle smile, "in the old days, the patrons decided and knew *everything*."

Mobile Communications: Entering the U.S. Market

Even while launching Europe's first digital telephone system, Nokia continued its aggressive acquisition activities. It also initiated supply relationships with L. M. Ericsson in Sweden, IBM in the United States, and Northern Telecom in Canada.

Soon thereafter Nokia engaged in strategic alliances, such as the joint venture with Tandy in Texas and South Korea, to learn more about flexible manufacturing and to ensure access in the U.S. market. Nokia was small enough to exploit new technologies more flexibly and quickly than its mass-producer rivals. Due to rapid international expansion, Nokia's young employees enjoyed great autonomy, especially in the new international businesses.[13]

Lessons from the Japanese

Through the postwar years, U.S.-based multinationals dominated world-wide competition. As Nokia began to internationalize and move into the technology sector, Japanese companies were challenging U.S. leadership across several industries, primarily in the electronics sector. Many people thought Nokia was a Japanese company, due to the sound of the company name. The Finns did not mind; they felt it was better to be misunderstood than unknown.

In addition, the Nokians studied the business models of Japanese industry leaders from Sony and Matsushita in consumer electronics to Toyota and Honda in the car industry. Unlike the Finnish Nokia, which had to compete for success, the Japanese mobile equipment manufacturers were the preferred suppliers of NTT (or Nippon Telegraph & Telephone Corporation), the national telecom giant. The Nordic mobile markets had a history of relatively high competition and they had been largely deregulated, privatized, and liberalized in the 1980s. In Japan, such reforms took longer.

"In 1979 when [Nokia's mobile communications business] was established, we were told that 'the Japanese will kill us.' Or 'Nokia doesn't have a chance in hell. By 1985, you will be chewed up and spat out,'" recalls Kari-Pekka ("KP") Wilska, Nokia's former senior executive. "But it didn't go that way."

Ambitious Growth Brings New Challenges

Years before Nokia's restructuring and refocusing, CEO Kairamo was already thinking about selling off some old, core divisions of the company to generate cash and capital to compete with major electronics giants. In Finland, skeptics thought Nokia was too big for a small country. Abroad, it was deemed too small for the big leagues. Still, it was slowly carving itself a market niche by its willingness to listen to the customer.

The problem was that as a European technology concern, it was a latecomer. When Nokia entered the TV business, the Japanese were already dominating the industry. When Nokia entered the IT business, Silicon Valley was already leading the sector. In order to survive, Nokia would have to adapt to a different future, once again.

Under CEO Kairamo's leadership, Nokia changed from an insular maker of pulp, paper, chemicals, and rubber into an international technology leader, focusing on TV sets and mobile telephones. Not only was the company growing fast, but it was also increasingly diversified. After the intense M&A period, even sympathetic observers wondered whether Kairamo was hedging bets "too boldly and too broadly," as one Nokia insider puts it. "Eventually it all did lead into a catastrophe."

In the early 1980s, the Finns conjectured about where Nokia was going. A decade later, they wondered whether it would survive.

Finland's Economy Plummets

"In the next ten years, Nokia will change more than in the preceding 120 years," predicted Kairamo to journalists in the late 1980s.

Despite the intense M&A drive, many took it as hyperbole, recalls Lauri Kivinen, Nokia's longtime corporate communications chief, who now heads corporate relations in Nokia Siemens Networks (NSN). "What's shocking about the statement is that it proved so true. With technology progress, economic globalization, and political liberalization, Nokia was not a large ocean liner that moves slowly, but agile and responsive."

Bank Bubble Bursts, Soviet Trade Collapses

As measured by gross domestic product (GDP) per capita, Finland in the late 1980s was one of the richest countries in the world, and the Finns thought of themselves as the "Japan of the North." But the happy days were about to end. Practically no fiscal or monetary policy measures were taken to moderate the expansionary effects of the economic boom. At the same time, Finland's trade with the Soviet Union amounted to 25 percent. As the bank bubble burst, Finland was swept by a recession unlike anything it had seen since the 1930s. At first, things got really bad. And when the Soviet Union collapsed in 1989–1991, so did Finnish-Soviet trade. It was then that things got a lot worse.

The Finnish economy went into a tailspin and plunged into a recession, which proved exceptionally severe in the history of the industrialized world. It was caused by a combination of economic overheating, depressed markets with key trading partners (particularly the Soviet and Swedish markets), and the disappearance of the Soviet barter system. Stock market and housing prices declined by a whopping 50 percent. In the booming 1980s, the growth was based on debt, and when the defaults began rolling in, GDP declined by 13 percent and unemployment increased from a virtual full employment to one-fifth of the workforce. In 1989, the Finns' standard of living had been 80 percent of the U.S. level; four years later, it was less than 70 percent. For all practical purposes, fifteen years of prosperity dissipated into thin air.

Initially trade unions opposed reforms, which served to amplify the crisis. Politicians struggled to cut spending, but the public debt doubled to 60 percent of GDP. In the 1980s, much of the economic growth was driven by debt financing; now debt defaults led to a savings and loan crisis. A costly bailout of the failing banks led to the consolidation of the banking sector. The ghastly depression bottomed out only after devaluations in 1993; and with new foreign ownership laws, many Finnish companies drifted into foreign hands.

After 1991, Finland got its first nonsocialist government since 1966. In 1991, the centrist-conservative government of Prime Minister Esko Aho (who became Nokia's chief of corporate relations in 2009) formulated an export-oriented economic strategy to revitalize Finland's exports and industrial production.[14]

Nokia Struggles for Corporate Control

At the same time, the struggle for Nokia's corporate control escalated. In order to prepare the company for international markets, Nokia's CEO Kairamo initiated organizational reform in the late 1980s to increase flexibility and cooperation while delegating responsibility. He wanted to demolish the old hierarchies that prevented the company from "listening to the customers." The legendary decentralization and teamwork found today at Nokia (discussed in detail in Chapter Three) resulted from these efforts. However, the external stakeholders—particularly banks and insurance firms—had their own ideas for what the future of Nokia held.

Nokia Loses Its Leaders

Concurrently, the hectic pace of the M&A activities began to affect Nokia's seemingly invincible executives. In April 1988, Timo Koski, who was managing director of Nokia's electronics and potentially Kairamo's successor, suffered a cerebral hemorrhage on a plane in Heathrow, London.

Meanwhile, Kairamo was unable to achieve some of his goals. He had been introduced to the Roundtable of Industrialists, the elite CEOs of European big business, by Pehr G. Gyllenhammar, who was then CEO of the Swedish carmaker Volvo. Together Kairamo and Gyllenhammar proposed the most expensive Nordic business deal in history, but when Kairamo introduced the plan to Nokia's board of directors, which at the time comprised growth-driven directors and more conservative banks and insurance firms; he lost the vote. "The banks don't want it," Kairamo said later about the proposed Volvo/Nokia deal.

Through its entire history, Nokia had been controlled by two rival banks: the Union Bank, which initially dominated the rubber business, and KOP (Kansallis-Osake-Pankki, which today is a part of Nordea Bank AB, a Nordic giant), which initially dominated the forestry business. Kairamo thought that the leading Finnish banks were conspiring to spin off pieces of the empire he had been building. The banks denied the allegations.

Only eight months later, on December 11, 1988, Kairamo was due to travel to Thailand for a vacation. But he had had enough: that afternoon, he hanged himself. In a letter, he indicated that his death was due to a manic-depressive condition and gave recommendations on how to deal with the issue without harming Nokia's interests. The suicide, he said, had to do with him, not with Nokia. He signed his letter, "Sick."[15] Perhaps he also felt that he had failed to bring Volvo into Nokia and was weary of the board's opposition and frustrated with the banks and insurance firms. An empire was coming down and there was little he could do.

From Great Visions to Severe Restructuring

So began Nokia's restructuring and financial rollercoaster. New players were encircling Nokia, among them Pentti Kouri, a controversial Finnish investor and a onetime advisor of the international investor George Soros. Despite the severe recession, Nokia recovered quickly as its new CEO, Simo Vuorilehto, began to streamline business in 1988–1992. Vuorilehto was a tough-minded engineer who rose through the ranks of Finland's big pulp and paper industry. He lacked experience in electronics and he did not share Kairamo's ambition to make Nokia a more international company. As long as Kairamo and Vuorilehto had played together, one drove the vision, the other executed. With the vision gone, Nokia's strategy became one of restructuring.

Can Nokia Be Saved?

Throughout the twentieth century, Finland had been defined by its relationship with the Soviet Union. In 1995, the Finns joined the European Union (EU) and later the European Monetary Union (EMU). "My objective was to contribute to new employment opportunities and thereby reduce the high level of unemployment after the recession," says Martti Ahtisaari, Finland's president (1994–2000), who won the Nobel Peace Prize in 2008 for his efforts to resolve international conflicts.

For two decades, Nokia had struggled to open the doors to Europe through Nordic cooperation and European integration. Its dramatic growth contributed to leading Finland out from the recession after 1992, when the forty-one-year-old Jorma Ollila was appointed CEO.

Discipline, Trust, and Hope

Through the prior years of chaos, Nokia had a circle of business leaders who trusted each other and tried to keep things going. As Ollila took charge of Nokia, he had two priorities: restructuring operations and promoting a culture of trust at Nokia. The economic situation was very challenging, and the company needed order, discipline, and systematic reporting. In Finland, Nokia is the oldest company listed under the same name on the Helsinki Stock Exchange (since 1915). Nokia's shares are also listed in Frankfurt (since 1988) and the New York Stock Exchange (since 1994). The latter meant a substantial change, by increasing visibility in the marketplace and fostering operational efficiency in the organization. While maintaining a long-term strategy, Nokia had to focus more on shareholder value.

Regarding the second priority, it was mutual trust that had supported the organization when it got close to the edge. "Jorma took seriously Nokia's culture and value base," says Nokia's former senior executive Sari Baldauf. "These brought cohesion after the hard and traumatic years, which meant the death of many and which we did not really talk about."

In fact, Nokia had been one of the key clients of Jorma Ollila, a Citibank banker and former student leader. In a 1984 meeting with Kairamo, Ollila had argued that in order to match the new competitive environment, Nokia needed a thorough organizational transformation. "Nokia had some really good people, and it had a lot of drive, more intense drive than a well-managed international organization," recalls Ollila today. "It was under a lot of transformation in 1985 when I joined in and there was a clear intent to go international."

Kairamo had hired Ollila as a vice president of international operations; soon thereafter, he became CFO and a member of the group executive board. Ollila got his first taste of the mobile industry operations in February 1990 by heading the small but strategic cellular phone division in Salo, a small Finnish city an hour's drive away from Helsinki.

The Great Turnaround

In November 1991, Nokia's then-chairman Casimir Ehnrooth called Ollila. "Can Nokia be saved?" he asked. If Nokia focused on mobile phones and opted for the digital GSM (the Global System for Mobile communications, which had become the new European technology standard), yes, Nokia could be saved, said Ollila. After all, Nokia was one of the key developers of GSM, which could carry both voice and data traffic.[16] Unlike the U.S.-based players, Nokia was able to seize a disruptive opportunity.

Ollila had only one condition for the proposed CEO job: he had to be free to pick the management.

There was a two-year quiet period when many observers thought that Nokia was on its way to the final resting place. "People were wondering why I wanted to destroy myself in this kind of a venture," recalls Ollila. "There were no expectations. But I took the job because I thought that we had great people and that, with the right focus, we could turn this company around and create something."

As the Finns were about to join the European Union, Nokia had in place a new CEO who was finally able to execute the kind of changes that Kairamo could only dream of.

Nokia's New Global Focus

In January 1992, Ollila got the job. "Look, you get six months to make a proposal on whether we sell it or what we do with this business," he was told." After four months, Ollila said Nokia should *not* be sold. Rather, he advised that "you must build a new company around mobile communications, handsets, and infrastructure. Get rid of the rest."

After a boardroom shake-up, Ollila, as CEO, and Olli-Pekka Kallasvuo, his CFO (who later became CEO when Ollila retired), began to envision Nokia's new strategy. "We had unhappy Finnish shareholders, unhappy international shareholders," says Ollila. "The only thing we could do is to start building the foundation for a meaningful stock performance." In August 1992, he was working on a presentation. He quickly scribbled a title, "Nokia 2000," and four headings that would become famous: "Focus, Global, Telecom-oriented, High value-added." The rest is history.

Focus on Core Capabilities

In the 1980s, Finnish companies were still growing horizontally as conglomerates. In the 1990s, they began to grow vertically by focusing on their core strategic capabilities. The collapse of Soviet trade served as a great catalyst for change in Finland. In addition, the severe recession accelerated the structural transformation of the economy. Finally, membership in the EU brought a new sense of optimism.[17]

Even in the 1980s only a few Finnish companies had an international orientation, and most were diversified conglomerates. "Those of us who did travel internationally had a hell of a job to explain why Finnish firms were so diversified," says a veteran executive. But they operated in a small country with a small marketplace. "If you wanted to grow and stay in Finland," he adds, "there was no alternative but to gain new legs."

Nokia got into mobile communications through R&D in digital electronics in the 1960s and Nordic cooperation later in the decade. But its mobile communications properties were decades older. In the 1970s, Nokia was able to consolidate Finnish electronics. In the 1980s, the business thrived in the analog cellular era. But the real boom era followed with digital cellular in the 1990s.[18] Deciding to focus on mobile communications globally, Nokia concentrated on its core businesses (Nokia Mobile Phones and Nokia Networks), leveraged both units worldwide, and divested the company's many noncore properties. During those troubled times, this was a bold strategy intent. "A lot of people had to go, and a lot of businesses would have to be sold," recalls Ollila. After the start of the strategy process in spring 1993, he proposed to the board that Nokia should sell everything except Nokia Mobile Phones and Nokia Telecommunications.

Nokia's board did not oppose the new course, but it wanted a second opinion. So Nokia hired the management consulting firm McKinsey to explore whether the proposed focus was too narrow. McKinsey's bottom line? "No, the focus isn't too narrow, but you'll have a lot on your plate." The mandate was made official at the 1995 board meeting in Hong Kong.

"It's not so difficult or dramatic to sell businesses. Western banks love to get such a mandate," says Ollila. "It's far more difficult to create something, to grow a global business—and that's what we wanted to do." By spring 1995, Nokia's executive team was fairly confident that it was on the right track. They believed that they could grow the core businesses—handsets and infrastructure—into something really good and strong, as long as they put all their energy into the effort.

However, focus strategies have different implications in big and small countries. In large advanced economies, the industrial portfolio is usually so large and diversified that a single company's focus strategy does not have a great impact on the broad economy. In small countries, however, the industrial portfolio is so small and narrow that a single giant's focus may have a tremendous impact on the broad economy. Nokia and Finland are a classic example of this. The great new opportunities came with great potential rewards and new risks.[19]

Repositioning of Nokia in Terms of Global Growth

In the early 1990s, Ollila and his executive team did not just refocus the company in terms of its mobile businesses; they also repositioned it in terms of global growth. The bold strategy had been explored earlier by several members of his executive team, including Matti Alahuhta, later Nokia's executive vice president who had written a dissertation on global growth strategies.[20] Led by the Nordic markets, the Europeans opted for the GSM digital mobile standard, which was pioneered by Nokia and Ericsson. In the European Commission, the triumph of the GSM standard, the Nordic cellular industry, and the global rise of Nokia and Ericsson showcased European competitiveness at its best: by summer 1998, Nokia was number one in handsets and number two in infrastructure.

At Nokia, success was attributed to the right strategy, organization, and culture. When asked about personal motivations and incentives, many Nokia executives refer to perseverance. "It was great to see the company come back from the crisis of 1992," recalls Jorma Ollila. "We felt we had the right concept until we hit the brick wall in 1995–1996 with the logistics crisis." It is this crisis that veteran Nokians describe as their defining moment and that inspired the *Financial Times* to declare Nokia to be history.[21] "We were written off," smiles Ollila: "Only two years later, our stock went through the ceiling. So what's most rewarding in this business? To come back from such an obituary, that's the best!"

32

Embrace of Globalization

"In the Ollila era, Nokia focused on telecom," says Arja Suominen, a Nokia veteran and currently chief of communications. "Now we live in an age of convergence. But one of our principles has been the faith in continuous change and that has not changed. We are addicted to change. It is energizing."

As a small-country multinational whose success is predicated on globalization, Nokia's legacy has been shaped by global economic integration, which occurs through trade, migration, and foreign investment capital.[22] Through its history, Nokia has embraced the waves of globalization.

Waves of Globalization

Starting around 1870, only a few years after Nokia's founding, the first wave of globalization was driven by the falling costs of transportation and communications. It was reversed in the early 1910s by a retreat into nationalism and protectionism. Between two world wars, transport costs continued to fall, but trade barriers rose as countries followed beggar-thy-neighbor policies.

During these decades, companies from European countries, especially those with extensive overseas empires, dominated the expansion of investment abroad. Many developed a *multinational* strategic mindset to emphasize differences among national markets and operating environments. It was during this period, too, that Nokia initially established a foothold in the worldwide markets through exports: first as a forestry enterprise, later as a diversified concern. But it was still a peripheral player and the multinational mindset never really took root in the company.

After 1945 governments cooperated to rein in protectionism, which led to the reduction of trade barriers and transport costs. In this second wave of globalization, U.S.-based companies, taking advantage of their new technologies and capabilities, were best positioned to exploit the postwar boom. They had an *international* strategic mindset. They developed products for the domestic market and only subsequently sold abroad.

In the Cold War era, leading Finnish companies, including Nokia, became intermediaries between the capitalist West and the socialist East. But at this time, the company was still imitating rather than innovating, and its electronics unit was still small and marginal in total revenues.

In the 1970s, globalization began to boost the fortunes of the Japanese multinationals. In an operating environment of improving transportation and communication facilities and falling trade barriers, these companies thought in terms of creating products for a world market and manufacturing them on a global scale in a few highly efficient plants. The Japanese multinationals had a global strategic mindset. It was their success that fueled Nokia's growing ambitions. Under the leadership of Kari H. Kairamo, the Finnish company engaged in a rapid series of bold M&As that transformed the company into a European technology conglomerate with daring aspirations to become a world-class manufacturer.

Since the 1980s, global economic integration has drastically accelerated as many developing countries have broken into world markets for manufactured goods and services. During this third wave of globalization, world trade has grown massively and markets for merchandise have become much more integrated than ever before.

Despite its long history and Finland's advanced level of economic development, Nokia has much in common with the "new globalizers" from peripheral countries. Like these late movers, it struggled for years to compete against established global giants from the United States, Europe, and Japan. And it has been transformed by strong leaders who led the company out of isolationism and parochialism.

The Balance Sheet of the Ollila Era

During Ollila's era, the company was transformed from an ambitious Finnish technology conglomerate into a globally focused mobile communications leader. When Ollila took the job of CEO in 1992, Nokia had some 27,000 employees, its net sales amounted to less than $3.5 billion, and it suffered from a net loss of $140 million. When Ollila retired in 2006, Nokia had more than 68,000 employees and its net sales amounted to $54.3 billion, with a net profit of $5.7 billion.

As Ollila himself sees it:

> In 1992 Nokia was a conglomerate. It was growth-driven and inno-
> vative in terms of finding new growth opportunities, but it had no real
> focus, a low level of R&D, and no heavy bets on new technologies. Geo-
> graphically, it was focused on Nordic countries and the Soviet Union,
> in addition to the home base. It had a very strong, healthy engineer-
> ing culture. A decade and a half later, Nokia did not operate in many
> businesses anymore. It was highly focused on mobile communications.
> It was innovative and growth-driven, with very heavy R&D spending in
> carefully selected areas. It was global and had a truly global perspective,
> which was reflected by both ambition and by reality. It had a very strong
> and innovative engineering culture, coupled with unique capabilities in
> overall manufacturing and supply chain, as well as exceptional brand
> strength.

Nokia's senior executives are deeply aware of the fact that they have greatly benefited from globalization. If, however, globalization made Nokia, it could also break Nokia. During the 2008–2009 global economic crisis, the third wave of globalization collapsed. Unsurprisingly, CEO Kallasvuo occasionally spoke about his unease with signs of potential protectionism. As a global company, Nokia has sales in most countries of the world and consequently its sales and profitability are dependent on general economic conditions globally and locally.

Nokia has been successful because of its ability and willingness to take advantage of its unique legacy while embracing globalization. And it has succeeded with this approach not only as a result of its external orientation—for example, its embrace of environmental change—but also because of its internal collaboration, as we shall see in Chapter Two.

Nokia's Lessons

- Not all companies have a legacy that has evolved through several eras and reincarnations. However, as Nokia's success indicates, it is vital to embrace change and adapt to the future, even when it requires a thorough transformation.

- Since its founding in 1865, Nokia's market focus has been abroad, but its global triumph originates from strategic decisions in the early 1990s. Today, the world is its home. Success requires building on legacy but taking advantage of globalization—not just in the proximate markets but all potential markets worldwide.

- While Nokia has embraced global integration since the nineteenth century, it opted for a truly global strategy amid the peak years of the third wave of globalization. As Nokia's success indicates, timing matters. Strategy must rhyme with the requirements of the changing competitive environment.

- When CEO Jorma Ollila and CFO Olli-Pekka Kallasvuo opted for Nokia's global focus strategy in 1992, they bet the future on new emerging industries and markets and began to divest all noncore properties. Most bold strategic decisions encompass both constructive creation and creative destruction. The lesson? Acknowledge the facts and never shun bold strategic decisions. The bolder the decision is, the greater are the potential rewards. Risk comes with the territory.

- The ability to embrace change, take advantage of globalization, and make bold strategic decisions does not automatically imply willingness to execute all three. As Nokia's success indicates, seizing global opportunities requires an ambitious vision and bold leaders to guide a company out of isolationism and parochialism.

2

STRATEGY THROUGH THE EXECUTIVE TEAM

Operating in a technology- and marketing-intensive environment, Nokia is a global company that seeks to be externally oriented but internally collaborative. As we saw in Chapter One, it has embraced globalization, but unlike large-country multinationals it cannot rely on a large home market. Nokia's strategy is determined by the executive team, which is driving its transformation from products into services and solutions.

Globalization Without a Home Market

Operating in a rapidly changing environment, Nokia and its rivals are all thought of as global companies. In reality, they have substantial differences, depending on the size of their home markets. In comparison to these rivals in the United States, Western Europe, Japan, and emerging economies, Nokia's regional revenue distribution is much more even:

- More than one-third of Nokia's net sales originates from Europe.

- Nearly one-third comes from Greater China and Asia-Pacific (including India).

- The remaining net sales come from the Americas, the Middle East, and Africa.

Although the United States dominates the technology sector, it accounts for only 4 percent of Nokia's sales. Most important, Finland (Nokia's home market) accounts for less than 1 percent of net sales.[1]

Figure 2.1 shows the striking contrasts between Nokia and Motorola, Apple and RIM, Microsoft, Google, Yahoo, and Alcatel-Lucent.

- Motorola, Nokia's historical rival, obtains half of its revenues from the United States, its home base.

- Until recently, Apple's iPhone has been primarily an American innovation for Americans in America: the U.S. home base accounts for 60 percent of Apple's sales.

- The United States also accounts for about 60 percent of sales for Google and Microsoft (and even more, 68 percent for Yahoo).

- RIM (read: Blackberry) may be produced in Canada, but its primary market is America, which accounts for 63 percent of the total (sales to the United States, United Kingdom, and Canada amount to 77 percent).

- Palm's domestic share is even higher: More than 75 percent of its sales originate from the United States.

Among leading infrastructure players, the competitive situation is not that different:

- More than half of Cisco's sales originate from North America.

- Alcatel-Lucent is headquartered in the United States and France, which account for half of its sales.

- Home market accounts for 22 and 46 percent of the sales of Korean Samsung and LG, respectively;[2] the two have a regional rather than a global focus, with Asia accounting for some 50 to 70 percent of their net sales.

- Interestingly, the share of international sales at Huawei has soared to 75 percent: China, its home market, accounts for only one-fourth of its sales.

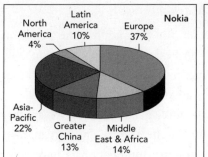
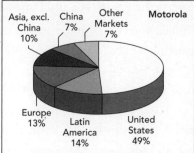
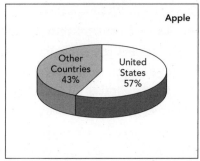
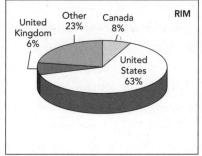
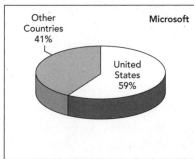
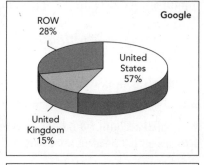
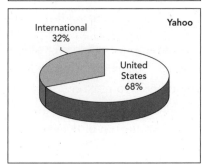
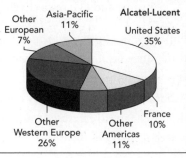

FIGURE 2.1   Role of the Home Market: Nokia and Rivals—Geographic Net Sales (2008)*

Home market in white

Succeeding with a Tiny Home Market

"When you come from a small market, you're typically quite flexible in working locally," says Nokia's CEO Olli-Pekka Kallasvuo. "You don't say, 'This is the way we do things at home.' You say, 'How do you do things here and how can we serve you?' You are responsive."

To large-country multinationals, foreign markets are yet another source of revenues. To small-country multinationals, foreign markets are all they have. Moreover, large-country multinationals have most of their critical activities—from headquarters to R&D—in their home base, whereas small-country multinationals have many of their critical activities dispersed worldwide. "Nokia is a global company, the most global company in the world," says Richard A. Simonson, Nokia's former CFO and currently chief of mobile phones, who has worked for some of the most global companies in the world. "Most view themselves as domestic companies that have overseas operations, whereas I have never heard anybody here talk about 'overseas operations,' or 'foreign operations,' or 'multinational operations.' It just doesn't exist in our lexicon."

Small-Country Multinationals Are More Adaptive to the Rest of the World

Without a commercially viable home market, Nokia is dispersed worldwide. "Both Australia and Finland understand that the world is not going to adapt to them, they have to adapt to the world," says Colin Giles, Nokia's global head of sales, who is of Australian descent. "And I believe that has helped us a lot."

Even Australia's population of 21 million is four times higher than Finland's, but both are located in remote geographic extremes, and as a result, they both need openness to reach out. Conversely, America has a very large homegrown market, so it doesn't need to reach out so much. Accordingly, U.S. companies are less inclined to perceive a comparable need to adapt to the rest of the world, whereas the rest of the world has a need to adapt to them.

The Future of Business Is Multipolar

Big- and small-country multinationals may look alike, but they are different, and they compete globally in a different way. To the extent globalization will continue through trade, investment, and immigration, it will be driven by multiple power centers worldwide. In such a future, Nokia's example is far more than an isolated curiosity of interest to few; because it is totally reliant on global markets, it serves as a bellwether case of the future of multinational companies in an increasingly multipolar world.

In his former life as a Finnish veteran politician, Esko Aho, currently Nokia's chief of corporate relations, was chairman of a European group that looked into European competitiveness. "Some said there that it's hard for Europe to do the right thing because there are so many small countries," he recalls. "I asked them, 'Look at the competitiveness rankings of Europe. Which countries are leading? Finland, Sweden, Denmark, Norway, Iceland, Switzerland.' " In global competitiveness or globalization rankings, the leading nations are often small countries. The secret is not so much the Finnish or the Nordic model. Rather, small countries understand that they are not setting the rules. They are adjusting to the changing world.

To Nokia, that's extremely important. It cannot set the rules but it can be very flexible in adjusting to changes. In small countries, nothing has been given. They have to work harder; they have to fight for their share.

Strategy Driven by the Executive Team

"When you participate in Nokia meetings, these differ from comparable meetings in other multinationals," says D. "Shiv" Shivakumar, head of Nokia India. "You'll never figure out who are the leaders. It is decision making by consensus, not by force. So when the Nokians decide to go for something, they go for it by 110 percent, with the intent to win. It is not easy to replicate."

Finnish culture has a strong legacy of egalitarianism, which is reflected not just in Nokia's people, values, and legacy (described in more detail in Chapter Three) but also in its executive team's emphasis on team-work. This is not always understood outside Nokia, as illustrated by the preparation of the first major cover story on Nokia in the United States.[3]

It Is Not the CEO but the Executive Team

In many other multinationals, a CEO might fight for such a moment in the sun, but at Nokia the opportunity of being featured so prominently by a major U.S. business publication was seen as a potential pitfall. The senior executives were only too familiar with the practice of U.S. business media of personalizing success, primarily with the CEO, and they found it appalling.

"Why is everyone here so skittish about profiles?" asked *BusinessWeek* in 1998, when Nokia was conquering international markets but still relatively unknown in America. "We want to stress the team effort," said Jorma Ollila, Nokia's then-CEO. "I don't want to personalize Nokia with me. [Grandstanding] is not very Finnish, it's not very Nokia." Recalling the story, Ollila says now, "Usually I don't ask for conditions in giving interviews, but this time I did. " 'You can't write an article just about me,' I told them. 'You have to include the team.' "

Nokia's senior executives believe that routine business coverage that tends to associate a company's success or failure with one individual is conceptually flawed and potentially damaging to the team spirit. Compared to aristocratic business elites and larger-than-life egos, Nokia's senior executives may be a refreshing exception. "A profile is a lie," said Nokia's then-President Pekka Ala-Pietilä. "American CEOs are in many cases saying 'I.' It's a false picture...instead of 'I,' it should be in most of the cases 'We.' The omnipotence of a leader does not serve well the purpose of building self-motivating and long-lasting organization."

During his Nokia era, Ala-Pietilä was known as a humble leader. To make a strong statement was a stretch, especially to him. Yet it reflects the underlying conviction of many in the company.

Strong Teamwork Reduces Internal Tensions and Politics

The emphasis on teamwork has important side effects as well. Due to the driving role of the teams in the company, Nokians say they have less of the kind of political intrigue or departmental friction that characterizes many other companies. "The company is focused on achievement and winning, which it seeks to do in an uncompromised way and with integrity," says Ollila. This has been a purposeful effort ever since the great restructuring of the early 1990s.

Typically, Nokia's senior executives continue to prefer to use "we" when they talk about the successes of their company. This issue is very close to their mind and heart because it pertains to what is most critical, different, and distinctive about this company in which they have served most of their life. "Today, the media personifies everything," said Jorma Ollila to Finnish journalists in 2006, as he was preparing to retire from Nokia. "This company is not the achievement of one person; nothing is." In fact, such personifications prevent even informed observers from understanding the true importance of Nokia's leadership innovation—the senior executive team as an *amalgam* of diverse assets and capabilities and united for a common end.

At Nokia, the "power of we" reigns. The Nokians believe that as a team they can achieve more than as individuals.

Humility Deters Complacency

"We believed in teamwork," explains Matti Alahuhta, Nokia's former executive vice president and currently CEO of KONE, one of the world's largest and most global elevator companies. "It is about realism, egalitarianism, and trust. No titles are significant. As Finns, we are big on humility. That attitude is vital in a technology-intensive sector, where today's winners can be tomorrow's losers. You take pride in the past, but you don't project it into the future."

This humility is partly cultural, and partly a built-in resistance. "We do not just sit back and say, 'Boy, we did a very great job!'" says Nokia's chief of services Niklas Savander. "We have a higher degree of built-in resistance to feeling too good about ourselves. It's a work ethic of a mixed Finnish, Nordic, and Lutheran legacy." But it is certainly not the monopoly of northern Europe and it can also be trained. Today many of Nokia's leading executives, and country and functional chiefs, have changed and an increasing number of them are no longer Finnish, but the emphasis on humility remains. Along with other country operations, Nokia India is no exception. "One of the common characteristics of Nokia and its leadership is humility, they just don't get arrogant or carried away by success," says D. Shivakumar. "They do not rest on their laurels. They question success and ask, 'How can we make this better?'"

At Nokia, humility is not just a moral ideal but also a pragmatic guideline. Modesty is not about meekness, but about purposeful determination. Nokia's executives are painfully aware of the fact that the fall of great companies is paved with complacency and arrogance.[4] Paraphrasing Intel's Andy Grove, the Nokians also believe that only the humble survive.

Nokia's Collective Mind

Since the late 1990s, Nokia has been literally transformed, from the top to the bottom. When Simon Beresford-Wylie, former CEO of Nokia Siemens Networks (NSN),[5] joined Nokia in 1998, it was still evolving and had a relatively tight national identity. "This was the era when the great Finns were sort of parachuting to countries that they had not heard of," he says. A trusted group of people had the ability and was empowered to move quickly and fast. "To the credit of Jorma [Ollila] and the executive team, they enabled the company to grow in a way that allowed them to bring in external DNA. That has served the company well in its years of globalization."

Today, Nokia has 126,000 employees, which is three to four times more than only a decade ago. Strategy is more multidimensional. The organization is more complex. And values are ever more critical (as we'll see in Chapter Three). In this rapidly changing environment, it is the group executive board (GEB) that is responsible for managing the operations of Nokia.[6]

In Finland, the careers of the GEB members are followed with the same awe that the speculations of the Sovietologists attracted during the Cold War. In both cases, the primary motivation remains the same. In the past, Finland's geopolitical fate was intertwined with the Soviet Union; today Finland's innovative capacity is vitally aligned with Nokia.

What the Group Executive Board Members Have in Common

Most GEB members were born in the 1950s; the "newbies" are from the 1960s, so many are in their early fifties. Most Finnish members are alumni of the Helsinki University of Technology (HUT), the country's premier technology institution, or the Helsinki School of Economics (HSE), the country's leading business school, or both.[7] Typically they have a degree in technology or an MBA, or both. As a group the GEB members personify the tough work ethic that Kari Kairamo, Nokia's CEO from the 1980s, brought to the company after his years in the United States. That ethic is not just about ambitious goals, but also about relentless execution.

Along with values, the Nokians share certain personal characteristics. The Nokia executives may seem nice and unassuming, but they are also bold, tough, and ambitious. Like most Nokians, they are soft-spoken, dislike bragging, and shun office politics. "We are human and we understand that people make mistakes," says Arja Suominen, Nokia's chief of communications, who has been in the company for some twenty years. "But we are not softies, and we work very hard."

The Nokians emphasize teamwork and consider personal agendas a distraction. Although critical of aristocratic personality cults, they admire flexible and innovative U.S. companies. They are deeply impressed by and follow developments in the Silicon Valley, which has increasingly become their mindset headquarters. They work hard and will continue to work even harder to emulate the best of American innovation, entrepreneurship, and venture capital.

While they feel pride over their European legacy, they also believe that many European multinationals are too slow and inefficient to succeed in rapidly changing and increasingly global industries. And they think that many Japanese multinationals can be fast and efficient but have been too unresponsive to markets beyond Japan. Where most corporate giants in North America, Western Europe, and Japan tend to benchmark each other, these executives see future challengers also in large emerging economies, such as China and India. They are impressed and genuinely intrigued by the dramatic rise of Asia. And like many Asian corporate giants, their strategic thinking tends to emphasize long-term objectives rather than short-term market pressures.

Most GEB members keep their distance from publicity. They are loyal and have worked much or all of their work lives for the company. This loyalty reflects their private commitments, and their private loyalty works for the company. Most are married and have two to five children. They are committed to Nokia's ways and values. Of course they are driven by success and money, but also by more intangible rewards, such as prestige, lifelong learning, and professional respect. Until recently, these were the staple of Finnish values.

Deep in their hearts many also have dreams that cynics would call idealistic; they desire success, but they also want to do good things in life. They see affinities with Google's ingenuity and ethos, the idea of doing new and good things in life. They want to improve not only their own personal lives, but also the ways of the world. Their mission is not just individual, nor is it collective. It is not some sort of abstract humanism; it is very concrete and practical, and at times almost stunningly bold. They sincerely hope and want to change the world—for the better.

The Inner Circle Works as an Integral Whole

In the late 1990s Jorma Ollila delegated substantial autonomy to an inner circle of a handful of GEB members: his right-hand man Pekka Ala-Pietilä, international business specialist Sari Baldauf, globalization expert Matti Alahuhta, and then-CFO Olli-Pekka Kallasvuo. The four became known in Finland as Nokia's "dream team." Despite the central role of the executive team in Nokia's strategy making, however, their role was hardly even noticed outside the country until the late 1990s. Ala-Pietilä, Alahuhta, Baldauf, Kallasvuo, and Ollila formed the nucleus of the executive board and worked together about fifteen years or even more. "We knew each other well enough to use a kind of shorthand in conversations," recalls Alahuhta. "It was very compact, dense communication. You didn't hear so much talk about 'Jorma this' or 'Jorma that.' It was more like 'Olli-Pekka and Jorma,' 'Sari and Matti,' or some combination."

The team members knew each other from the mid-1980s. They had informal communications between each other. Certainly, they were different personalities, their ways of working were different, and their minds worked differently. But what united them was the underlying understanding of what the company could do. "We believed we were doing something very meaningful, internationally competitive, and with real staying power, not just a flash in the pan," says Ollila. "We shared values that we all understood and which radiated through our own personal management styles."

With their diverse backgrounds in finance, industry, R&D, engineering, manufacturing, and international business, the GEB members complemented each other and functioned as an integral whole. Ala-Pietilä focused on future challenges. Baldauf's name was synonymous with international expansion, particularly in Asia. Alahuhta wrote a dissertation on global strategies. Key members of the GEB also included Anssi Vanjoki, the marketing wizard who turned Nokia into a global brand in just a decade; Yrjö Neuvo, the legendary technology chief who many still see as one of Nokia's spiritual founding fathers; and Veli Sundbäck, the accomplished diplomat who played a vital role in Finland's talks about EU membership before he joined Nokia.

The Nokians believe that in a rapidly changing and highly complex technology and marketing business, a broad and diverse executive team can provide stability, flexibility, and simplicity in decision making.

Informality, Quick Decision Making, Freedom to Act

Most major corporations had more CEO-driven processes than Nokia. Conversely, the members of Nokia's executive team had more leeway and more freedom of action than typical in major multinationals. And that's very much the way Ollila wanted it: "You have enormous decision making power, but you better perform because that's the best guarantee of getting your colleagues and the CEO in alignment." Of course, the executives could just use phone and e-mail or the GEB meetings as their sounding board, but that is on the slow side. Rather, the point is to optimize time, actions, and decisions. Due to the their joint internalized norms and values, they can move ahead relatively quickly, independently, and as a team. "The point is that you must maintain the *trust* of your colleagues," Ollila says.

It was this quickness in decision making that was critical during Nokia's hectic high-growth period in the latter half of the 1990s. There was a clear willingness and readiness to take positions and responsibility, and then to lead in a way that not only demonstrated but also positively formulated the values of the company. "The key people gave their 24/7 to the company," says Ollila. "They were always available. No exceptions, no compromises, no holidays."

In any well-managed global organization, an element of the GEB—the informality, quick decision making, freedom to act—is vital. What varies is how you play together in getting the agreement and trust of your colleagues. You can have a formal process, you can have big meetings, small meetings, or you can have a very powerful informal way of communicating and interacting—and Nokia is relatively advanced at that end of the scale.

"The objective at Nokia has always been to have decisions made by the people who have the best knowledge," says Nokia's former senior executive Matti Alahuhta. The company is not only less hierarchical than most large corporations, but decidedly antihierarchical. The objective of meritocratic management is to encourage creativity, entrepreneurship, and personal responsibility.

"Externally Oriented but Internally Collaborative"

The strategic goal of Nokia's CEO Olli-Pekka Kallasvuo—who the Nokians call either "OP" or "OPK"—is a multinational company that is both externally oriented and internally collaborative. "In Finland, there isn't much in the way of market," he says. But the other side of Nokia's high degree of external orientation is an equally high degree of internal collaboration. In both cases, the common denominator is the same—market creation.

Going Beyond Traditional Strategy Frameworks

In the late 1980s—even before the days of the dotcom revolution—many companies that had risen to global leadership began with ambitions that were out of proportion to their resources and capabilities. In the early 1990s, some management thinkers portrayed Nokia among the winning companies that were building gateways to the future through an "obsession with winning at all levels of the organization."[8] These ideas had an immense appeal at Nokia, although a case can be made that they just reinforced what the Nokians already knew and were doing.

As a result of their legacy of a tiny home market and a strong and diverse executive team, the Nokians cannot take at face value strategy frameworks that have evolved in or been tailored to large-country multinationals with top-heavy CEO offices. A decade ago, Ollila and his senior executives began to develop a strategic response to the growing complexity in their competitive landscape. In January 1999, Ollila first lectured on "Nokia's strategic intent."[9] The new management paradigm was portrayed as an effort to combine and transcend two dominant strategy paradigms:[10]

- According to the *resource-based view* (which is often associated with Prahalad and Hamel), firms compete by leveraging their unique competencies on old or new market spaces. At Nokia, this paradigm is seen as too slow, too much driven by the past, and focused on history.

- According to the *market-based view* (which is often associated with Michael Porter's ideas of competitive advantage), firms compete for attractive industry segments by differentiation, low cost, or specialization. The problem with this paradigm is that it takes the market as a given, is driven by the present, and places too little emphasis on renewal.

At Nokia, both paradigms are perceived as necessary but insufficient. In order to succeed in dynamic markets, it is vital to develop layers of competitive advantages. The real challenge is to build on existing capabilities while developing new advantages. In developing such "market-making strategies," the emphasis is on the successful combination of foresight and execution. One must have reasonably accurate scenarios of the future and an ability to execute the strategy in a highly competitive environment, where timing and speed truly matter.[11]

So from the beginning, Nokia's senior executives learned to think of competitive advantage in a plural sense. Operating in a technology- and marketing-intensive market, they also understood the importance of *time*, which is not just about *timing* and *speed*, but also about *rhythm*. It all starts from the timing decision—from the strategic assessment on the ripeness of the market opportunity. You cannot come into the marketplace too early or too late. In other words, you must prepare for the *mass* market. "Through a few bitter experiences, we understood that you cannot make a market if it is not adequately mature," says Pekka Ala-Pietilä, one of Nokia's leading executives in the Ollila era. "From the standpoint of the end user, maturity means a market which offers great benefits but requires only incremental changes on the behavioral side."

Certainly, Nokia must create new products and be a pioneer and a thought leader, but if the market is not mature, it should have only limited resource stakes. Conversely, when the window opens for a mass market, *then* Nokia should scale up investment resources quickly and adequately. This is how right timing will pave the way for *speed* in implementation. "In our business, the volumes have been very high since the mid-1990s," acknowledges Ala-Pietilä. "So it is really important to time right investments, product, product development, and suppliers. If, for instance, we misestimated the timing of the volumes, we could select the wrong supplier, [one with] no ability or capacity to scale up fast enough in the marketplace."

Nokia's speed in implementation is often seen as embedded in its organizational capabilities and in the passion of the Nokians to move fast in everything they do. Hence speed—or the capability to be faster than their competitors—was and remains one of the Nokians' obsessions.

The third time-related dimension is *rhythm*, which refers to the inherent renewal cycle of products and services. It varies by market and is not easy to execute. "If you bring to market new products too frequently and with incremental improvements, the threat is that consumers do not appreciate the effort and you will not get an appropriate return for your R&D investment," says Ala-Pietilä. Conversely, if you seldom bring new products but seek for great onetime changes, you end up with a product line that lacks competitiveness for a long period of time. Among Nokia's rivals, this rhythm varies a lot from one competitor to another; it is usually heavily influenced by the product renewal cycle of the competitor's home market.

When Nokia opted for its critical strategic choices, these made little sense to an entire generation of managers that had been brought up with a steady diet of traditional strategy frameworks. "We saw very early on at Nokia that it's not enough to have either cost advantage or differentiation advantage," says Matti Alahuhta, Nokia's former senior executive. "You need both." And most internationalization strategies are based on a process in which a company goes abroad in stages. That made no sense at Nokia, which sought to go "directly global," as Alahuhta puts it. In their efforts to cope with rapidly changing markets and disruptive innovation, the company has been particularly ingenious in taking advantage of industry transitions.[12]

Kallasvuo's "Just Do It" Ethos

Today, the GEB chairman is Olli-Pekka Kallasvuo, Nokia's CEO. His precursor, Ollila, was known as a hard-driving and high-profile executive; Kallasvuo prefers a lower profile in public. Yet both weigh their words carefully. Behind the façade, Kallasvuo is as ambitious, hardworking, and disciplined as Ollila. It was these two who developed Nokia's winning strategy in 1992. "OPK is very pragmatic and has a courage to challenge old dogmas," says Nokia's communications chief Arja Suominen. "If you can prove your case, he's OK with it."

When Kallasvuo joined Nokia in 1980, he was a twenty-eight-year-old lawyer. He was working for a major Finnish bank that "loaned" him to Nokia for a year. But he really liked the "just do it" atmosphere. He joined the board in 1992, "ten years too early," he acknowledges. Those were tough years: things weren't that organized. "There was a great drive for international business, but the skills were not there. We worked with Jorma quite intimately in that phase and got a green light for the new strategy. We had a team that could make decisions."

Since the 1990s, Kallasvuo's responsibilities have increased year by year from corporate finance to country chief in the United States to CFO and chief of Nokia Mobile Phones to CEO of Nokia. "I see it all as an evolution," he says. "Nokia has changed a lot very fast." As a senior executive or CEO, you must change as well. In the company, a lot can happen in just one year. As a result, people must constantly learn and change.

"If Nokia is to continue to thrive, it must be externally oriented," Kallasvuo emphasizes. "It must have the kind of humility that makes it listen and seek ideas from outside." This humility in the face of complexity requires strong internal collaboration, which ensures a fast, flexible, and appropriate response.

Diverse Team Drives Transformation

In the late 1990s, Nokia was still relatively Finnish, especially the top executives. Today, it is more diverse and international. Kallasvuo believes that the diversity of the leadership—not just in the sense of nationality, but also in terms of overall background, training, gender, and so on—is a critical contributor to Nokia's success.

Diversity Facilitates Better Decisions

Diversity ensures a positive mix. It provides better means to make good decisions. It means different backgrounds, skill sets, and perspectives.

Taking into consideration the large size of Nokia, it is hard to find such diversity elsewhere. "We have greater diversity and different skill sets," says Kallasvuo, who compares Nokia's executive team and corporate governance with Dutch multinationals. It highlights the importance of cooperation. The more diversity you have, the better it is for the company and the less you will have the "not invented here" syndrome, which he considers very detrimental. "Nokia has always had to fight hard against complacency," says Kallasvuo. "The bigger and older we become and the more we age, the harder we must struggle against complacency."

In a sense, the problems have only begun. Once the Nokia Siemens Networks merger was completed, the number of Nokia's consolidated employees soared from 60,000 to more than 126,000. That is a great concern to those executives, such as Kallasvuo, who want to keep Nokia agile and responsive. "Today, Nokia is a big company, a really big company," he says. "Yet we cannot become an incumbent. Then we'd lose our soul. We just can't have it. In a big company, it's very easy to lose the focus because there's simply so much going on internally. We must be externally oriented and internally collaborative, but we can't lose our soul."

Dream Teams Are Diverse Teams

The original dream team created a strong base for success. The longevity and stability in the management team in those formative years from the 1990s to early 2000s was unheard of in comparison to many other multinationals. Despite different roles, the group executive board demonstrated strong collective leadership. "So many people in Nokia saw that and experienced that, and it became almost a self-fulfilling positive force," says Niklas Savander, chief of Nokia's Services unit.

CEO Kallasvuo launched his own dream team in early 2008. Until recently, the core members of the GEB were Anssi Vanjoki, Kai Öistämö, Niklas Savander, Richard A. Simonson, and Mary T. McDowell. The first three head the core units (Markets, Devices, Services). The latter two are based in Nokia's corporate office in New York. Former CFO Simonson focuses now on mobile phones, while McDowell's task is to ceaselessly refine Nokia's strategy for growth.

Like other senior executives at Nokia, Anssi Vanjoki has held a wide array of senior executive positions in the company. As executive vice president and general manager of the Markets unit, Vanjoki is responsible for consumer insights, sales, marketing, manufacturing, and logistics across all Nokia products and services. He has been a member of the Nokia group executive board since 1998. As Vanjoki sees it, "Since we are a living organism, we have got to be all the time very sensitive to what's going on in our competitive environment, what's happening in different market areas, and what's happening in technology."

A veteran of Nokia since 1991, Dr. Kai Öistämö is a former head of the Mobile Phones and is now responsible for the new Devices unit, that is, Nokia's device portfolio, R&D, sourcing, and related strategy. With Nokia's organizational transformation, the GEB has taken on more joint responsibility and interdependencies. "Now, there are more shared issues, and that builds commitment," says Öistämö. "The new setup ensures the support of the peer group in solving problems."

In fall 2009, Nokia augmented its key units (Devices, Services, Markets) with the Solutions unit, headed by Alberto Torres, previous head of the Devices category management. Concurrently the Venezuelan-born McKinsey alumni joined the group executive board as well.

Born in Middletown, Ohio, Richard A. Simonson joined Nokia in 2001. "More than most multinationals, Nokia is focused on achievement and success and doing it in an uncompromised way and with integrity," he says. "It has less of the kind of debilitating politics that waste time in petty conflicts or personalities." As head of the Mobile Phones subunit within the Devices unit, he is based in New York and also heads strategic sourcing for Devices and reports to Kai Öistämö, head of the Devices unit, while Jean-Francois Baril, senior vice president of Sourcing, reports to him.

A seventeen-year veteran of HP-Compaq, Mary T. McDowell joined Nokia in 2004. She is executive vice president and chief development officer (CDO) leading the Corporate Development unit. As CDO, she is responsible for optimizing Nokia's strategic capabilities and growth potential. Among other things, McDowell oversees corporate strategy, the Nokia Research Center, corporate business development, and solutions portfolio management. She has played a critical role in Nokia's increasingly integrated business model.

54

These core members are supplemented by other GEB members. After a twenty-two-year career at Hewlett-Packard, Hallstein Moerk has had global responsibility for all human resources activity in Nokia. Tero Ojanperä, the newbie of the GEB, has played a defining role in the R&D work of Nokia's business groups and the Nokia Research Center, has served as CTO, and currently oversees offerings in music, video and TV, games, software distribution, and social networking services.

Since November 2008 Esko Aho has been Nokia's executive vice president, corporate relations and responsibility, as well as a GEB member. Prior to joining Nokia, Aho had a long and distinguished career in Finnish politics, holding the post of prime minister in the early 1990s and most recently president of the Finnish Innovation Fund (Sitra).

Niklas Savander is in charge of the new Services unit, while Timo Ihamuotila, who used to be responsible for Nokia's global sales within the Markets unit, is now the CFO. In addition to being Nokia corporate treasurer, he has held several other senior positions over the years in, for example, risk management and portfolio management. The most recent member of the GEB is Alberto Torres, executive vice president of Solutions, responsible for defining the portfolio of Nokia's solutions across the company.

Currently, the GEB has some dozen members. A decade ago all were Finnish citizens. Today half are foreign citizens. In addition to the Finnish Nokians, the group includes two Americans (Simonson and McDowell), a Norwegian (Moerk), and a Venezuelan (Torres).

Smooth Generational Change

These Nokia insiders work well together, and each adds to the board something unique. Every second member has been in the company barely a decade, and most joined the GEB only in the past half decade. During these years, the GEB went through a generational transformation, which was managed smoothly.

Despite the critical importance of the large emerging markets to Nokia, the GEB members do not yet include Chinese or Indian members. That should and is about to change as Asian senior executives are rising in the organization. As Colin Giles was transferred from his position and promoted as Nokia's head of global sales, Chris Leong, formerly heading marketing GTM (go-to-market) operations, took over as head of Nokia Greater China, Japan, and Korea SU, reporting to Giles. In fall 2009, NSN CEO Simon Beresford-Wylie was succeeded by Rajeev Suri, a telecom veteran of Indian descent who handled the NSN Services business.

Nokia appreciates longer-term commitment. In general, organic evolution tends to favor insiders rather than those who have been recruited from outside the organization says one former Nokia executive. Already in the 1990s, Jorma Ollila used to say that every tenth appointment should come from outside Nokia; take, for instance, the GEB's Aho, McDowell, and Torres. Yes, incremental and internal evolution is important. But so are external appointments, which ensure new ideas and perspectives—diversity.

However, after a slate of recent executive appointments and years of intense recruiting in the BRICs, the boundary between inside and outside has grown blurry. Nokia likes to implement change without drama, says head of Mobile Phones Richard Simonson. "It shows to the entire organization that we can evolve and change and have new organizational structures without causing turmoil in the company."

How the Executive Team Works

Right before she started to work at Nokia, Mary McDowell, who is currently Nokia's corporate development officer, had dinner with Jorma Ollila, who said that he had two pieces of advice for starting her Nokia career. "The first one is that there's no swearing in my meetings," Ollila said. That was interesting, McDowell thought. Despite occasionally intense internal debate, people were expected to be civil to one another. But the second piece of advice was absolutely to the point. "Just because I approve something," Ollila said, "doesn't necessarily mean it's approved. This is a very networked culture, and you need to have a broad buy-in in order to get anything done. So don't fall into the trap of coming to me for support. You're going to have to work across the organization and across the network."

McDowell discovered the advice turned out to be true and remains so today. Nokia's executive team is not just an organization; it's more like an organism, in that it may reject things that are not in keeping with the strategy or the culture.

"Things Argue, Not People"

Ever since 1992, the group executive board has had a key role in strategic decision making. It sounds like a formal structure, but it is very informal. As a whole, the GEB is more valuable than its individual parts. It remains Nokia's collective mind. Efficient teamwork, however, does not mean absence of leadership. Through his era, Ollila alternated his role as a facilitator and leader. "Everybody could participate and talk," recalls Yrjö Neuvo, Nokia's former technology wizard. Strong personalities led Nokia's core units, especially Nokia Mobile Phones. Often the team took a lot of risk and debated hard on the available options. During those intense debates, says Neuvo, "Jorma [Ollila] was willing to listen a lot and openly, but in the end, he would take charge and say what to do."

The tradition lives on. CEO Kallasvuo will listen, support, and facilitate, but he will also make decisions, including difficult decisions when they need to be made.

The executive team has formal meetings at least once a month and more often when needed. The meetings are structured. Critical decisions are debated and agreed upon as a group. There is a shared understanding that if there is a very important issue, for instance, a change in the way Nokia operates or an acquisition, the key GEB members need to know. "Never was any formal decision brought over as a fait accompli to the GEB," says Ollila. The staffs of the GEB members also often have a great interest in the team's activities.

Trust Enables Fast Decisions

Formally, decisions are made in the GEB. But the setup also enables substantial flexibility. For example, if a Nokian executive in Australia stands in front of a customer who asks something impossible, he obviously cannot always consult others in the next thirty seconds or two hours because of regional time zone differences. Therefore, each GEB member knows that if he or she is in a comparable situation, others will understand the need for a quick decision and give the mandate to go beyond what one would normally do. There is trust that the judgment will be in the best interest of the company. When you have such trust, others will be ready to support, even if there is no time for a formal meeting.

Yet the GEB does not hide from debate. Every now and then there have been some efforts to limit the discussions, but the team is a group of very strong and opinionated people. "The way the Nokia management debates things differs from its British or U.S. counterparts in that the debate is very free," says KP Wilska, Nokia's former chief of Americas. "However, when the board decides something, everybody will stand behind the decision. People won't throw stones afterwards to make life unpleasant."

Although the individual members of Nokia's executive team can be very opinionated and engage in tough debate over every major strategic decision, Nokia is led by values. The executives try to listen to others. They try to do things that are a little riskier. They talk openly and are not afraid to challenge, but when they decide on something, everybody pulls behind the joint effort. The Nokians like to paraphrase a Finnish saying, *"Asiat kiistelevät, eivät ihmiset"* (Things argue, not people).

Rotation Broadens Experience

Like their predecessors, Nokia's senior executives have served in a diverse set of positions. The company likes to remove people from their comfort areas to keep them from becoming complacent. Rotation also helps people learn from one another in different businesses; it enables them to better identify synergistic opportunities among businesses. It is seen as fostering a kind of cross-fertilization. The assumption is that holding various roles prepares one for a broad set of perspectives, which is vital in a global, complex, and rapidly changing landscape. Internally, the emphasis is increasingly on cooperation, interdependency, and synergies.

Take, for instance, the current CEO Olli-Pekka Kallasvuo. The young lawyer joined Nokia in 1980 as corporate counsel. In the late 1980s, he was appointed assistant vice president of the legal department, but only two years later he was senior vice president of finance. As Nokia focused on mobile communications, he was named executive vice president and CFO. In some companies, he might have remained in that position for the rest of his life. But after half a decade, he left Helsinki and moved to the United States, being responsible for all Nokia's business operations in the Americas. Some two years later, he returned to the CFO position. But as Ollila prepared his departure from Nokia, Kallasvuo became executive vice president and general manager of mobile phones in 2004–2005, until he was named president and COO and, finally, CEO. "I never studied finance or mobile communications in the university," he says. "But I have always learned on my own what I need to know."

Of course, such career evolution reflects the impact of promotions, but it is predicated on rotation; in Kallasvuo's case, from legal positions to finance, country, and regional management and ultimately to industry operations. Today, this rotation is taken for granted at Nokia, especially with younger demographics.

Take the newbie of the GEB, Tero Ojanperä, who started as co-head of Services in January 2009. After Ph.D. studies in northern Finland and the Netherlands and several senior management positions in the former Nokia Networks, he headed the Nokia Research Center in 2003–2004, driving Nokia's technological competitiveness and renewal. A year later, he held the position of executive vice president and chief strategy officer, and thereafter as chief technology officer, in a wide-ranging role spanning corporate and technology strategy, strategic alliances and partnerships.

Before his current job, Ojanperä served as executive vice president, entertainment and communities, with overall responsibility for Nokia offerings in music, video and TV, games, software distribution, and social networking services. In his case, senior positions in telecom infrastructure led to R&D, executive roles in strategy and technology, entertainment and communities, and ultimately services. Somehow a career that started with technology studies in the dark and near-arctic Oulu led to cooperation with colorful Eurythmics founder and Nokia consultant Dave Stewart and meetings with Bono at his house in the south of France. As Kallasvuo says of Ojanperä, with a gentle smile: "Tero sure looks more and more like Dave Stewart every day."

How Teams Drive Strategy Throughout Nokia

Nokia has a very strong culture for effective teams to operationalize the strategies for mobile devices, services, solutions, and infrastructure, all of which are different. "The strategies are divided by high-level business objectives, which each consists of a handful of initiatives," says Heikki Norta, Nokia's senior vice president of corporate strategy. "Some of them cut across units, and some across the entire company. The latter are more important because their impact covers the company, not just the units."

Teams—in Nokia's official parlance, "programs"—are tasked to bring results in each of those initiatives. Historically, these programs were first called concurrent engineering and later product development.[13] In product development, various functions (engineering, design, manufacturing, etc.) are integrated to reduce the time required to bring a new product to the market. Overall success relies on the ability of engineers to effectively work together.

Nokia has also made a significant impact on teams that service customers by pooling people together from marketing, product customization, quality, product development, and of course sales. Another team concept that plays a vital role in Nokia involves teams that have been deployed to build vision and strategy.

The Program Way of Working

What is central to Nokia's organizational structure and matrix is its program way of working; in other words, the many and different teams working on projects. This operational mode is typical to Nokia's people and organization, its management and leadership practices, as well as processes and conduct. It is also why a simple structural chart of Nokia in no way captures the richness of the teams working in and across the organization, creating value by running portfolios of projects and programs.

To Nokians, the program way of working means *integration*. After all, the company seeks to mobilize optimal knowledge, experience, and resources, whether they match the organizational structure or not. It also means setting and *achieving common targets* as a team. At Nokia, it is neither the individual nor the collective that truly counts, but the team. The Nokians also believe that the program way of working allows them to *prioritize*. The teams make possible the focus on the best opportunities through portfolio management and "executing right things at the right time with the right resources." Finally, working in this way makes Nokia *unique*. The Nokians believe that it is primarily the teams that allow them to convert ideas to innovations and engage in continuous learning.

At the broadest level, then, the benefits of the program way of working far outweigh the costs, while allowing teams to

- Bring order, structure, and goal orientation to chaos
- Deal with unique and transient goals
- Align and integrate activities toward common goals
- Provide resource mobility across line structures
- Provide cross-organization visibility to activities through portfolio management

Portfolio management is good for making prioritizing decisions because it fosters cross-functional knowledge and learning, as well as social networks across organizations.

The Role of the Board Is Supportive

In the late 1980s there was still a great deal of friction between Nokia's chief executives and the board of directors. Since 1992, the board has been more sympathetic toward the strategic objectives of the company. As a former banker, Jorma Ollila was liked by the board and he spoke their language. In 1999, he was elected chairman of the company. Prior to Ollila, Nokia's chairman was Casimir "Casse" Ehrnrooth, a Finnish magnate whose career had begun in forest industry. Ehrnrooth did not intervene with Nokia's operational activities; that is the job of the CEO.

The tradition has prevailed in Ollila's board. "As a CEO, Jorma was, and as the board chairman he is, first and foremost, a professional," says an influential Nokia board director. "In his era, leadership has been very systematic and conversational at Nokia."

Led by Ollila, who is currently also chairman of Shell, Nokia's board of directors has some dozen members. The veterans were appointed prior to 2002; the others joined were appointed in 2007 or thereafter.[14] Their function is primarily supportive and facilitative.

At Nokia, values and culture are seen as the glue that keeps the complex organization together. Values are not perceived as simple rhetoric or PR; they are considered the most effective instrument of strategic management. They are also seen as a commitment to make money by doing good things. As a Nokia slogan puts it:

> When Nokia changes, the world will change
> We can impact lives, make the world better
> The success of Nokia depends on it

Nokia's strategy of internal collaboration is further enhanced by the company's values, culture, and people, which are described in detail in Chapter Three.

Nokia's Lessons

- When Nokia recently entered another new country market, CEO Kallasvuo said that "it's wonderful to have a new home." Large-country multinationals achieve international scope through scale economies in large home markets; they leverage domestic strengths internationally. Small-country multinationals achieve scale economies through global scope in critical markets. Small home markets do not preclude global competitiveness.

- Nokia seeks to be externally oriented but internally collaborative. It is not driven by a single CEO and his office. Nokia's successful strategy is driven by a diverse and increasingly global executive team with diverse capabilities. In this team, fast decision making is facilitated by strong trust.

- Today many multinational companies operate in an environment that is both technology- and marketing-intensive and extends across the world. Simple strategies no longer match the complexity of their environment. The resource-based view of core competencies is too slow, too much driven by the past and history. The market-based view of competitive strategies takes the market as a given; it is driven by the present and places too little emphasis on renewal.

- Success requires dynamic strategies that can also shape and create markets, sense and respond to environmental change, and are driven by the future and place emphasis on ceaseless renewal.

- Traditional strategy frameworks are necessary but insufficient in dynamic and rapidly changing global environments. In order to succeed in dynamic markets, it is vital to develop layers of competitive advantages. The real challenge is to build on existing capabilities while developing new advantages.

3

HOW NOKIA'S VALUES, CULTURE, AND PEOPLE CONTRIBUTE TO SUCCESS

Nokia's success emerges from its strategy, legacy, and ability to take advantage of globalization (as described in Chapters One and Two). However, what truly animates Nokia are its values, culture, and people. In this chapter, we take a closer look at how perseverance and increasing diversity drive Nokia's efforts to build a shared purpose through values. We also examine how Nokia develops global human resource management, recruits diverse team players worldwide, and builds managers and leaders.

Perseverance as Driving Force

In January 2007, *Harvard Business Review* interviewed executives on their "moment of truth" challenges. "If Nokia is to continue to prosper," said CEO Olli-Pekka Kallasvuo, "the company must be externally oriented and have the kind of humility that makes it listen to its customers and seek ideas from outside." "Having humility does not mean that you are quiet or that you lack the courage to say what you think," he added.[1] Courage and humility are more complementary than contradictory. But by courage, he means *sisu,* or perseverance, which is the key to Finnish history and culture.[2]

At Nokia, *perseverance* means strength of will, determination, and purposeful action in the face of adversity. Like "having guts," *perseverance* also alludes to something that reflects the inner character. In Finland, it is intertwined with strong egalitarian aspirations, an overwhelming sense of unity, and a deep desire for peace—values that reflect the historical yearnings of a small population in a cold geographic region, often at the mercy of neighboring empires. Perseverance is deeply rooted in the Finnish culture and remains one of Nokia's driving forces.

Today, *sisu* may be more subtle and diffuse, but it continues to have an integral role in Nokia's ways and values. In the early days, the company was inspired by an immense desire to show what the Nokians could do. "We wanted to prove that even a company coming from a small, peripheral region could compete against and win over the big guys," says Kari-Pekka "KP" Wilska, Nokia America's former president.

Nowadays, it is no longer just a Finnish drive, but something that animates Nokians worldwide through their shared purpose. For example, like its rivals Nokia wanted to have a presence in India, but unlike its rivals it was more determined. Nokia saw the potential of India and wanted *to win* in India. "You must have *sisu* to win," says D. "Shiv" Shivakumar, head of Nokia India. "Unlike many other multinationals in its industry, Nokia, from the very beginning, had this tremendous determination to win in India."

Everybody Is in This Together

Held in reserve for hard times, this spirit of persistent determination is seized in the moment of adversity. As the Nokians describe it, that is when Nokia's formal structure dissolves and the organization becomes a living organism and does what it has to do to win. The values, the organization, the strategy, even the brand come together. "You put aside other things, the bureaucracy and the rest, and you focus on the task at hand," describes Keith Pardy, Nokia's former head of strategic marketing.

The sense of "everybody is in this together" is not limited to crisis situations. It is signaled on a daily basis and reflected by the accessibility of the executive team. In many multinationals, the executives work apart.

But at Nokia, they do not live in an ivory tower but with other Nokians. This is not a company whose executives rush across the world in private jets. "Olli-Pekka [Kallasvuo] and Jorma [Ollila] and they're all in the cafeteria or the lunch room, not in official private dining rooms," adds Pardy. "They're where everybody else is. It's exceptional and important when you consider the challenges ahead."

Like Apple, the Nokians promote a strong corporate culture. But in stark contrast to Apple, Nokia works hard so that the organization is not personified by a single executive, which the Nokians consider detrimental to teamwork.

Nokia was a relatively Finnish company in globalizing markets, until the late 1990s, which saw the rise of Nokia's leadership transformation and increasing expansion in large emerging economies. As shown in this chapter (especially in Figure 3.1), Nokia today is an increasingly global company whose headquarters remain largely, but no longer exclusively, in Finland. In the past, Nokia was driven by the Finns. Today, it is increasingly driven by Nokians from Finland as well as many other countries.

To emphasize the international outlook, everyone is required to speak English in Nokia. At home, however, they no longer speak just Finnish or Swedish, or French and German, but also Mandarin and Hindi, Arabic, Spanish, Portuguese and Russian, Urdu and Swahili. Despite all these differences of nationality, language, and culture, what unites Nokians and what they all must have is *sisu*.

Increased Diversity from Across the World

Some companies are driven by their strategy, others by their organization. Nokia's primary force is its people. Every successful organization claims to invest in its people, but not every successful organization truly *empowers* people. As Thomas Jönsson, Nokia's chief of regional communications, puts it, "This is a company that creates and benefits from people power."

With globalization, the nature of this power has shifted; Figure 3.1 shows how the company's personnel has changed and grown by comparing how it looked in 1991, 1997, and 2008.

How Nokia's Values, Culture, and People Contribute to Success

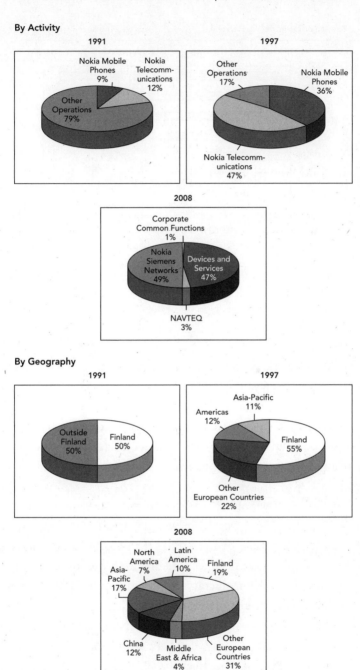

FIGURE 3.1   Distribution of Nokia's Employees from 1991 to 2008

Ten Major Countries by Personnel

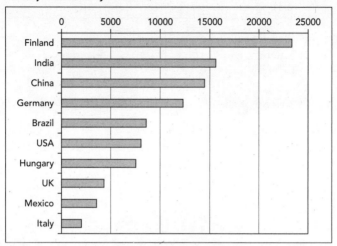

FIGURE 3.1   (*continued*)

As Nokia's markets have soared globally and the company has been transformed internally, the Nokians have grown increasingly global and diverse by origin. Since the early 1990s, Nokia has evolved pretty organically; it has not engaged in high-profile corporate acquisitions (although it could have). It has only been active in incremental and relatively small M&As, which has reinforced its culture and values.

Nonetheless, Nokia never expected to grow so large. Former CEO Ollila said in the late 1990s, "We will not become a company with more than 100,000 people." Unlike IBM's then-CEO Lou Gerstner, Ollila thought that elephants can't dance, and that the bigger the company, the more cumbersome the bureaucracy would be. So instead of hiring more people, Nokia outsourced more processes.

But after partnering with Siemens in 2006, Nokia's infrastructure unit almost tripled overnight. Today, there are some 126,000 Nokians: more than 65,000 in Nokia and more than 60,000 in Nokia Siemens Networks. Half are now in Europe, and more than 28 percent in Asia-Pacific (including 12 percent in China). At the country level, most (20 percent) remain in Finland. And although Nokia operates in the technology sector in which Silicon Valley remains the trendsetter, only 7 percent of Nokians are in North America.

Emphasis on Diversity

Nokia pays special attention to diversity and corporate responsibility. The goal is to enable men and women of different cultural or ethnic backgrounds, skills and abilities, lifestyles, generations, and perspectives to contribute their best to the company's success. Diversity is seen at the heart of Nokia's business success and values.

But it was not always this way. In the 1990s, a few people had not even heard the word *diversity,* recalls Hallstein Moerk, Nokia's executive vice president of human resources. "When you are in a global company and your home base represents less than 1 percent of your revenues, there is just no way that you can operate a global company without having an inclusive environment."

Today, Nokia is increasingly global and diverse:

- It has device manufacturing in nine countries, infrastructure equipment manufacturing in four countries, R&D in sixteen countries, and sales in more than 150 countries.

- Of Nokia's overall workforce, less than half of employees are European (49 percent).

- The rest come from Asia-Pacific (17 percent), China (12 percent), Latin America (11 percent), North America (7 percent), and the Middle East and Africa (4 percent).

Nokia's management diversity is reflected by the fact that general management is dispersed in fifty countries and represents almost as many nationalities.

- Of the middle and senior management, the majority are still Finns (52 percent) and Europeans (24 percent).

- However, a proportion of the rest—North Americans (13 percent), Asian (7 percent), Latin American (1 percent), and Middle Eastern (less than 1 percent)—is growing more rapidly.

- Nokia has localized very quickly and successfully, especially in large emerging economies.

- In India, for example, practically *all* middle and senior management positions are occupied by Indians. In China, roughly one of every two managers is Chinese.

Gender Diversity Matters

At Nokia, egalitarianism is not just about equity in general, but also about equity among men and women. "That's why Nokia is very attractive among Indian women," says Nokia India's head D. Shivakumar. "In our Chennai facilities, almost three of four are women," he points out, referring to India's fifth most populous city (formerly known as Madras), located on the coast of the Bay of Bengal.

In this regard, the company also reflects its Nordic roots. Like Norway, Sweden, Iceland, and Denmark, Finland is among the world leaders in closing the gender gap between men and women, according to the overall rankings by the *Global Gender Gap Report 2009*. In stark contrast, the United States and the largest European economies (such as Germany, the United Kingdom, and France) are not even among the top ten, and Japan remains far behind (ninety-eighth in 2008).[3]

Much work remains, but Nokia and Nokia Siemens Networks (NSN) are committed to promoting diversity and inclusion in the workplace and providing rewarding career development opportunities for all employees.[4] "I never experienced [a glass ceiling] in Nokia," says Sari Baldauf, Nokia's former leader and one of the most influential female executives worldwide until she stepped down in 2006.[5]

If, however, culture is central to Nokia's success, how can the company sustain its drive as it becomes increasingly global? This dilemma accounts for the Nokia executives' almost obsessive preoccupation with values—the global glue that can drive, energize, and inspire Nokians from the CEO and his senior executives to the frontline employees.

A Shared Purpose Through Values

When Nokia's rivals attract new talent, many talk about professional challenges, money, and stock options. In contrast (and to the surprise of their interviewees), Nokia's executives often talk about life and values. "I thought Pekka Ala-Pietilä would ask me about marketing," recalls Keith Pardy, former head of Nokia's strategic marketing, who had his job interview during a dinner. "Instead, he asked me about life and my values. It was amazing! If the company was anything like the values Pekka talked about, I felt I wanted to be a part of it." Pardy's story is not an exception.

"A company that is led by values has the best chance to become the most effective one because when people have thought through these values and share them, they will want to give the best they have," says Pekka Ala-Pietilä, former president of Nokia (1999–2005) and Nokia Mobile Phones (1992–1998). Every company has values, regardless of whether those have been created consciously or unconsciously. However, few companies, including Nokia, have created common values that people can commit to. In other words, it is a corporate culture that has been purposefully created on the basis of values. In the 1990s, some associated value management with "soft values"; in reality, it is probably the most demanding management style for leaders but it generates great results. A leader needs to lead by example: to "walk the talk." Shared values and leadership by example nurture a culture in which people can become more committed and personally exposed. As an outcome this means higher creativity and better results than expected. Interestingly enough, there is *no room* for fear as a management tool in this kind of culture. That's very different from a "command and control" culture in which most employees instinctively protect themselves and are more cautious and calculative with their commitment.

Stretch, Trust, Humility, and Teams

If you had looked for a job in Nokia," says Ala-Pietilä, "I would have asked you simply and sincerely: 'What's the meaning of life for you?' This simple question opens the door to the world of personal beliefs and values and also gives the opportunity for me to explain Nokia values at a very personal level."

In building the corporate culture only "walking the talk" counts, says Pekka Ala-Pietilä. "Hence the nomination of people for new jobs—regardless of whether they are internally promoted or externally recruited—became the cornerstone for our cultural (r)evolution."

There was a set of core personal attitudes that played an important role in the selection process. First was the capability and keenness to set stretch goals that exceeded the current individual and organizational performance. Next was the individual's capability to create trust-based relationships so that the networking-based organization could work effectively. This kind of trust was tested daily in interactions among people and teams. When you manage to create a trust-based culture you have also produced one of the best medicines against corporate politicking. Both intellectual and emotional honesty are key ingredients in harnessing trust-based teams. The third attitude is best described by the Finnish word *nöyryys,* which doesn't translate well to English. The best way of defining it would be a nonarrogant, noncomplacent way of working. This humility was equally important when Nokia achieved great successes and when it faced its failures. And finally, Nokians expect you to be able to work in and as a team. You must be able to think of yourself, your team, and the company as a whole. "When a team truly shares these values of stretch, trust, and humility," says Ala-Pietilä, "then if anything can be done, they *will* be able to do it, as a team."

Values Motivate the Shared Purpose

"What Nokia has done very well is that it has built a great value base," says Hallstein Moerk, Nokia's HR chief. The success of Nokia relies on attracting, developing, and retaining the most talented people. It requires an environment that nurtures creativity and the collective realization of individual ideas. People are inspired and energized by purpose, but ultimately they are committed to the values that motivate the purpose. "Values keep an international company together, like glue," contends former CEO Jorma Ollila. "In building commitment, they are a far better instrument than money or options."

As Nokia's strategic task has become increasingly complex, its organizational units have become more dispersed. The importance of the shared understanding of the broad direction and priorities has grown accordingly. As Nokia opted for the global focus strategy, it also began to develop a strong sense of purpose, which is communicated effectively to managers and employees worldwide; initially top-down but today bottom-up as well.

Clarity, Continuity, and Consistency

Indeed, building a shared vision has relied on the clarity of purpose, continuity in pursuing it, and a consistency in interpreting it across the organization. It is a shared vision that is reflected well by Nokia's slogan, "Connecting People." The seemingly simple statement focuses managers' attention on the company's broad strategic thrust.[6]

Nokia's managers are almost on a mission. They want to make a contribution. The vision of "Connecting People" is a very strong motivator. It is not just about mobile products and services but also implies values that drive growth and prosperity. After all, higher mobile penetration and usage is typically associated with a higher level of economic and human development. Like Google, Nokia has grown very fast; it has a strong mission and people who like to do good things. "You can make money without doing evil" is one of Google's slogans. "That's a very strong mission, but Nokia is not that different," says Sari Baldauf. "It has a good leadership, and a good cause."

During the organizational transformation in 2007, Nokia's chief development officer Mary McDowell and her colleagues began to reexplore the company's slogan. Initially, "Connecting People" meant making a phone call. Now Nokia is in an era of mobile devices and Internet-based services and solutions. Voice will remain a vital part of the portfolio, but there are new services and new capabilities that are going to be accessed through mobile devices. The content of the corporate mission is shifting, but the foundational values remain largely the same.

Despite dramatic changes in the global operating environment and organizational requirements, Nokia has remained committed to a core set of strategic goals and organizational values. It is this continuity that accounts for the endurance of the unifying vision. Conversely, it is the consistency of the purpose across diverse and dispersed organizational units across the world that ensures that this vision is truly shared by all. Continuity and consistency augment change and disruption. Enduring principles go hand in hand with the willingness to make bold strategic moves. "Creative destruction means the end of the old," says Lauri Kivinen, NSN's chief of corporate relations. "This is not seen as fatal or detrimental to Nokia's legacy and continuity. In this regard, Nokia and Intel are similar."[7]

Despite its rapid growth, Nokia continues to emphasize a corporate culture of an independent, innovative, and creative startup.[8] On the one hand, the objective has been to maintain this culture no matter how large Nokia might become. On the other hand, the Nokians understand that corporate cultures evolve and especially in fast-changing environments, such as theirs. In the past two decades, Nokia's culture has changed, and Nokians have changed their culture. The best way to achieve these dual objectives is to impart Nokia's values to everyone in the organization globally, with local emphasis on different aspects depending on national culture.

How Nokia Promotes Its Values Around the World

The importance of Nokia's values has only increased over time, just as they have grown "less Finnish" and "more global," as one senior executive puts it. "Now that the organization is so much larger, the real question is: How should the culture evolve?" says Sari Baldauf, Nokia's former senior executive.[9]

Nokia is coping with massive geographic shifts as the majority of the user base is migrating to large, emerging economies, along with increasing economic power. Due to its global strategy, Nokia does not want to have practices that vary by country. The company recognizes and celebrates differences between cultures, but it seeks to cultivate basic values that are common and provide a foundation to all Nokians, including those in the large emerging economies. "It's very easy to underestimate the human capital in China; it's a huge force and it's developing extremely fast," says Moerk.[10]

Some Nokian executives believe that its values are actually better understood in emerging economies, whose rapid economic development is contributing to the rapid pace of overall modernization. In China, such values as engagement, passion for innovation, and achieving together have worked well. "As everything is changing in China, people are open to change and innovation," says Colin Giles, Nokia's former China chief. "We have used both 'Connecting People' but also 'Human Technology' [as slogans]. Both work well in China. Our technology comes from humanity."[11]

In India, Nokia grew into the largest multinational in barely a decade and a half, leaving behind multinationals that had been in India for ages, such as British Tobacco and Unilever. Today Nokia is India's most trusted brand. "What Nokia has done right is that it is consistently recruiting people strictly for Nokia values," says Nokia's head of India D. Shivakumar. "Values come first, and so does the perspective for the future. For instance, when I was recruited, I was told that 'today we may be a $1 billion firm, but we want people who can run a $5 billion company in India.' You're competing for the future."

Because of increasing prosperity and higher education in emerging economies, the Nokians expect that over time diversity will become less of a cultural issue and more about differences in perspectives.

Nokia currently has employees from 120 countries. For many—particularly those in large emerging economies—working at the company means a world of new opportunities. In turn, Nokia seeks to create an environment in which all employees can fulfill their potential by leading or participating in projects that have global impact. Values are not seen as "just words"; the shared philosophy is to *live* them on a daily basis. When Kallasvuo took charge of Nokia as CEO in 2007, there was a natural opportunity window to review the values.[12]

Nokia and Nokia Siemens Networks are separate entities. Their values are similar, but not identical.

Values of Nokia

Today, Nokia's set of values, developed by employees around the world, reflects and supports its business and changing environment. The values act as a foundation for Nokia's evolving business culture and form the basis of how it operates:

- *Achieving together,* to reflect how the Nokians reach out to others, encouraging them to work together and share risks, responsibilities, and successes

- *Very human,* to reflect how the Nokians do business and work with each other

- *Engaging you,* to reflect how Nokia engages its customers, its suppliers, and its own employees in what it stands for

- *Passion for innovation,* to reflect Nokia's curiosity about the world around us and the Nokians' desire to improve people's lives through innovation in technology

Nokia's values and culture cultivate a strong emotional affiliation. "Nokia is my life," says Colin Giles, current head of global sales, who has been with the company for close to two decades. "This is an organization of like-minded people who are all driven by similar values aiming at the same objective. I feel I am part of a family, with intense loyalty and with a very emotional attachment."

Like a family, the company provides a supportive foundation for agreement *and* disagreement. People can talk about things openly and bottom-up. Finnish openness is often a cultural shock to many. "We have had employees from firms which have almost literally the same values as Nokia," says KP Wilska, Nokia's former chief of Americas. "After six months in Nokia, they will say, 'Wow, we have the same values, but in Nokia these values are *really* alive. If you disagree with your boss, you won't be laid off next week.' That's what makes Nokia different."

Nokia encourages open discussion and debate within the business. An annual global employee survey is conducted as a way of getting feedback from employees on a range of important issues, and the company does act on this feedback when designing its people policies and practices. In spring 2008, Nokia even set up an intranet soapbox known as Blog-Hub, which was opened to employee bloggers around the world, and a company-sponsored social networking side encourages employees to offer product ideas or to post critiques. The blogs and recommendations are not ignored. When a sales rep in China asked why the styluses sold with touchscreen handsets should be just gray and why customers should not be offered a palette, Nokia soon began shipping phones with spare styluses in different colors.[13] The premise is that internal debate can contribute to consumer welfare because smart ideas will prevail.

Values of Nokia Siemens Networks

Nokia Siemens Networks also has a set of values that reflects and supports its business and the changing environment. In 2007, NSN defined values to reflect the business objectives and values of its people:

- *Focus on our customer,* to reflect the importance of helping customers succeed in their business

- *Communicate openly,* to reflect the importance of speedy, fact-based, and transparent communications

- *Inspire,* to reflect the importance of building excitement within the business, especially about the needs of customers

- *Innovate,* to reflect the focus on innovation to succeed

- W*in together,* to reflect how trust, respect, honesty, and openness form the workplace

"What a contrast it was to come to an open-environment company that had leaders that were engaged and actual managers," says Simon Beresford-Wylie, former CEO of NSN. "Unlike your classic telecom bureaucracy, there was no hierarchy in Nokia. The youthful energy was almost infectious. But the most striking thing was the international value-centric culture." Today, similar values form the basis of how NSN operates.

Certainly, Nokia alone cannot lay claim to modern egalitarian management, but, unlike many of its rivals, it has not gotten stuck in the past. "Nokia's management is driven by a no-bullshit, apolitical, non-hierarchical, open communications, pragmatic, and R&D culture," says Beresford-Wylie. In this, the values play a key role in normative integration, which is critical to the merger of Nokia and Siemens infrastructure units, vis-à-vis NSN. "Culturally, it was a complicated merger of Finnish and German employees as well as those from the rest of the world," adds Beresford-Wylie. "When the Finns looked at Germans, they saw a very formal culture. When the Germans looked at the Finns, they saw a bunch of very reckless people. And when the rest of the world took a look at Finns and Germans, they saw Europeans."[14]

Values Come Before Strategy

At Nokia, values take precedence over strategy and form the basis for the company's globalization activities. Unlike values, tactical plans may change on a very short-term basis, but not values. Unlike strategy, values cannot be changed or even easily revised on an annual basis.

Values also provide guidance for good days and bad days, including for the restructuring necessitated by the global economic crisis. Nokia's HR professionals highlight the need to acknowledge the facts and react quickly. "You need to send a message that restructuring is necessary because otherwise we'd all be in an even worse situation a few months down the road," says Moerk. If some layoffs prove necessary, you have to think carefully how to do that without breaking the values.

Values are Nokia's anchor point for globalization. They are particularly important with partners and officials in emerging economies. "Through your values, you are showing people what kind of organization you are and want to be," says Robert Andersson, Nokia's head of corporate alliances and business development. "That's inherent in your values and how you live life."

At Nokia, values are not taken lightly. Nokia is its values. Nokia's brand is its value proposition. Ultimately, these values are more important than strategy. If strategy is wrong, you can fix it. If values are wrong, nothing can be built on them.

Commitment to Corporate Responsibility

In the Anglo-Saxon tradition, executives increasingly see themselves as caught between critics demanding ever higher levels of corporate social responsibility (CSR) and investors applying pressure to maximize short-term profits. In the past, philanthropy has been used as a form of public relations or advertising, promoting a company's image through high-profile sponsorships. More recently, companies have begun to emphasize a strategic way to think about philanthropy by using charitable efforts to improve their competitive context, particularly the quality of the business environment in the locations where they operate.[15]

Social Dimension Is Only a Part of Corporate Responsibility

The Nokians are pragmatic enough to understand and occasionally apply a strategic way to think about corporate responsibility, but they tend to feel uncomfortable with the idea that philanthropy is all that there is to social responsibility. These views reflect Nokia values and code of conduct, which have been shaped by the Lutheran influence and egalitarian legacy in the Nordic countries.

After all, Nordic Europe is far less polarized than the United States, leading European nations, or Japan in terms of wealth distribution. A rough measure of equity is the so-called Gini coefficient, as illustrated by Figure 3.2. In Finland, polarization is relatively low, as reflected by the coefficient of 27.5 percent, which is 3.5 percent less than the EU average. In the United States, the comparable figure is as high as 45 percent, about the same as in Cambodia or Rwanda.[16] Such differences tend to reflect in the daily activities of companies, their values, and the enforcement of those values.

As the industry leader, the Nokians believe that the best contribution they can make to the global community is to conduct their business in a responsible way. Accordingly, Nokia's corporate responsibility agenda is

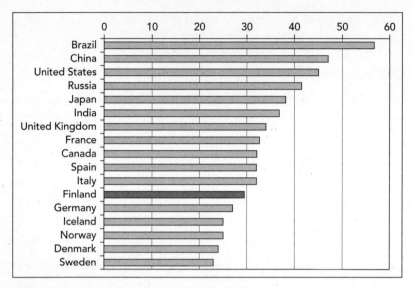

FIGURE 3.2   Home Base: Degree of Inequality*

The Gini coefficient is commonly used as a rough measure of inequality of income and wealth. A low Gini coefficient indicates a more equal distribution, while higher Gini coefficients indicate more unequal distribution. Most developed Nordic countries and Germany have Gini indices less than 30, but the Gini indices for Russia, the United States, China, and Brazil are above 40, reflecting greater inequality.

framed around the Nokia values. The company believes that management of corporate responsibility issues is most effective when sustainability policies and programs are embedded in every aspect of its operations. "Our code of conduct is the way we do things at Nokia globally," says Esko Aho, Nokia's chief of corporate responsibility. "It's a highly valued asset in Nokia and based on our values."

Way to Promote Growth in Emerging Economies

In comparison to U.S. and many Japanese multinationals, Nokia's view of its responsibility as a multinational is broader, more egalitarian, and more proactive. It can be illustrated by the company's pioneering efforts to accelerate economic growth in emerging economies (see Chapter Eight) and at sustainable development (environmental protection, energy efficiency, and climate change). For example, the company supports the

Grameen Bank Foundation on the Village Phone project to bring mobile access to unconnected communities across Africa through microfinance. A major part of the volume and value growth of the global mobile device market is expected to come from low-income segments. Making products and services affordable is essential for this next generation of mobile technology consumers.

Way to Promote Sustainable Development

In fall 2009, the Dow Jones Index named Nokia as the world's most sustainable technology company. Indeed, Nokia considers its stakeholders to be the people who affect or are affected by its business, including investors, customers, governments and regulators, nongovernmental organizations (NGOs), industry organizations, and universities. Instead of seeing the NGOs as adversaries, Nokia often cooperates with them. In particular, it works with a number of NGOs specializing in community and youth development projects around the world. After all, seen from Nokia's headquarters—literally and physically—climate change is not something abstract or distant. The Arctic sea ice cover continues to shrink and become thinner, providing more evidence that the region is warming more rapidly than anticipated.[17]

Nokia has a track record of doing business responsibly while trying to reduce its environmental impact, as reflected by its role in the FTSE4Good and Dow Jones Sustainability indices. It is among the favorites of Greenpeace International.[18] Through the 2000s, environmental policy making in Nokia has been characterized by a very proactive posture.[19]

At Nokia, sustainable development means an environmental strategy, a climate strategy, and energy efficiency. The environmental efforts focus on substance management, energy efficiency, and recycling. Nokia's climate strategy targets all relevant areas that contribute to its direct or indirect CO_2 emissions. "Nokia's strategy is not just about growth, and the convergence of mobile and Internet technologies," says CEO Olli-Pekka Kallasvuo. "It is also about doing business in ways which benefit people, communities, and the environment."

Development of Global Human Resource Management

In 1999, when Hallstein Moerk, Nokia's chief of human resources, joined the company after twenty-two years at Hewlett-Packard, the Norwegian noted that Nokia "used to have many HR tools and systems and nobody could tell how many employees we actually had."

Putting the Basics in Place

Moerk's first step of developing global human resource management at Nokia was all about getting the basic HR tools and systems in place. A good example is Nokia's Performance Management Process (called "Investing in People") and a tool linked to that process, which supports Nokia's employees, managers, and HR globally in administrating the objective setting, performance evaluation, and incentive payout every half year. Performance management in Nokia is based on half-year, short-term planning periods. Other examples are a global recruitment process and tool, equity programs, global mobility (i.e., national and international transfers), recognition plans, retirement plans, and so on. All these processes are guided mostly globally in Nokia, but also need local adaptation and management because Nokia operates in so many countries.

Maximizing Commitment and Engagement

Once the basics were in place, the second step was to maximize the commitment and engagement of the employees. In effect, engagement remains one of the pillars of Nokia's 2009–2010 People Strategy with a focus on development, recognition, and well-being of employees.[20] For years, the company has used the "Listening to You" process, an annual employee satisfaction survey that provides continuous feedback on how employees feel about their work, their team, and their relationship with their manager and the company. Nokia also has an extensive process in place to disseminate the results of this yearly survey to all management levels so that managers improve their achievements and take specific actions on increasing the performance and engagement of their teams. Based on the outcomes of this survey, the Nokians continually study the best practices of highest-scoring internal teams on engagement and benchmark employees internally and externally vis-à-vis industry rivals.

What ultimately drives engagement is Moerk's view that "if you do good things for the employees, you do good things for the company and the society, for the family and dogs and cats and everybody."

Maximizing Organizational Capabilities

When the basics were solidly in place and efforts had been initiated to maximize the employee commitment and engagement, the third step was to begin to maximize the organizational capabilities. That has required a lot of time working with the line management in all of these elements and looking at all drivers that build organizational capability.

For instance, recently the Organizational Development & Change (OD&C) Department in HR has been focused on several initiatives. First, with increasing competition and the rise of mobile computers, Nokians need to be even more innovative and flexible. Second, as Nokia is becoming more of an integrated company, organizational capabilities are enhanced by moving away from silos and breaking down the organizational barriers. Third, the program way of working (see Chapter Two) is becoming more significant as it provides the capability to be flexible and ramp up or ramp down programs more easily than with traditional business units. Finally, Nokia is putting into practice combinations of program-focused and community-focused ways of operating. For instance, the Nokians work with students, designers, and other experts outside the company for product design, business model innovation, and development of Internet services, such as services for millions of phone users in India and Africa, where cultural sensitivity is especially important.

Optimizing the Basics, Engagement, and Capabilities

The fourth step is about continuing to work on these stages and optimizing the basics that are now in place, motivation and engagement, as well as organizational capabilities. Moving forward, a lot of emphasis will be on the new ways of working. "The key question," says Moerk, "is how does a large global company like Nokia actually maximize the best new ways of working *together?*"

Nokia operates in a technology- and marketing-intensive industry, where industry boundaries are often blurry and change is rapid and occasionally discontinuous. In the dynamic environment, even the key competitors may change significantly in a matter of months. Obviously, these drivers must also play a vital role in the human resources function.

Focusing on Flexibility and Global Mindset

In such a fast-changing industry, it is impossible to sit down and devise a neatly structured long-range plan for employees' personal development. Rather, Nokia focuses more on the ability of developing flexibility in individual teams and leaders. The same goes for the staffing function. The premise is that you are not hiring a person for a given job but someone who will be flexible enough to work in different programs.

As organizations have moved from the multinational to international to global stages of corporate evolution, global managers need different skills to lead global companies. Nokia's experience is that people with global mindsets seek to continually expand their knowledge and have a high conceptual capacity to deal with the complexity of global organizations. They are flexible and strive to be sensitive to cultural diversity. Finally, they are able to intuit decisions with inadequate information and have a strong capacity for reflection.

A person with a global mindset thinks and sees the world globally, is open to exchanging ideas and concepts across borders, and is able to break down his or her provincial ways of thinking. The emphasis is placed on balancing global and local needs and being able to operate cross-functionally, cross-divisionally, and cross-culturally around the world.

Focusing on Action Learning, Not Courses

Past limitations and shortcomings in global leadership development have caused many organizations to seek more effective ways to develop leaders. In the process, action learning has quickly become the leadership development methodology of choice for thousands of organizations, including Caterpillar, Novartis, DuPont, and Nokia. In the 1990s, Nokia's employee development was still largely focused on training. It was about which courses an employee would take this year and which ones he or she wanted to take next year. Those days are gone. In their businesses, Nokians have discovered that learning comes from action, experiences, new jobs, living in a new country, and participating in new projects. The emphasis has gone from training to action learning settings.

As Nokians need to increase their agility and capacity for change in a fast-moving and highly competitive world, they seek to improve the capacity to learn fast and act on the challenges that face them. To improve and expand their approach, they have been using an inquiry process to understand what has worked well with action learning in the past and how they can improve the linkages among business strategy, learning, and organizational development. They have also clarified the "Nokia action learning" approach to make it more consistent when implementing it more widely in the organization.

Recruitment of Diverse Team Players Worldwide

With Nokia's global expansion and the importance of large emerging economies, recruitment processes have become worldwide by nature. The company puts a great emphasis on teamwork—not only at the executive level but at all levels of the company. "This emphasis is very prevalent in looking at who's hired into Nokia, who succeeds, and how people rotate in Nokia," says Rick Simonson, head of Nokia Mobile Phones.

Targeting the Best and the Brightest

Nokia's HR professionals say they do not target particular universities. They claim to recruit from good universities across the world. Because the Nokians believe that they can develop good people to be really excellent, they feel they don't need to recruit only in the highest-ranked universities. If the aim is to hire good *team* players, you do not always try to hire the stars because sometimes the stars are not good team players.

In terms of hiring, the Nokians do go after the younger candidates, though not exclusively, seeking passion, energy, and good values. Will these people enjoy working in teams? Do they have high integrity? Those are the characteristics they are looking for. But they also want to have a lot of diversity in the organization, along with basic values.

Attracting Talent Worldwide to Ensure Diversity

In terms of recruiting and geography, Nokia has deep roots in Finland and thus an overrepresentation of Finnish nationals (as mentioned, 20 percent of its employees are Finnish). First of all, in order to ensure adequate diversity in the organization, Nokia continues to hire worldwide and quite aggressively in critical areas. For example, London-based Symbian Foundation, which builds the operating system used in most Nokia smartphones, has an office in the Silicon Valley and was recruiting heavily, even amid the global economic crisis and the U.S. recession. "People say, 'What do you mean—you're hiring?'" says Larry Berkin, Symbian's head of global alliances.[21]

Second, Nokia recruits for creativity and innovation. If most employees come from the same neighborhoods, live in the same type of houses, and drive the same cars, preconditions for creativity and innovation will be weak.

Third, Nokians want to build one of the best consumer-driven companies in the world, so it recruits locally, around the world. "We want to understand the consumers," says Moerk. "And it's easier for a Chinese national to understand the Chinese consumers. You want a cut of your people to be similar to your customer base."

Although Nokians are working to scale up the relative role of Asian middle- and high-level managers in the company, they see diversity as a long-term exercise. "If you try to achieve appropriate diversity in a very short period of time, you end up doing the wrong things," says Moerk. "You end up creating quotas, not hiring the right people, and the right caliber. You need to have time."

Using Rigorous Interviews and Behavioral Interviewing

To ensure the "right stuff," Nokia's interviewing process is rigorous, with extensive interviewing by executives and employees to ensure proper fit. The interview techniques are not that different from other large companies, but Nokians like to do a series of interviews and have a long, thorough interviewing and selection process.

Like many other large companies, Nokia is also using behavioral interviewing. When hiring people, the Nokians try to find out how they will behave in different situations and how they will fit with the culture and values. "If we have a 'command and control' type of a person who likes to yell and so on," smiles Moerk, "we'll probably say, hmm, you have the kind of leadership skills that will probably not be a fit with us. We are looking for leaders who generate energy in a different way."

Development of Managers and Leaders

Once the company has identified managers that are more sensitive to the requirements of international business, it can begin to develop their potential through management training and development processes. Training and development emphasize professional and personal growth.[22] Today, Nokia's great brand name and reputation for culture help attract talent. "The better the leaders, brand, and reputation, the more you attract good leadership talent," says Moerk. "It's a virtuous circle."

On the development side, Nokia has been acknowledged as one of the top players worldwide.[23] As to the retention of the executive talent, the Nokians know that the number one reason employees leave the company is that they do not like their boss. The second reason is that they do not like their team. And the third is that they do not think that they are working on the right things. Therefore, Nokia can retain its talent with good bosses that the employees can like and respect, good teams that they enjoy participating in, and work that focuses on the right areas.

Nokia's distinctive management and leadership approach is based on its culture and values. Personal growth through self-leadership provides the foundation for successful management and leadership practices. "Career development in Nokia is driven by a set of key principles, which comprise career 'self-reliance,' our '70–20–10' philosophy, as well as career drivers and development paths," says Rita Vanhauwenhuyse, a Compaq-HP veteran who headed Nokia's HR strategic solutions globally.

The implementation tools include career development workshops and personal development plans.

Philosophy of Real-Life Experiences

Around 2003 Nokia started to work with action learning, the "70–20–10" approach, a concept that immediately captured Nokia's attention because it built on something the Nokians truly believe in. It is based on the idea that:

- 70 percent of your learning derives from actual experience and concrete applications and is by nature experiential (here learning-by-doing is what really matters)

- 20 percent of your learning is gained by increasing self-awareness through personal evolution, which is gained by reflecting constantly on how one is evolving as an individual (this is done through coaching, assessments, and mentoring, which are a form of experiential learning, too)

- 10 percent of your learning comes from adding knowledge by participating in e-learning, lectures, seminars, and workshops where someone talks and you learn by listening (this is more passive by nature but can be useful for enhancing professional skills in the early days of your career)

In the development of managers and leaders, individual balance depends on the seniority and experience of the program participants. For example, less experience requires more "10" type of training and more seniority will require a higher use of "70," but the weight of "20" is always equally important. The overall aim is to shift the balance in the overall portfolio toward the 70 and 20, but still provide top-notch quality 10.

Career Drivers and Development Paths

Overall, Nokia empowers its management and executive talent through career "self-reliance."[24] However, different career development paths are supported by different personal characteristics. For example, employees

88

who value expertise, stability, and security gravitate toward lifelong focus on one specialty, that is, expertise. In contrast, employees who are more driven by power, achievement, and influence tend to be more competitive and seek fast progression up the career ladder. Overall, certain personal drivers tend to reinforce associated career development paths that emphasize expertise, competitiveness, learning, and entrepreneurship.

Since the early 2000s, Nokia has also paid increasing attention to mentoring. Each member of the executive team mentors two to six young and upcoming leaders. The intention is to have mentoring aligned with overall strategy and other initiatives.

Transitions in the Leadership Journey

Working closely with Nokia's corporate strategists, the management and leadership development (MLD) team also cooperates with a small pool of international consultants and top-quality international business schools, such as Wharton and Duke, which have often been selected on the basis of experience and experiential learning. As Nokia has been implementing its most recent structural and cultural organizational changes, the team has been renewing its leadership development portfolio.

This portfolio provides a set of learning initiatives, interventions, and approaches that the company implements in order to develop great leaders. The focus is on four transitional moments in the leadership journey, and certain key capabilities and behaviors characterize each of these transition moments:

- The first transition occurs when the future Nokian leader serves as a line manager or in project teams.

- The second transition takes place when he or she is managing other managers.

- The third moment of transition follows when he or she is a leader of a business or a function.

- The last transition takes place at an executive level, as a leader of multiple businesses.

The goal of management and leadership development is first to build a strong "Lead Yourself" awareness, which will pave the foundation for building the "Lead Your Team" capabilities and, ultimately, for building the "Lead Your Business" capabilities.

The portfolio comprises transition solutions and complementary solutions. There are many such programs, from "Voyager" to "Compass."[25] At the highest level, the "Panorama" program has had a special role. In one way or another, most executives are involved with it. "People wanted to take it, they were motivated, and GEB members served as mentors in these programs" says Matti Alahuhta, Nokia's former senior executive. "When I participated, it had pioneering speakers, project presentations that were viewed by members of the executive team. It enabled higher management to think holistically."

The Four Leadership Functions

Nokia's leadership model starts from creating a vision, having a strategy, and making sure that the goals are shared. The management and leadership development team has developed a framework of twenty leadership competencies, which are grouped under eight dimensions and described in behavioral terms. The framework is predicated on strong values, culture, and teams. The focus is on four leadership functions.

- In the strategy domain, developing the vision is a core function of leadership. It is about defining the direction and setting out how to get there. Leaders need to accurately analyze the facts and to establish a sense of urgency where change is required. They also need to establish a mission, develop a convincing and appealing vision of the future, and outline the strategy by which it can be achieved. Developing the vision is not about a lone leader having an idea; it is about bringing together the relevant and necessary "forces" and getting the buy-in of that team to lead the change related to the vision.

- In order to share their goals, leaders need to be able to communicate them, along with the vision. They also need to set objectives and take decisions that embody the strategic direction of the organization.

Interacting with internal and external stakeholders ensures that everyone is on the same page and understands the new goals. Leaders have to establish coalitions and networks and influence people to get goals accepted and internalized, which also implies that leaders themselves model the necessary behaviors.

- In order to gain adequate support, leaders need to motivate others to achieve the goals. This requires leaders to recognize concerns and reconcile people with the change agenda to get full engagement and support for the vision and strategy. Leaders need to empower broad-based action and remove barriers to change while keeping support even when under pressure or facing setbacks.

- In order to deliver success, the effective implementation of strategy requires operational efficiency and commercial understanding. This means clarifying for people the links between their behaviors and the goals and changing the structures that influence peoples' behaviors, through drivers and barriers. Delivering success requires a fine balance between leadership and management to ensure operational efficiency and growth in the organization.

In the past, the management and leadership development programs targeted primarily Nokia's high-potential managers. The team now regards everybody as a potential leader in the organization.[26] Individual Nokians understand the ramifications, as evidenced by a simple anecdote:

Amid the integration of Nokia Siemens Networks, the Nokians and Siemens got a team together to talk about the cultures of the two companies. They were asked to draw a picture of the company. It was a powerful ship that featured the captain at the top, his lieutenants at the next level, then the crew. In this amazingly structured hierarchy, each level and each person had a specific function. Then the Nokians were asked to draw a picture of Nokia. Instead of a ship, they drew a group of fish swimming together. At one point, the group seemed to have a leader, but when something changed in the environment, the fish took an altogether different direction with a different leader, depending on which fish had the best instinct at the time.

That's the story of Nokia's values, culture, and people in a nutshell. Increasingly diverse Nokians are building a shared purpose through values. And they are doing so in teams whose leaders alternate in terms of the strategic task at hand—or "best instinct at the time."

In addition to current challenges, including demographic changes,[27] Nokia's human resources must cope with extraordinary challenges around the world. Ultimately, Nokia must develop employees, managers, and executives who can deal with autonomy, empowerment, and diverse responsibilities in a highly distributed organization while it is producing tens of millions of mobile devices each month. That requires a high degree of *empowerment*—individual responsibility within a distributed organization that emphasizes the role of teamwork.

Nonetheless, making use of legacy and globalization, an appropriate strategy, values, culture, and people will not be enough unless the organization is structured in a way that will support strategic goals worldwide. That is the story told in Chapter Four, which describes how Nokia's far-flung global network can work effectively.

Nokia's Lessons

- In the early phases of its globalization, Nokia was driven by Finnish perseverance (*sisu*), which still drives its values worldwide, along with humility. Perseverance allows people to fulfill highly ambitious yet realistic strategic goals, while humility deters complacency in triumph and resignation in failure.

- To a small-country multinational, diversity of the workforce (e.g., ethnicity, nationality, gender, and so on) is not a recipe for failure but the precondition of success. However, it must be achieved patiently and through market-based incentives, not by quotas.

- To paraphrase the old maxim, "man doesn't live by bread alone": material rewards are not an optimal motivator. As illustrated by its slogan "Connecting People," purpose and values play a great role at Nokia, along with perseverance and humility. As the success of the company indicates, shared purpose that is achieved through values can be highly effective.

- The specifics of such values vary across industries. The broader lesson is in the process by which they are formulated and implemented. Nokia's success is based on a shared purpose that is driven by values that are negotiated by the entire company—top-down by the executive team and bottom-up by individual employees.

- Nokia's success is based on corporate responsibility that permeates all aspects of the company's activities, from innovative ways of promoting growth in developing countries to sustainability (protection of environment, struggle against climate change, and energy efficiency).

- In the early days of rapid growth, success often breeds success and attracts great talent. In the long term, success requires sustained efforts to develop global human resource management by putting the HR basics in place and maximizing commitment and engagement, as well as through organizational capabilities.

4

BUILDING A GLOBALLY NETWORKED MATRIX ORGANIZATION

To cope with rapid environmental change, the ability to take advantage of globalization, the right strategy, and the right culture is necessary, as we have seen in Chapters One, Two, and Three. But this capability is insufficient unless it is supported by the right structure. Historically, Nokia's executives have paid special attention to building organizational capabilities. While seeking a balance between business and geography, the Nokians have moved from an area structure to a worldwide product structure, with their flat, team-driven, and globally networked matrix organization.[1] In the past, geographic regions were important because technology standards were regional; today, business rules at the expense of geography.[2] Let's take a closer look at how this networked organization has developed and how it works.

Building Organizational Capability for Changing Markets

"We've always been in a changing environment, and thereby a changing organization," says Robert Andersson, who until recently was Nokia's chief of manufacturing and logistics and now heads its corporate alliances and business development, including cooperation with Microsoft. Initially

Nokia had several business units, and each was responsible for its own business. The executive team simply confirmed the unit-based strategies. When Nokia focused on mobile communications globally in 1992, then-CEO Jorma Ollila created business group boards, which comprised both corporate and group executives. In this transitional form, the executive team got closer to the strategic business unit. Concurrently Nokia began to divest all noncore properties (as described in Chapter One). Over time, Nokia has evolved from a highly decentralized structure to more of a centralized organization.

Typical Stages of Company Growth

In the past, much managerial focus in multinational companies has been on the organizational structure and trying to find a "fit" between competitive forces and strategic imperatives. In the popular "stages model," the organizational structure is determined by the number of products sold internationally and the relative importance of international sales to the company. The model can be used to illustrate Nokia's path toward a matrixlike organization.[3]

At the early stage of foreign expansion, worldwide companies tend to manage their international operations through an *international division*. Over time, those companies that expand internationally without substantially increasing their foreign product diversity prefer an *area structure*. Other companies that expand internationally by increasing foreign product diversity tend to adopt a *worldwide product division* structure. These stages are descriptive, not prescriptive. Each company has its own unique path. However, when both foreign product diversity and foreign sales increase, companies may try a *global matrix*.

From the early 1990s to the early 2000s, most of Nokia's sales originated from just two divisions (infrastructure, handsets). As it completed the divestments in the late 1990s, it also sought to improve its local and regional responsiveness and to harmonize internal processes and management systems by implementing a groupwide area organization in the Americas and in Asia-Pacific in 1997. The global profit responsibility, however, continued to be assigned to the key business groups. Since the late 1990s, Nokia has steadily engaged in efforts to stimulate synergies among various emerging business segments.

Initially, then, Nokia's emphasis was on an area-based structure. Over time, it has shifted toward a worldwide product structure. More recently, it has moved closer to a global matrix.

Tradeoffs of Working in a Matrix Organization

Like other matrix cases, Nokia invests substantially in R&D, and expenditures for new product development continue to climb. Mobile devices and networks are fairly standardized and require high-volume factories. At the same time, Nokia's operations require much cross-border coordination. Individual countries do not design and manufacture their own mobile devices. Rather, the business units manage development and manufacturing. "Coordination" would not be an optimal term for this management; as Jorma Ollila used to put it, when people are coordinating things, they usually aren't doing anything. There is an important cultural point to the anecdote: Nokia has little use for people who tell others what they should do; the Nokians tend to be people who take responsibility for what they do, so that intermediary levels of "coordinators" are not needed.

In brief, Nokia has a very broad and diverse portfolio of products, and its key rivals are global players. Strong businesses dominate over strong geographies.

In truly dynamic and global competition, most Nokians see the matrix as often cumbersome but practically inevitable. It is a means, not the objective. "What's most important for us is the teamwork," says Nokia's HR chief Hallstein Moerk. At Nokia, the matrix is a way to bring together the right people for the right results. The tradeoff with a matrix organization is that it simply takes more time to conclusion, but the Nokians believe that ultimately they get better results because more people have been involved and committed.

Another tradeoff with a matrix has to do with murky reporting relationships. Those Nokians who value individualism, autonomy, and entrepreneurship struggle most with the structure. "Due to the open atmosphere, Nokia has thrived with and without the matrix," says a former, skeptical Nokian executive.[4] The matrix can make decision making ambiguous and thereby grind the whole process to a halt, as Nokia discovered in the early 2000s. "In the past, there was a lot of ambiguity as to how we would work and live together," says Nokia's corporate development officer Mary McDowell. In the new structure, the priorities are clearer, all the way to device R&D.[5]

Nokia is not alone. In the past, many companies have been frustrated by the matrix and, by the late 1970s, several firms concluded that a "matrix doesn't work," typically citing the following reasons:

- Instead of diversity of perspectives, it has aggravated dissension within the organization.

- And instead of greater flexibility, dual reporting has cultivated conflict and confusion on multiple levels of organization, which has often been escalated by the basic ingredients of international business: geographic distance, different time zones, languages, and cultures.

For example, Jack Welch, former CEO of GE, admires what Nokia has achieved but does not like the matrix structure. "Matrixes sound great in theory but are hell to put into practice," he says. "For all the good they can do in terms of productivity and knowledge-sharing in multiproduct-line companies, they can really fuzz up reporting relationships."[6]

Why Nokia's Matrix Works

Often the pitfall has not been the matrix itself but an incomplete or inappropriate implementation. In too many cases, matrix implementations have focused on structure rather than on supporting changes in processes, incentives, or people. The secret of Nokia's success in implementing the matrix is its culture, and the secret of its success in instilling its culture is its matrix. "If you have global ambitions, you have to have an organization that can support that goal," says Nokia's Chairman Jorma Ollila. "It's a cultural issue that you must drive into the DNA."

A matrix organization also requires complementary changes to the IT system, planning and budgeting processes, performance management, and other systems.[7] In contrast to companies with costly matrix failures, Nokia does not have reporting systems that are built and run as separate instances among different geographies or countries. In fact, Nokia was one of the first to globalize an electronic reporting system (ERP) that runs its supply chain, factories, and the resulting billing and accounting system. With SAP's system, Nokians are running what they believe is one of the largest single integrated electronic reporting systems in the world. "It makes the organization much more efficient, gives us scale, cost advantage, and timeliest information," says Nokia's former CFO Richard A. Simonson. Typically, when Nokia acquires or integrates a company, it rolls those systems into its own.[8]

Balancing Business and Geography

The core structure of the matrix can be simplified to a business-geography matrix. In a typical business-dominant matrix, business unit managers are responsible for more decisions, control more of the budget, and have a stronger voice. In this structure, the balance of power tilts the matrix toward the business and functional axes. The determinants that influence power are

- A high degree of cross-border coordination (high fixed costs, relatively homogeneous markets and standardized products, global customers, competitors, and suppliers, as well as high transportability)

- Relatively passive local institutions (government, unions)

- A high diversity of the international business portfolio (because of multiple businesses and different business systems)

In contrast, in a typical geography-dominant matrix, it is the country chiefs who have the key role, and the determinants that influence power are the reverse of those in a business-dominant matrix. Figure 4.1 illustrates this comparison.

The flexibility of the matrix was vital to Nokia amid the dark days of the great global economic crisis in 2008–2009. Instead of costly

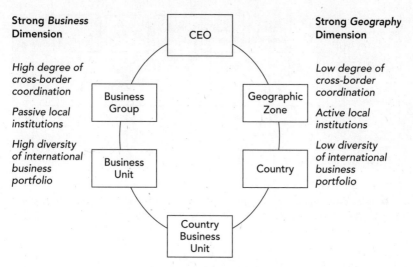

FIGURE 4.1 Core Matrix: Balancing Business and Geography

restructuring, Nokia was able to sense and respond to rapidly changing events by recalibrating the balance of power through its matrix. The simple rule of thumb is that during periods of rapid global growth, rising trade, and investment, business reigns over geography; whereas, during periods of stagnating global growth and protectionism, geography reigns over business, as shown in Figure 4.2 (although different patterns apply differently in different countries).

From the standpoint of the Nokians, a rigid, heavy-layered, and non-communicative organization is simply incompatible with the strategic imperatives of contemporary international business. You can't have more than seven to eight layers from the CEO to the front line in the factory or sales force, says Nokia's Chairman Jorma Ollila. "Thin layers enable efficient communication and learning from your mistakes. If you don't learn, what's the benefit of global reach?"

Today, Nokia, strictly speaking, has a functional/matrix organization. The adoption of a business-dominant matrix does not mean that geography is entirely subject to a strong business dimension. More recently, there has been a shift in Nokia to be more centralized and, in that sense, a more globally driven organization.

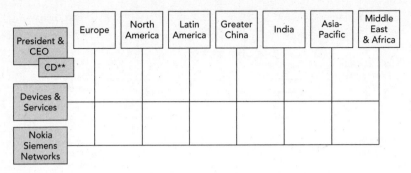

FIGURE 4.2   Nokia's Core Matrix*

*The figure features Nokia's core matrix. It does not portray the horizontal units of Nokia's digital mapping unit, NAVTEQ, or the wide array of project teams.
**CD, Corporate Development Unit

In certain regions, Nokia does localize. For example, since the early 1990s, the importance of the local dimension has steadily increased, especially in large markets, such as China, India, and, more recently, the United States. With increasing global competition, local competition has grown more intense. "You must have modular structures so that you can optimally take advantage of local markets," says Matti Alahuhta, Nokia's former senior executive. "Local sensitivity has increased in the business."

China is one of these priority markets as Nokia's largest market, greatest revenue base, expanding R&D site, and one of the largest employee locations. Overall, Nokians continue to apply the global approach in China, but localization is also necessitated by cultural differences in terms of empowerment and assertiveness. In Nordic countries, the basic approach to matrix is *empowerment,* but this is not always received well in China and much of Asia. "In a matrix organization, empowerment means that a Finnish boss in Finland would expect that solid-line directions come from him. But in China the subordinate is looking for daily, detailed directions that are better given by someone working closely with them. So they start to treat their local boss as the solid-line manager. It doesn't always work too well," says Colin Giles, Nokia's former Greater China chief.

The other challenge is *assertiveness*. In order to be successful, Nokians are expected to argue for their case. "The Finns are direct, straight, and assertive in their own way, especially the Nokia Finns," says Giles. "The assertiveness can be a contrast to Chinese and Asian values that are more indirect, diplomatic, and generally aren't assertive."

Typically, Nokia also needs strong country managers. After all, an increasing proportion of its sales originates from large emerging economies, which often have active host governments and customers. To serve these customers, Nokia wants to be seen as a local player, but in a specific sense. Unlike Ericsson, Nokia does not want to have manufacturing in many host countries. It does not want to be a traditional manufacturer; but it wants to be a strong local player, with local presence and, as CEO Kallasvuo likes to put it, many homes. It seeks to have core production facilities in key regions, in order to be close to the customer.

Obviously, senior executives cannot be expected to be knowledgeable about all these geographies. From the regional or country perspective, there remains a strong line element in Nokia. For example, consider the role of the Greater China chief (Chris Leong) in Nokia's matrix organization. In that role, she has a direct line manager, and targets are set globally. She runs a regional management team which is cross-functional, and many members of that team do not have a working relationship with her. Like her, they have a global reporting responsibility. Still, everybody accepts that she is the focal point and provides common direction for Nokia's activities in China. In turn, she accepts that these team members have their local target that they need to adhere to and that when they meet, they focus on the regional level.

As a formal organizational structure, the matrix can be complicated. But when it is built on common understanding over values, strategy, and culture, it can work. "In practice, most Nokians don't *feel* that they're working in a complex structure," says Thomas Jönsson, who heads Nokia's regional communications. What makes Nokia distinctive and where it also differs from a pure matrix organization is the great emphasis on teamwork and diverse task groups.[9] Trying to develop a matrix on a structural basis only—that is, without the kind of values, culture, and people that are the necessary supporting foundation—is a recipe to failure.

In Nokia, the culture and the values support the matrix, which provides a flexible structure to the values. "The good news with the matrix is that you must take into account the benefit of others, too," says Lauri Kivinen, NSN chief of corporate relations. "It differs from a pure competitive organization in which it is more difficult to strengthen or optimize the interest of the whole."

Nokia's Structure Today: Toward the "Pure" Matrix

In 1992, Nokia initiated its global focus strategy, but the governance structure remained largely intact. Instead of some dozen business groups, now there were only two, mobile phones and networks (later these were augmented with the venture organization). Until 2004, these groups were led relatively independently. In practice, then, the strategic and operative leadership of the company involved the heads of the business groups, while the technology standard GSM (Global System for Mobile communications) kept them united. As these businesses grew bigger and more global, they also became more independent. Meanwhile, GSM was augmented by new standards. As a result, the glue that kept the whole together began to give in. In the past, Ollila provided the goals to the business groups. Nokia did not yet have an integrated business model. Complexity was in the business groups.

With increasing competition globally, Nokia moved toward a more integrated model in 2004. That meant a strong and multidimensional matrix structure, with horizontal and vertical units. From the standpoint of the organization, this was a dramatic change. The good news was that the implementation began during a time when the business was again thriving, especially in the large emerging economies. Concurrently, change sped up the generational change. The old structure rewarded independent managers; the new one cultivated leadership that emphasized interdependency. "It was a huge, huge change," thinks Mikko Kosonen, Nokia's then-head of strategy and CIO. "It had important implications not just for the structure, but for the culture as well."

From this perspective, the organizational change of 2008 was "more of the same." Independent business groups were replaced by a massive single unit. The mobile phones and services were partly presented as solutions, just as Apple did. However, Nokia operates now both in solutions and products. While it continues to produce traditional mobile communications products, it is increasingly developing solutions (mobiles plus services). Ultimately, the Nokians know that if they can get the solutions game right, they will be able to support it with global high-volume capabilities that are unlike those of their rivals, including Apple.

Since April 2007, Nokia results include those of Nokia Siemens Networks (NSN) on a fully consolidated basis; NSN is effectively controlled by Nokia. Another transformation followed in 2008, when Nokia's three mobile device business groups (Mobile Phones, Multimedia, and Enterprise Solutions) and the supporting horizontal groups (Customer and Market Operations and Technology Platforms) were replaced by a single integrated business segment, Devices and Services. This unit is "Nokia's purest matrix," says Nokia's CEO Olli-Pekka Kallasvuo. A year later, Devices was further differentiated into mobile phones, smartphones, and mobile computers. At the same time, the company augmented services with solutions.[10]

In the past, Nokia had a group of relatively independent businesses, which individually had a great freedom and few dependencies on each other. In the executive team, each group chief concentrated on his or her own matters, while the CEO and the staff focused on the big picture. Today the organization is built for interdependencies, which characterize the executive team itself. In the past, group chiefs updated each other; now, they are working on solutions together. Nokia's strategy builds on strategic capabilities to protect existing markets and to create new markets.

Nokia used to have relatively independent business groups, even though it shared a lot of technology, and much of its sales were going through a common set of customers, through operators and distributors. Now there is a single team working for a common objective, whereas in the past, there were multiple teams working for often conflicting goals. "Now that we have gone into a functional organizational structure, what makes us different is that today we really have to collaborate with each other," says Chief Development Officer Mary McDowell. "You may want to manufacture all the beautiful devices you want, but you will have to work that one out with Anssi [Vanjoki]," she adds referring to Nokia's chief of markets.

Instead of a business group structure, the current Nokia structure has a functional organization. It is led by the group executive board, whereas Corporate Development focuses on strategy and future growth and provides operational support for integration across all the units. Figure 4.3 illustrates this relationship.

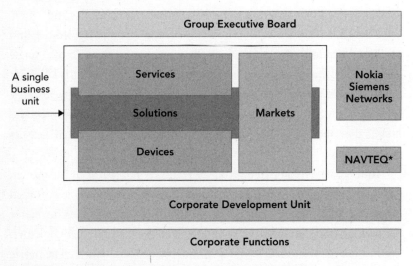

FIGURE 4.3   Nokia's Core Organizational Structure (2010)
*NAVTEQ is Nokia's digital mapping unit.

In the new organizational structure, the singular profit and loss statement (P&L) is no longer attributable to one senior executive but several: the chiefs of mobile devices, services, solutions, and markets. That suppresses independence and dependence, but it provides a strong incentive for *interdependence*. It also requires structural changes in how the executive team collaborates as a team.[11] "Sure, we might have competing ideas, but we don't have competing resources," says Anssi Vanjoki, chief of Nokia's Markets unit. In comparison to a traditional business group organization, the tradeoff is that if these chiefs make the wrong bet, the unit will go wrong all the way. However, when the bet is right, they'll go right all the way.[12]

Integrating multiple business units into a single unit to reinforce interdependencies is critical to success in solutions. "Devices will not be successful without services, services will not be successful without devices," says Nokia's chief of services Niklas Savander. In turn, solutions will not be successful without success of the market. Today, the networks (NSN) are maturing, and only a handful of global players dominate the landscape. Nokia's portfolio of mobile devices continues to dominate the global business, extending from the low end (cheap, entry models) to high end (expensive smartphones), even as the business is rapidly maturing. The future is in mobile service solutions.

The downside of the new organizational setup for software and services is that when you marry a twenty-four-*month* cycle of the mobile device business with a twenty-four-*week* cycle of the mobile services business, you need to be careful not to disjoint both inadvertently. When markets are transformed, the organization must also change globally. "As we're transforming the company into a solutions organization, *we* must change as well," says Colin Giles, Nokia's former chief of Greater China.

At the surface, this may sound trivial. Surely, the change of any organizational structure requires change among employees. In practice, however, the required change is dramatic because the business model that matches the needs of the device business would be inappropriate in the solutions business; in fact, it requires a different mindset. And although Nokia's businesses are global, each country—and particularly the largest markets—always requires some tweaking and tailoring.[13]

From the standpoint of NSN, Nokia is more tightly managed and Finnish than NSN, which is perceived as less tightly managed and less

Finnish. "Nokia is a very global company, but very centrally run. We're a bit more multidimensional," says NSN's former CEO Simon Beresford-Wylie.[14]

How Nokia's Headquarters Work with Its Country Units Around the World

The Nokia House, the head office, is located by the Gulf of Finland in Keilaniemi, Espoo, only a fifteen-minute drive from the center of Helsinki. In most multinational companies, headquarters are in close proximity to capital cities or commercial metropolitan centers. At Nokia, the dispersal of the HQ is increasing as some members of the group executive board are primarily based in Finland (Kallasvuo, Aho, Ihamuotila, Moerk, Savander, Torres, Vanjoki, Öistämö) and others in the United States (Ojanperä, Simonson, McDowell). Furthermore, those GEB members who are in Finland can hardly be compared with typical large-country executives who remain in the headquarters most of the time; rather, they travel much or most of their time. Finally, many functional chiefs—take, for instance, Henry Tirri, the head of the Nokia Research Center— is located in Silicon Valley, while traveling extensively from Helsinki to Beijing.

What is true of strategic management is also true of investor ownership. In the early 1990s, Nokia's ownership was still relatively Finnish. Today, only about 10 percent of the company is owned by the Finns. Although the United States accounts for less than 4 percent of Nokia's net sales and just over 6 percent of its personnel, U.S. investors own almost 50 percent of the company—which is nearly as much as Europe as a whole.[15] Hence, Nokia has a corporate office close to the financial center of New York.

Like other cost-conscious multinationals, Nokia did not locate to Manhattan. It is in White Plains, New York, not far from Armonk, the home of the global headquarters of IBM, Nokia's partner. Head of mobile phones unit Rick Simonson has an office in both White Plains and Espoo. By his own estimate, he spent 40 percent of his time in New York City, 40 percent in Helsinki and northern Europe, and the remaining 20 percent around the rest of the world. "I don't know any other major global corporate or Fortune 100 or 500 company where the CEO and CFO aren't sitting right next to each other," says Simonson. "It's an unusual arrangement, but it worked with Jorma [Ollila] when he was CEO and it works with Olli-Pekka [Kallasvuo]. That says a lot about our culture, our trust, and our relying on each other to do what's necessary for the company."

Culture is vital to Nokia because it grew very rapidly into a global network. It is the glue that keeps the complex structure together, but flexibly and through empowerment. "Nokia's organization is a jazz band, not a symphony orchestra," says Nokia's former chief technology officer Yrjö Neuvo. "A symphony orchestra is very hierarchical and everybody has strict guidelines that must be obeyed. In a jazz band, the musicians play the same song, but there is not often a clear leader and each must have the opportunity to improvise. That's the Nokia way."

With their large domestic marketplace, U.S. multinationals have traditionally favored a command and control culture, which is based on a strong headquarters and a top-down approach to the country units. In contrast to these companies, which internationalized gradually over decades, Nokia grew global rapidly. Therefore, it developed a different kind of organizational capabilities, and it has relied on a sense-and-respond culture. Nokia's holistic culture and values support and simplify what at first sight seems like extraordinary complexity.[16] However, when the organization grows, there is an inevitable dilemma, says Sari Baldauf, a former Nokia executive. "In order to be efficient and take advantage of scale, you must have global processes, but in a big organization, it's just harder to see meaning and purpose."

Until recently, most multinationals were located in the large and advanced economies of North America, Western Europe (Germany, France, United Kingdom, Italy), and Japan. As growth moves from the advanced economies to the large emerging economies, this shift is reflected in Nokia's key locations. More than a fifth of Nokia's total personnel remains in Finland, more than a third is already in the BRIC economies, and barely a fifth remains in the advanced economies (i.e., the G7 nations). Nokia's production, R&D, and venturing sites reflect these realities. Except for the mobile phones factory in Salo, close to Helsinki, no major production facility remains in the advanced economies; instead, they are primarily in the BRICs and in Eastern Europe's transitional economies (e.g., Hungary, Romania). Although the Nokia Research Center has several locations in Finland, it is globally networked and particularly active in cutting-edge university locations in the United Kingdom, Switzerland, New York, Los Angeles, and Silicon Valley, as well as Beijing and Bangalore.

Overall, the output of national operations is determined by two dimensions. The primary strategic consideration involves the overall importance of local environments to the company's global strategy. Large market size is very important, but so is a market that is highly advanced technologically. The major organizational consideration is the importance of the country unit's resources in any given value activity, such as technology, production, marketing and branding, or any other area. Depending on its positions along these dimensions, the country operation may play different and changing roles, as described in detail in the following paragraphs.

Leaders

The country units in the United States, China, India, and the United Kingdom are the "leaders"—that is, these organizations have a relatively high degree of internal competencies and are located in strategically important markets. They are natural partners of the headquarters in developing and implementing broad strategic themes. In addition to detecting early warning signals for change, they participate in analyzing the resulting threats and opportunities while developing appropriate organizational responses. Nokia's leading country operations are in the United States, the largest European nations, and the BRICs.

Scanners

The country operations in Korea, Finland, Israel, and Japan possess a relatively high degree of local competencies, but they are located in strategically less significant markets. They are the "scanners." By scanning the sophisticated marketplace, they may anticipate the needs of strategic or large markets. They may provide critical intelligence. Through them, the headquarters may try to capture the benefits of certain local competencies and capabilities in order to apply them to broader worldwide operations. Nokia's intelligence scanners include Japan and Korea.

Potentials

These country units in Brazil, Russia, and Indonesia have a relatively low degree of internal competencies, but they are located in strategically important markets—the "potentials." In such markets, the company's global leadership tends to require a strong local presence. These markets include large emerging economies that are following in the BRIC footprints, such as Indonesia and Vietnam. On the other hand, such markets are often fluid. They could be strategic leaders, but they lack the resources for the position. Conversely, if their strategic importance is reduced, they will be demoted to contributors.

Contributors

Finally, some country units do not enjoy important local competencies, nor are they located in strategically important markets (Mexico, Hungary, Spain, and Italy). Typically, the resource commitments of the headquarters reflect the target market's limited potential. In most companies, the majority of country units play the role of a contributor. Individually, these country operations are dispersed and low-value executors of the company's global strategy. In Eastern Europe, Hungary and Romania serve as contributors in production, and Italy and Spain have a similar role due to their relatively large markets. In the Americas, Mexico has a comparable role in production. Collectively, however, they make it possible to capture economies of scale and scope, which is an issue of life and death to small-country multinationals.

How Nokia's Country Units Localize Global Strategies

Ultimately, the secret of success for any multinational is the quality of the relationship between the headquarters and the country units. This relationship should be positive, relatively stable, and even surprises should be moderate rather than big swings that constrain credibility. The ability to translate the global mandate to a local execution plan and to win is critical. From the standpoint of the country operations, you truly need to understand the global mandate and how it applies in the local environment, and then execute. You need to find a common win-win area and keep on expanding it. The operating country units of the multinationals are like ambassadors of this company in their respective countries. People may have a bad day; however, an ambassador cannot. "As an ambassador, you must be emotionally engaged but still diplomatic," says D. Shivakumar, head of Nokia India. "As long as multinationals keep that in mind, they will win. Otherwise, as the old saying goes, you may be either hopelessly global or mindlessly local."

In the past, multinationals' strategies have been assessed primarily vis-à-vis their headquarters. The underlying assumption has been that the overall corporate strategy is reflected by the entire organization. The assumption is valid primarily in the case of the interwar European large-country multinationals, which sought to replicate their home-base organization in host countries. "There's no way to describe Nokia as replicating national operations," says Nokia's chief of Mobile Phones Richard Simonson. "We did not take a model from Finland and then just replicate it. We have a global operation."

With increasing organizational, environmental, and technological complexity, contemporary strategies tend to be far more differentiated. This is the case with Nokia because its home market is practically insignificant in terms of revenues (though hugely important strategically), and its key markets are located in large emerging economies. To be successful in a global technology- and marketing-intensive industry, it is vital to have a presence in many different locations worldwide. The smaller the multinational's home base and the larger the market and strategic importance of the host country, the more likely are the pressures to localize the overall strategy. Certainly Nokia's regional and country chiefs consider the overall strategy important and have no intention to belittle it. However, the chiefs that represent the largest and strategically vital markets do not necessarily think that this strategy alone is the foundation of success in their respective host countries.

An Organizational Case Study: Nokia China

Due to differences between the headquarters and the country unit, Nokia's China organization provides interesting insights. The company has some eighty offices in China's large marketplace. Although the matrix has been responsive to the market and added to flexibility across the organization, Nokia's China unit must also have solid line reporting systems. That's the area where Nokia's senior executives find themselves struggling, because Chinese people are educated in an environment where they are given strong direction by teachers or parents. Nokia's former Greater China chief Colin Giles believes that a Chinese manager is much more like a general than an international or Western manager, who operates more in a team environment. "When you have one kind of a manager in Finland and another in China, that's something you often have to cope with in the organization," he says. As such, this is not a matrix issue, but solid line reporting is needed domestically. "After many discussions in the organization, one finally rationalizes that in Asia, you need stronger guidance, so you set up strong line reporting domestically," Giles concludes.

Another matrix challenge is its inherent complexity. It can be very difficult to actually identify the person responsible for a certain decision. "You almost need to have been close to two decades in the organization, as I have, to know what you need to do to get support," says Giles. "Still, [the] matrix does work. It is almost inherent to our culture."

The matrix is as much about a structure as it is about a culture. Although the built-in conflicts in matrix structures may pull managers in several directions at once, developing a matrix of flexible perspectives and relationships within each manager's mind allows individuals to make the judgments and negotiate the tradeoffs that drive the organization toward a shared strategic objective.[17] Furthermore, time may be on Nokia's side. Unlike many large-country multinationals, it has a more social culture, and a more social approach, which comes in handy in the 2010s as the technology sector is moving toward social media.

Although most of the strategic work is done on a global basis, in China Nokia's culture and organization is perceived as more important than the overall strategy as such, and it has been stretched to become more local. "While strategy has been important, it has not been the foundation of success in China," says Giles. "Our success in China has had much more to do with culture."

In addition to localization inspired by the HQ's overall strategy, it has also been able and willing to localize new business models of its Chinese competitors. Around 2003, Nokia, along with other multinational technology giants, was temporarily beaten by Chinese equipment manufacturers in the Chinese marketplace. While its Western counterparts tried to do better what they were already doing, Nokia took a closer look at its Chinese rivals to understand better what *they* were doing. As a result, Nokia's China operation went from being a centralized organization, essentially based in Shanghai and Guangzhou, to expanding more to the West and then partnering with local distributors. This localization became the foundation for its future success.

The real dilemma is not structure versus culture, but finding an appropriate balance between the two.

A Globally Networked Organization

For two decades or more, the matrix structure has frustrated many multinational companies. Yet Nokia has embraced a relatively complex multidimensional matrix. Today, this global grid enables the company to be centralized and decentralized, global and local, big and small. If former CEO Kairamo first understood how important it was to "listen to the customers," his successor Ollila took this learning to a new level by divesting noncore properties and moving from an area organization toward a matrix. Recently, current CEO Kallasvuo has built on these foundations by globally networking the matrix and reinforcing interdependencies within the company's organization. This is the structural and cultural foundation for the externally oriented and internally collaborative Nokia. "For us, the question has not been *whether* to adopt a matrix, but *how* to make it effective," says Kallasvuo.

At Nokia, as shown in this chapter, the matrix has not been seen as the primary goal, but as an instrument to realize a globally networked organization. And it is Nokia's legacy as a small-country multinational that accounts for its effective execution. In turn, the globally networked matrix organization provides the structural and cultural foundation for Nokia's strategic capabilities and advantages, which we shall explore more closely in the next two chapters.

Nokia's Lessons

- As most companies today base strategy on costs, quality, innovation, or combinations of the three, new sources of success are vital. With increasing competition across global markets, it is imperative in the long term to build strong and unique organizational capabilities.

- Typically, all multinational companies seek a balance between business and geography. Truly global strategies are based increasingly on a matrix structure. As Nokia's success indicates, organizational charts—including highly complex structures—only scratch the surface. Ultimately, it is people, values, and culture that drive any organizational structure. They are the glue that keeps the whole together—even in a complex multidimensional matrix organization such as Nokia's.

- Global success is almost impossible with fragmentary, country-specific IT systems. Increasingly complex and highly distributed operations rely on efficient, global, and centralized IT systems and networks.

- Nokia has operations in more then 150 countries worldwide. A truly global company has a wide array of country units in different countries that are characterized by different local capabilities and a different local environment. Whereas corporate success is based on global strategy, the success of country operations is often based on a degree of localization, especially in the largest and most strategic markets.

- Nokia is concentrated in terms of business, dispersed in geography, and distributed organizationally. This highlights the importance of a flat, team-driven, and globally networked organization.

5

INNOVATING GLOBALLY VIA R&D NETWORKS

Global success never comes easily. The right legacy, ability to embrace globalization, a team-driven strategy, culture, and organization are necessary elements of success, but not enough. In order to create, develop, and generate attractive products and services, a successful multinational must build the right strategic capabilities. At Nokia, these are seen as the priority areas where the company is investing in order to build layered competitive advantages. And innovation is Nokia's most critical capability. This chapter shows how Nokia's emphasis on sustained innovation is reflected by the rapid expansion of the Nokia Research Center (which engages in long-term research); unit-based R&D (which focuses on short-term development); and globally networked university cooperation, open innovation, and venture funds. Let's see how Nokia's R&D has evolved to be successful in all parts of the world.

The Rise of Nokia's Innovation

In 1960, Nokia entered the telecom equipment market, and an electronics department was established to concentrate on the production of radio transmission equipment. Nokia's "digital gurus," including Björn Westerlund and Kurt Wikstedt, maintained good relations with universities and had a strategic vision of the digital future. For instance, Wikstedt's vision of the future relied on American management approaches years before these were widely employed in Finland, including the experience curve and portfolio analysis. "Electronics has been right for the company," he acknowledged. "Its profitability is not as good as we'd like it to be."[1] Strategically, the long-term vision made sense; financially, it was horrible, initially.[2] Only when Wikstedt was about to retire did the unit become profitable. It had been in the red for seventeen long years until 1977.

It was only through years of investment and hard effort that the unit turned into a cash cow. While paper and cable made the money, funds were often allocated into electronics, which seemed to be driven by a bunch of wild mavericks. "Occasionally, there were muted complaints: 'Why should they always get the money?'" recalls Sari Baldauf, Nokia's former senior executive. As a diversified conglomerate, Nokia had a different kind of R&D in different units, even if telecom R&D was growing most rapidly. It was involved with many technologies, but they were business-specific and shared little in terms of interface between business units.

In the early 1990s, when Nokia bet its future on the digital mobile vision, R&D was quickly ramped up in three major Finnish cities: Helsinki, the capital; Tampere, the industrial center; and Oulu, near the Arctic Circle (and later a fourth city, Jyväskylä, has been in the picture as well).

Rise of the Finnish Innovation System

Until the early 1990s, Finland's innovation institutions gave a powerful boost to Nokia's R&D, which now dominates Finnish R&D. Due to the Cold War, Finland, unlike other Western European countries, missed the Marshall Plan and the ensuing technology transfers and associated capabilities in managerial and international business know-how. Until the 1970s, it lagged behind most European nations in innovation. By the 1980s, the Japanese MITI and technology development strategies served as models for Finnish industrial policy architects.

Finnish innovation investments began to climb in 1983, through the establishment of the Finnish Funding Agency for Technology and Innovation (Tekes). Still, even in the mid-1980s, Finland's R&D was less than 1.5 percent of the GDP, about half as much as the cutting-edge innovator countries and well behind the Organisation for Economic Co-operation and Development (OECD) average of 2.2 percent.

It was only after the collapse of the Soviet Union that the OECD and thereafter the EU—and, in the technology sector, the United States—have served as models for Finnish policies. As the new national export-led strategy and national innovation became a key priority in the government agenda in the early 1990s and Nokia's expansion took off, Finnish R&D expenditures increased to more than 3 percent of the GDP. Meanwhile, the Science and Technology Policy Council embraced the idea of innovation-driven competitiveness.

Yet Finnish leadership in innovation is the accomplishment of Finnish companies. In relative terms, the private sector accounts for over 70 percent of total R&D. The role of the public sector has declined to 10 percent and that of the academic sector is about 20 percent. Much of the R&D increase accrues to Nokia, whether measured by input indicators (R&D) or output indicators (patents). For example, since the late 1990s, Nokia has dominated more of the "stock" of Finnish patents issued in the United States than all other Finnish companies together, as evidenced by Figure 5.1.

Judging on the basis of R&D allocations, Nokia probably benefited from the R&D support of the Finnish innovation institutions until the early 1980s.[3] During the past two decades the relationship has turned upside down. It is the Finnish innovation environment that benefits from Nokia. "Nokia distorts the statistics of Finnish innovation system, R&D, and competitiveness in a positive way; without Nokia, our success story in innovation would look a lot worse," acknowledges Mikko Kosonen, Nokia's former head of strategy and CIO who is now president of the Finnish Innovation Fund (Sitra). "We may now be less dependent on Nokia than in the 1990s, but an exceptional dependency of the national economy on a single company remains."

Nokia's Knowledge Networks Are Pervasive Globally

As Nokia focused globally on mobile communications, the refocus drove R&D into mobile communications as well. Nokia delivered its first GSM

Patents

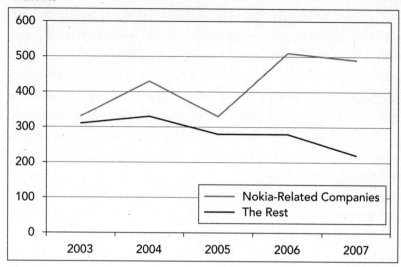

R&D

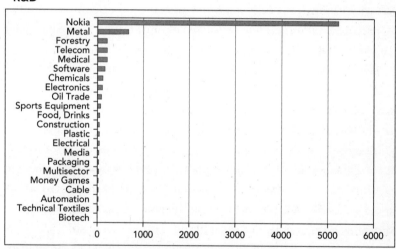

FIGURE 5.1 How Nokia's Innovation Leads in Finland

Source: *Patents (USPTO 2003–2007). R&D (EUR million, Top 100 R&D Investors by Talouselama 2007).*

network to the Finnish operator Radiolinja already in 1989, and the world's first commercial GSM call was made on July 1, 1991 in Helsinki over a Nokia-supplied network, by then Prime Minister Harri Holkeri, using a prototype Nokia GSM phone. Still, the company was and remains "technology agnostic." The point has never been this or that technology, but what the technology can do for people—not just executives or yuppies but ordinary people in both advanced and emerging economies.

Through the 1990s Nokia strengthened and solidified its market positions, not only in Europe but also in the United States, Asia-Pacific, and Latin America. Focusing on the fragmented U.S. market, Motorola continued to pump research into analog technology, which left Europe and the growing digital markets in Asia largely to Nokia and Ericsson. Nokia participated in the work of standardization bodies and international R&D projects in cooperation with universities, research institutes, and other telecom and mobile companies. Figure 5.2 provides an overview of how various divisions of Nokia work with these outside organizations; more specific information on each type of organization is provided later in this chapter.

In these activities, the Nokia Research Center sought to embody the entrepreneurial spirit of a small organization expanding to meet the needs of a global environment. "It was a great time to be in Nokia, there were new ideas, a real effort to make things happen, a sense of spring," recalls Yrjö Neuvo, Nokia's former CTO, who many Nokians consider something of a "technological, spiritual father figure."[4] There was always the concern over time and where the competitors were going. As Nokia moved ahead, so did its rivals. "We were not always the first," recalls Neuvo. "But we were often right in time, just when the business was taking off."

Nokia's R&D expenditures grew fivefold in the 1990s. As the Nokians point out, these figures should be seen in their context. In the 1990s, Nokia divested all noncore properties. The increases reflect changing revenue sources, particularly increasing R&D on digital electronics. Nokia was moving from low R&D industries to high R&D industries. In relative terms, Nokia's R&D as percentage of net sales was less than 5 percent through the

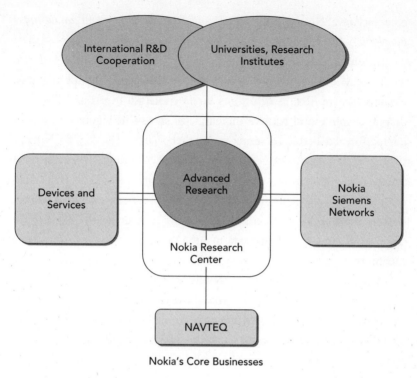

FIGURE 5.2   How Nokia's Knowledge Networks Interrelate in Innovation Activities

1980s, but climbed to 9 percent in the 1990s. R&D expenditures in mobile handsets exceeded those in mobile infrastructure as value migrated from the infrastructure to the devices.

In the early Ollila era, Nokia set as its objective a 20 percent market share. In the early 2000s, even 40 percent was seen as possible to achieve. Concurrently, it began to follow competitors more closely, particularly Ericsson, Motorola, and the Japanese producers. The Nokians saw themselves like Avis struggling with the entrenched Hertz and other big car rentals. "We were the underdog, the challenger," says Neuvo. "Like Avis, our mentality was that 'we'll try harder.'" As certain designs and concepts—particularly the groundbreaking cell phone models 2100 series, 5100, and 6100—succeeded, Nokia got ahead but had no time for complacency. "Now one of the key issues became, *How small can we make the phone?*" recalls Neuvo.

Although technological innovation was necessary to Nokia's success in the GSM era, it became insufficient by the late 1990s. Even today, Nokia's relative R&D is behind its direct rivals, Motorola and Ericsson, despite absolute and relative increases, as shown in Figure 5.3; still, it has performed better in terms of market share.[5] The key to Nokia's success is not the relative level of its R&D funding. Over the past three decades, Nokia has almost consistently invested *less* in R&D than most of its direct rivals, such as Motorola, Ericsson, and Qualcomm. Rather, the key to Nokia's success is how it is using the funding in the overall context of innovation—that is, innovation as a strategic capability.

As Nokia is morphing into a mobile Internet company, its R&D is no longer very far behind that of Microsoft and Google, and it has already left Apple and RIM (Research in Motion, the company that makes BlackBerry) far behind in R&D expenditures. From Nokia's standpoint, the global competitive picture has been distorted by the success of smartphone in the United States. There is some validity in the claim; just consider the statistics:

- In 2008, according to estimates, the global device market volume grew by 7 percent to 1,213,000 units.[6] At the same time, Nokia's mobile device volumes reached 468 million units.

- The new converged mobile devices (or smartphones), however, represented a small fraction of the total volume: sales of iPhone handset units soared to 11.6 million, whereas RIM estimated its BlackBerry account base at 26 million.

- Nokia's converged mobile device volumes amounted to 60.6 million units.[7] In 2008, Nokia's consolidated R&D expenses were approximately $1.45 billion.

In 2008, Nokia and NSN employed 39,350 people in R&D, or 31 percent of the total workforce, and had a strong R&D presence in sixteen

(a) Mobile Manufacturers (1980–2008)

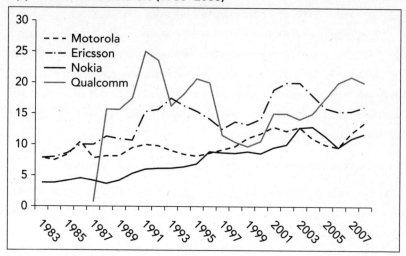

(b) IT Enablers (2000–2008)

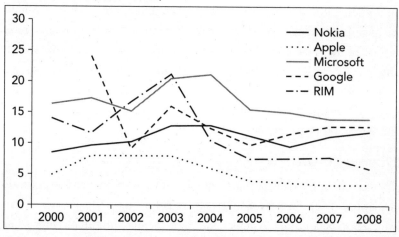

FIGURE 5.3   R&D Expenditures: Nokia and Rivals

countries. As Nokia continues to invest on its worldwide R&D network and increase collaboration with third parties, understandably its R&D has been climbing. But as Nokians point out, these gains should be seen in the context of the NSN merger. Prior to the fusion, R&D at Nokia mobile phones was close to 10 percent, whereas R&D at the networks amounted to almost 15 percent. Consequently, the NSN merger further contributed to the consolidated R&D, which increased from 9.5 percent in 2006 to 11.8 percent in 2008 as a percentage of net sales.

As Nokia and its rivals soon found out, technology innovation is a necessary but insufficient requirement for success. It must be accompanied by complementary *market creation*. Industry leaders have been successful in developing new technologies *and* new markets. The rise of services and solutions has amplified these preconditions for success.[8] Let's take a look at how R&D is done at Nokia.

The Nokia Research Center Drives Nokia Innovation

The key role in Nokia's long-term innovation belongs to the Nokia Research Center (NRC), which was founded in 1986 from the Nokia Electronics R&D unit with just eighty-six people on staff. That unit has grown dramatically. Today it employs roughly 400 researchers from forty-three countries and a wide variety of fields. As a small-country multinational, Nokia's home base has a population of only 5.3 million people, about the same as Minnesota. Although Finland continues to rank as one of the most competitive and innovative economies in the world, the talent base is inevitably narrow. In order to surpass such resource constraints, Nokia works with some one hundred universities globally. Even in Finland, NRC is hardly just Finnish; the workforce has already more than fifty nationalities.

Dispersed Center

The very name Nokia Research Center is both a misnomer and an accurate depiction. It is a misnomer in that there is no single NRC center. But it would also be accurate to depict NRC as a "center without a center." For historical reasons, the NRC has the largest laboratory in Helsinki, but it has globalized very rapidly and expanded particularly in Silicon Valley in the past few years.[9]

The idea that Nokia's R&D is somehow limited to Finland and Nordic Europe was dated already in the late 1990s, when Dr Yrjö Neuvo, who got his Ph.D. at Cornell and has served as visiting professor at the University of California, Santa Barbara, began to cultivate an international mindset. The same goes for his successors: Tero Ojanperä, who is currently

122

based in New York; and Bob Iannucci, a veteran of Compaq and IBM, who spent much of his time in the Valley, where the current NRC head Henry Tirri lives.

NRC's mission is to renew Nokia through strategic and long-term research. It is a global network of research centers and laboratories that Nokia maintains, in many cases in collaboration with outside partners. Except for Microsoft, HP, IBM, or NRC, few research organizations exist in the broad IT sector anymore. Apple does not have a comparable center. Even Google has intertwined research. Among mobile handset companies, few leaders (including Sony-Ericsson and the Korean players) have mixed structures rather than pure research. They do not have a global organization like NRC, says Tirri.

What makes Nokia different is that NRC is the only global research organization of its era. Bell Labs had its period, when telecom paced the prevailing trends. The era of Microsoft research peaked with applications research in the PC business. "We're now in the wireless era of mobile computers," says Tirri. "Nokia research matches the requirements of this era. We've developed a research agenda around the latest trends in mobile computing."

NRC works closely with Nokia Devices and Services and NSN. It has a unique mission to lead Nokia into the future. Looking beyond the development of current products, services, platforms, and technologies, Nokia's corporate research center creates assets and competencies in technology areas that it considers vital to future success. NRC has played a central role in standardization issues, says former CTO Yrjö Neuvo. "It has pioneered new areas of research, while influencing international cooperation. NRC has had a pretty important role in resource allocation internally and the orchestration of external evolution. Organizationally, it's now more decentralized than before."

NRC's Research Priorities

Nokia's current R&D objectives are twofold:

- In the short and medium term, Nokia researchers support the product development units to master key technologies and their evolution, which enables the company to develop competitive products efficiently.

- In the long term, Nokia's research aims to disrupt the present. Research in different sciences with global participation is a prerequisite for creating these disruptions.

NRC's strategic agenda is updated annually. It aims to portray the world and mobility three to seven years into the future. It has developed a vision of how the physical world will fuse with the digital world in the future through mobile technologies. In the past, it relied on two kinds of research centers, which collaborated with each other:

- The work for core technology breakthroughs supporting Nokia's existing businesses took place in the Core Technology Centers (CTCs). All of these four CTCs were located in Finland. They focussed on computation structures, interaction, Internet, and also included the Wireless Systems and Services Laboratory.
- More visionary, exploratory systems research that went well beyond any current business model was conducted at eight System Research Centers (SRCs), which were dispersed worldwide.

At the beginning of 2009, NRC adopted a research agenda that consolidated and halved its core areas into four focus areas: rich context modeling, new user interface, high-performance mobile platform, and cognitive radio.[10] By pursuing a narrower research program, NRC is targeting areas that, besides being the most viable investments financially, seem to offer the best potential for strengthening Nokia's position in the converging Internet and communications industries in the long term.

NRC also represents Nokia in many standardization bodies and large international cooperation projects, such as the European Union Framework programs and EUREKA cluster CELTIC (Europe's only R&D program in ICT dedicated to end-to-end telecom solutions).[11]

Accumulating Intellectual Property

In addition to safeguarding its technology advantage, Nokia believes that IPRs protect the unique Nokia features, look and feel, and brand. Indeed, one of the main targets of NRC is to create intellectual property rights or IPRs (which include patents, design registrations, trade secrets, trademark registrations, and copyrights). NRC researchers represent only about 4 percent of Nokia's R&D employees, yet they produce about half of Nokia's essential patents and a third of all Nokia invention reports. As a leading innovator in mobile communications, Nokia has created one of the strongest and broadest patent portfolios in the industry, investing some $60 billion in R&D during the last two decades. It owns 11,000 patent families. Much of this intellectual property has been declared essential to industry standards.

In late October 2009, Nokia filed a complaint against Apple with the Federal District Court in Delaware, alleging that Apple's iPhone infringes on Nokia patents.[12] In Silicon Valley, such patent rivalries come with the territory, but the high stakes of the smartphone rivalries gave this complaint higher visibility. "By refusing to agree to appropriate terms for Nokia's intellectual property, Apple is attempting to get a free ride on the back of Nokia's innovation," said Ilkka Rahnasto, vice president, legal and intellectual property at Nokia. Some two months later, Apple filed a countersuit claiming that Nokia was infringing on its technology.[13]

The iPhone enthusiasts saw Nokia's complaint as a defensive tactic to stall Apple's smartphone march to glory. After all, since the iPhone's launch, Nokia and other handset makers struggled to keep pace with Apple in the fast-growing, high-margin smartphone segment. In 2009, Nokia's share of the global smartphone market slipped to 35 percent in the third quarter, from 41 percent in the second, while its competitors Apple and RIM gained. Concurrently, Apple announced a 47 percent jump in third-quarter profits, while Nokia's gains were significantly lower. In this narrative, the maturing of the traditional cell phone industry and the emergence of the smartphone market meant escalating IPR friction.

However, there is also another narrative. Like IBM and Microsoft, Apple has played the patents game for decades. In the mobile communications business, the established players, led by Nokia, have licensing agreements with each other and few are net payers of royalty fees. As a latecomer, Apple can hardly avoid being a net payer in the intellectual property game. Further, Nokia is a global leader, but it has coped with patent struggles only since the late 1990s.[14] Even in the early 2000s, the company's IPR unit was relatively small. Furthermore, until Nokia's complaint, Apple was often perceived as the aggressor in smartphone patents. In early 2009, it threatened to sue Palm's Pre over its multi-touch interface.[15] In this narrative, Nokia has matured. It is no longer willing to sponsor a free ride.[16] In fact, something similar took place in the semiconductor and desktop computer businesses during competitive times. As margins deteriorate, companies seek to put up barriers to protect their positions.

How R&D Is Done in Nokia's Units

In addition to NRC, Nokia conducts R&D in its business units. The former has a long-term technology perspective; the latter is driven by short-term business needs. With scale, resources, and insight on the future of the mobile world, Nokia has moved quickly toward services and solutions. In 2002, the company set up a dedicated business unit (called Imaging) to drive multimedia performance. In hindsight, it invested too much in the new areas, some Nokian executives acknowledge today. However, despite overshooting, the general direction proved right. "Besides," some add, "we felt that Microsoft was breathing down our neck."

In the early 2000s, Nokia chose Symbian as the smartphone platform because, according to Dr. Kai Öistämö, chief of the Devices unit, "We realized that it was time to move from product-based R&D toward a platform way of doing things." To the Nokians, that was the only way to manage the software. Outside Nokia, this vital shift was not well understood, due to Nokia's legacy as a manufacturer and the kind of value it had created thus far. "Even in devices, three-fourths, if not 80 percent, of the value, is in software today," says Öistämö.

Along with NRC, Nokia invests a substantial portion of resources in R&D activities within the integrated Devices and Services unit. Since January 2008, the bulk of Nokia's R&D has fallen within the R&D subunit of the Devices unit. A smaller portion of R&D efforts falls within the Services unit, and longer-term technology development comes under the scope of NRC.

How R&D Is Done in Nokia's Devices and Services Unit

In this integrated subunit, technology and research includes not just R&D, patents, and licenses, but also the following areas:

- *Component sourcing.* The unit sources components for mobile devices from a global network of suppliers. It also sources software and content.

- *Chipset platforms. Chipset* refers to a group of integrated circuits or chips designed to work together and usually marketed as a single product. The unit operates a multisourcing model for chipsets, working with some half a dozen chipset suppliers. Through *multiple sourcing,* Nokia deploys several suppliers for products or services, thus preventing reliance on any one supplier and ideally optimizing efficiencies.[17]

- *Software.* This refers to the platforms that enable the implementation of radio technologies and applications in mobile devices, and the applications or services that run on a mobile device. The key to Nokia's software strategy is cross-platform development environments, that is, layers of software that run across different device operating systems.

Led by Peter Røpke, Nokia's Devices R&D has a roadmap of about three years. Røpke's job is to get the execution risk under control. Whereas NRC only takes on projects where there is a major technology risk, what Røpke puts into his organization has got to work. Most of the technology risk has already been boiled out. The primary question for NRC is "Can we do this for the first time?" whereas the key question for unit R&D is "Can we scale this up and reduce the implementation risk?" Still, even in the operating units, says Öistämö, "productization plays a surprisingly small role in overall R&D investments."

In light of the transition to mobile computers and smartphones, Nokia's software R&D is particularly important. It deploys different software operating systems to balance usability, features, and cost in a flexible manner. These include software platforms developed in-house

(Series 30, Series 40, and Maemo), as well as S60, software built on Symbian OS, an operating system widely used by the industry.[18]

How R&D Is Done Within Nokia Siemens Networks

At NSN, R&D work focuses on wireless and wireline communication solutions that enable communication services for people and businesses. Where appropriate, NSN seeks to provide support for technologies that it does not produce itself.

In 2004, some 85 percent of its R&D was still done in Finland. In contrast, only five years later, in 2009 (about two years into the merger), about 40 percent of the R&D was done outside Finland, in Germany. "In a pace of just two years, we have balanced our R&D, which is becoming more 50–50," says NSN's former CEO Simon Beresford-Wylie. These figures and ratios, however, must be seen in the context of the NSN merger, which almost doubled the workforce and thus the proportion of R&D employees. At the same time, NSN also did begin to take R&D to Asia as well.

NSN's Research, Technology, and Platforms focuses on research, standardization, intellectual property rights, innovation, R&D services, and platform development. Like R&D in Nokia's Devices and Services unit, NSN cooperates with universities, the IT industry, and standardization and other industry cooperation bodies worldwide.

How Nokia's R&D Units Cooperate with Universities

In its R&D activities, NRC benefits from and contributes to extensive knowledge networks, which comprise universities and research institutes, as well as international R&D cooperation. Global R&D networking is a must to a small-country multinational, which cannot rely on its home base for R&D talent, ideas, and capital.

Recruiting R&D Talent

The United States has great universities and good basic research, but not all Nokians believe that these academics can talk with a company in operational terms as accomplished researchers are expected to do in Finland. For instance, Nokia used to have the Oxygen Project with MIT (focusing on pending developments in wireless networking and embedded computing), which cost about $1 million annually. Yet the actual benefits of the project were considered inadequate in proportion to expenditures. "It was too abstract, not really anchored in business realities," says one Nokia R&D executive. "Of course, there are greater resources in countries other than in Finland, but we too have well-paid and well-resourced research talent," comments Nokia's former CTO Dr. Yrjö Neuvo.

NRC recruits globally, but one reason for its interest in open innovation and collaboration with universities is the available talent pool. "We should not hire people who are famous now, but people who will be famous in the next ten to fifteen years," says Tirri. He would like to see NRC as a kind of future Xerox Park, the legendary research lab that was founded as a division of Xerox in 1970 and has contributed to many technology innovations, including laser printing, the Ethernet, the PC graphical user interface, ubiquitous computing, and advancing very large-scale integration. NRC likes talented R&D people who are hands-on, mostly Ph.D.s who write papers but have an industrial research mindset. The idea is to do great science and bring value to Nokia.

In the early 1990s, Nokia had no problems recruiting people. Its base was still very Finnish, and Finland was undergoing its worst recession since the 1930s. To most young researchers, any job was a good job. Now Nokia must compete intensively worldwide. Initially, Tirri thought that R&D recruiting would be difficult under these conditions. Now he believes that "just like with the Internet in the 1990s, people understand the mobile vision. So they gravitate toward us almost naturally."

Finnish Locations and University Cooperation

One symbolic milestone was passed in June 1999, when NRC's new main building was opened in Helsinki, Finland. It is located in the center of the city in close proximity to major universities. NRC cooperates intimately

129

with two Finnish universities (and in different ways with other leading Finnish universities as well):

- *NRC Helsinki and Helsinki University of Technology.* Located close to central Helsinki, NRC Helsinki is just a few minutes from Nokia worldwide headquarters in Espoo. Working in conjunction with the Helsinki University of Technology, NRC Helsinki projects are pushing forward the fields of user experience, mobile security, power management, and computing architectures, as well as intelligent context-aware radio or "cognitive radio."

- *NRC Tampere and Tampere University of Technology.* Located about 110 miles north of Helsinki, Tampere is the third-largest city in Finland. NRC Tampere is located about six miles from the city center. Collaborating with the Tampere University of Technology, NRC Tampere is chartered with exploring the areas of sensing and context, media representation, social media, user experience, mixed reality solutions, and 3D platforms.

Global Locations and University Cooperation

Nokia also has active exploration and teams on the ground from India and China to Africa and Latin America. In addition to Finland, NRC has some ten locations worldwide:

- It collaborates with leading U.S. research organizations in Palo Alto, Stanford, Hollywood, and Boston.

- It is also very active in Western Europe, from Cambridge in the United Kingdom to Ecole Polytechnique in Zurich.

- Along with advanced economies, NRC has its antennas in large emerging economies, including Tsinghua in Beijing and Srishti School in Bangalore.

- And in Africa's growth markets, NRC cooperates with universities in Kenya, Uganda, and South Africa.

According to Tirri, Nokia's head of NRC, the Beijing lab is one of the largest in NRC, in comparison to R&D investments in India and Africa. It is contributing to the China market, but it also does more global research. Like the Africa lab, India NRC is a technology developer on-site, but it also contributes as a thought and innovation' provoker. Indeed, Nokia pays special attention to local trends that could have global ramifications. What Nokia's R&D scientists do in China and India, in particular, may prove of great value not just domestically but also regionally and worldwide, says Mary McDowell, Nokia's CDO.[19]

NRC's labs are geographic labs and they operate worldwide. They are co-located with Nokia's innovation ecosystems, not with its operating units. Unlike Nokia as a whole (which, as described in Chapter Four, is a matrix of sorts), NRC's structure is a line organization. The heads of units report to Tirri. Even the lab heads have a very flat structure, just two layers before researchers. NRC is independently organized. It has an innovation pipeline to the operating units and to services and solutions. "We're seeding our technology," says Tirri. "Just as when you throw the ball over the net, we're doing everything we can on the technology that has matured, pushing the technology so that somebody can receive the ball as it falls through the net."

Today, Open Innovation Is Vital

Anssi Vanjoki, Nokia's brand wizard, likes to end his e-mails with a quote from Bill Bernbach, the legendary ad force behind the creative revolution on Madison Avenue in the 1960s and 1970s: "Knowledge is ultimately available to everyone." Today, open innovation is a fashionable catchword among leading technology innovators, but Nokia belongs to the pioneers of the approach. As a small-country multinational, its survival depends on networking. "Even though open innovation came from outside Nokia, primarily from R&D on software and Linux, Nokia has been intellectually oriented to open innovation," says Dr. Yrjö Neuvo.

Typically, the Nokia Foundation granted its 2009 award to Jimmy Wales, the founder of Wikipedia, the free, multilingual encyclopedia.

Wales was awarded for his contributions to the evolution of the World Wide Web as a participatory and truly democratic platform. "The theme for this year's award is Open Innovation, a way of working which is very important for our activities at Nokia Research Center, and a value which we believe is embodied in the participatory and inclusive approach of Wikipedia," said Henry Tirri, head of Nokia Research Center and chairman of the board of the Nokia Foundation.[20]

Nokia favors a sense and respond environment, whereas many of its rivals have a control and command environment. For decades, the latter was characterized by the paradigm of closed innovation, in which successful innovation meant the company had to control the generation of its own ideas. This kind of innovation originated in the early twentieth century, when universities and government were not yet involved in the commercial application of science. Companies sought to integrate innovation vertically, along with other aspects of their value chain. As a result, they launched their own R&D departments to control new product development in-house.

Over the course of time, the closed innovation paradigm crumbled, due to the increasing availability and mobility of skilled workers, the growth of the venture capital market, external options for ideas sitting on the shelf, and the increasing capability of external suppliers. In the new innovation environment, knowledge is no longer proprietary to the company but resides in employees, suppliers, customers, competitors, and universities.[21]

Today, the Nokians use the term *open innovation* in two ways based on complementary perspectives.

- One perspective refers to the open innovation ecosystem, that is, Symbian open OS platform, which is becoming open-source. This is a development-oriented view of open innovation.

- Open innovation also means broadly innovation in collaboration with Nokia's cooperative universities. In this sense, it refers to a mode of working.

By sharing resources, leveraging ideas, and tapping each other's expertise, NRC hopes to create vibrant innovation ecosystems. Nokia teams—co-located with leading universities around the world—are collaborating with a network of leading institutions.[22]

Nokia also drives innovation through its customers' ideas from around the world. Nokia's Beta Labs reflect the company's ambitions in the new service space. It is a lead-user community, which cultivates community-driven open innovation. The applications provided by Beta Labs are in development, but they are considered "mature" enough to be released in order to be tested by users worldwide.[23] Complementing Beta Labs, Nokia Pilots is an umbrella program that helps get Nokia users involved in the creative development process. It allows these users to share their ideas and suggest improvements that Nokia can put into action as it seeks to create the best products and services possible.

Even a crisis environment favors research, suggests Tirri. "Along with Rick Rashid, who leads Microsoft's R&D, I believe that the more there is uncertainty for the future, the more important becomes your innovation and the higher is your R&D investment."

Developing New Business

In order to boost innovations, Nokia also seeks to internalize venture capital approaches. The objective is ceaseless innovation, from its oldest offerings (mobile cell phones) to the most recent ones (services and solutions), and from short-term R&D (unit-based R&D) to corporate innovation (venturing) and, ultimately, long-term R&D (NRC), as shown in Figure 5.4.

New Business Development Internally

The Nokia Corporate Alliances & Business Development (NCBC) unit looks for breakthrough ideas beyond current conventions with which to expand the Nokia portfolio. It is interested in innovative business concepts and technologies that have a built-in disruptive element (i.e., in terms of a product's size, price, features, scale, or business model). It manages the

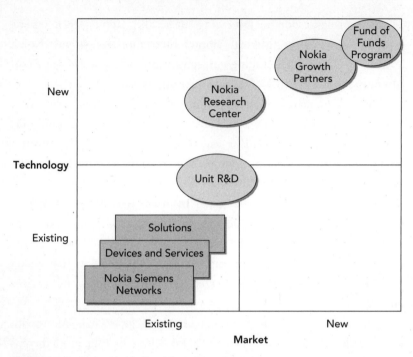

FIGURE 5.4 How Nokia Develops New Businesses

Nokia-wide business development funnel by coordinating activities with other Nokia business units. It creates new services and products that stem from the local needs of consumers and local expertise yet also benefit from global economies of scale.[24] The unit nurtures new businesses in their formative stages in order to integrate them with Nokia's core business or develop them as joint business with collaborating companies and strategic partners. Business and technology validation is crucial to the unit.[25]

Exploration and experimentation are at the core of Nokia's new business development activities. Technology scouting is the primary mode of discovery for early signals.[26] The company systematically scans emerging trends and disruptions across a variety of different channels and sources.[27]

Nokia evaluates proposals and allocates resources based on a variety of factors, including the project's cost and risk factors, its fit with Nokia's strategy, and the return on investment (ROI) it potentially offers. Nokia's Venture Capital Plus model involves using a dedicated team of technologists and designers who, at the due diligence stage, can validate the technology and build prototypes for different use cases. The aim is to eliminate technology risks by creating solution architecture for potential offerings, based on prioritized opportunities.[28]

New Business Development Externally

For many in the developing world, the Nokia device is their first Internet-connected device. It could also be their first camera, navigation device, or digital music and video player. Nokia now ships more cameras and digital music players than anyone in the world.

In addition to new business development internally, Nokia is partnering with external innovators to access and leverage competencies beyond its current core to maintain its competitive edge. "This is a fantastic time to be in the industry," says Paul Asel, partner at Nokia Growth Partners (NGP), who has spent two decades in global investment and has more than ten years on-the-ground experience in China, India, Russia, Europe, and Latin America.

Nokia Growth Partners is the premier venture investor focused on growth-stage companies in the mobile industry. With $250 million under management for direct investments in promising mobile companies, it also advises and manages $100 million for investments into other venture capital funds through Nokia's Fund of Funds Program. It offers portfolio companies a global perspective on the mobile industry and the strategic guidance, network, and platform to accelerate growth both domestically and internationally. It works closely with Nokia, its sole limited partner, to provide a superior return on investment while increasing the likelihood and magnitude of success in the companies in which it invests. It has offices in Silicon Valley in the United States, Finland, China, and India. "Innovation can happen organically through internal product development within Nokia, but it can also happen through acquisitions, or partnerships and investments," says Asel. "We play a specific role in just one of many roles that innovation can be achieved."

Among the technology leaders, the role of corporate innovation is common, but the way Nokia goes about it is different. The more normal approach is to have an investment entity that is basically part of the corporate investment arm within the company, without a specific funds structure, on an ad hoc basis, off the balance sheet. Instead, former CFO Rick Simonson opted for a different approach. Nokia has a separate fund that operates independently to bring in the best practices and yet work closely with Nokia. When it executes well, it combines the best aspects of a financial investor and strategic investor, while aligning both with Nokia's overall strategy. The expectation is that this should net Nokia a superior ROI from a financial point of view while also rendering a higher likelihood of successful partnerships that come from the strategic investments.

NGP manages its Venture Capital Fund to focus on investments in information and communications technologies ranging from components to services. It looks to partner with companies in growth-stage financing, with typical investments ranging from $5 to $15 million. "We are looking for companies that have a potential to grow to become a $100 million company," says Asel. NGP targets investments primarily in the United States, Europe, and Asia in companies that have a commercially available product or service; are ramping up revenues in large, growing markets; and are beginning to experience adoption by major industry participants such as Nokia. The first and foremost objective of Nokia Growth Partners is to partner with and support entrepreneurs in growing their companies into global leaders in their chosen field.

Ideally, business criteria and investment criteria overlap, which gives NGP an opportunity to work together in a business area. In this case, NGP and the business team hope to make a joint decision on both the investment and partnership. Integrity is vital so that each side can make its own unfettered business judgment. "If they come together *independently*, that's when the model really works," says Asel.

Since it began operations in 2005, Nokia Growth Partners has invested in companies in Asia, North America, and Europe.[29] The underlying assumption is that the talent that once was primarily in the United States, particularly in Silicon Valley, is now more dispersed.

Moreover, even the global economic crisis did not discourage Asel and his colleagues. NGP invests over a three-to-five-year period. In difficult markets, the strong get stronger while the weak fade away. In some sense, this may be a better investment environment. In 2008, global trade plunged for the first time since the early 1980s, but the latter was also one of the best periods to invest in U.S. venture history. "About half of thirty-three companies that were funded in 1983 went public," says Asel. "I'm a big believer that innovation happens regardless of cycles and that downturns can test determination, which actually yields better companies."

Nokia's Innovation Network Is Global

Until the 1990s, the value in the cell phone was in the radio and, in particular, miniaturization of the hardware. In the late 1990s, the value began to migrate toward added functionality, and Nokia followed in those footsteps. The challenge of combining mobility and the Internet has been immensely energizing to Nokia's R&D talent. "We're coming to the end of the GSM miracle growth phase of Nokia," says Nokia's former CTO Bob Iannucci.

Today, the Nokians struggle to come up with solutions that bring consumers the best user experiences. In order to ensure the consumers' voice in R&D, the unit is aligned with those organizational parts of Nokia that are close to the market. The goal is to make R&D decisions based on consumer needs, thus enabling the Nokians to envision complete solutions in which device, services, and content work are well aligned together.

Innovating Technologies, Creating Markets

In order to win, technology innovation must be coupled with market creation. Accordingly, innovation is today understood more broadly than before in Nokia. It comprises the activities of Nokia Research Center and unit R&D as well as new business development. These approaches include corporate innovation (along with the powerful brand, strategic approach to marketing, and global consumer insights, which are explored in the next chapter).

Nokia's global innovation network operates worldwide. The density of the network linkages is relatively highest in a handful of locations, particularly in Finland, the United States, and China. In each case, the nodal points do not cover multiple locations, only a few. In Finland, the key nodes are NRC locations in Helsinki and Tampere, open innovation research in the Helsinki and Tampere University of Technology, and Nokia Growth Partners in Helsinki. In the United States, NRC's key locations include Cambridge, Massachusetts; Santa Monica, California; and Palo Alto, California—in other words, research concentrations on Route 125, Hollywood, and Silicon Valley. In China, NRC has a new location in Beijing, which is also the home of Tsinghua University and research on open innovation. Nokia Growth Partners, however, is also located in Beijing. Figure 5.5 provides an overview of Nokia's international R&D partners.

Innovation Cushioned by a Strong Capital Structure

A less understood aspect of Nokia's innovation is the company's strong capital structure, which supports risk taking in technology research and market creation. During the worst days of the global economic crisis, for example, Nokia and its competitors faced comparable pressures, but not all were as well positioned to cope with them as Nokia was. From a financial standpoint, the company has always been managed in a way that outsiders have characterized as "very conservative." The Nokians consider that characterization flawed. Says Nokia's former CFO Simonson, "The reason we run with a strong capital structure and the reason that we run with a net cash balance as opposed to net debt is that we have a company that's valued on the basis of intangible assets." For all practical purposes, intangible assets are R&D that you have to make into product that you

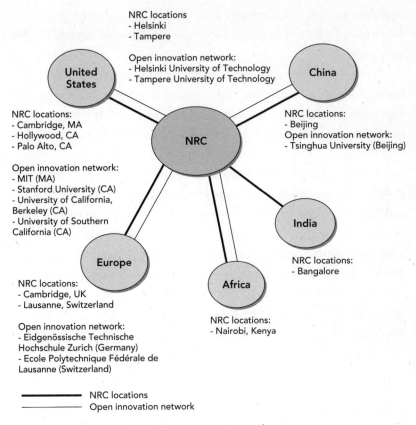

NRC locations
- Helsinki
- Tampere

Open innovation network:
- Helsinki University of Technology
- Tampere University of Technology

United States

China

NRC locations:
- Cambridge, MA
- Hollywood, CA
- Palo Alto, CA

NRC

NRC locations:
- Beijing
Open innovation network:
- Tsinghua University (Beijing)

Open innovation network:
- MIT (MA)
- Stanford University (CA)
- University of California, Berkeley (CA)
- University of Southern California (CA)

India

Europe

Africa

NRC locations:
- Bangalore

NRC locations:
- Cambridge, UK
- Lausanne, Switzerland

Open innovation network:
- Eidgenössische Technische Hochschule Zurich (Germany)
- Ecole Polytechnique Fédérale de Lausanne (Switzerland)

NRC locations:
- Nairobi, Kenya

———— NRC locations
———— Open innovation network

FIGURE 5.5   Nokia's Global Innovation Network

make a margin on. If you don't invest adequately in R&D, you have a product that isn't going to attract the value that allows you to make the margin, and there's nothing to fall back on.

The other intangible is the Nokia brand. It's one of the most valuable, trusted, and admired brands in the world. Running a business that has a technology risk and is based on intangible assets, the Nokia way is not to put a financial risk on top of that. In contrast, the idea is to have net cash, not net debt, that is, a strong capital structure. "Now you can manage cash flow so that, if for external reasons, you hit a tougher patch, you won't have a gun to your head because of the financial structure," says Simonson.

It was only with the global financial crisis that Nokia got its historical vindication. At the same time, the company is better positioned to cope with its historical transformation from a technology-intensive company to a technology- *and* marketing-intensive company.[30]

In the past, multinationals could gain competitive advantage by exploiting global-scale economies or arbitraging imperfections in the world's labor, materials, or capital markets. Over time, these advantages have eroded. Today, most multinationals compete primarily with a handful of other giants, comparable in size and diversity. These new winners are companies that are highly attuned to market evolution and technological trends no matter where they occur. In addition to innovation, companies that will continue to succeed, like Nokia, need to build layered competitive advantages through other strategic capabilities, which are described in Chapter Six.

Nokia's Lessons

- Any company that operates in a technology-intensive environment must view innovation as a critical capability.

- In order to create, develop, and generate attractive products and services, a successful multinational must build the right strategic capabilities. At Nokia, these are seen as the priority investment areas, which can be shared across functions and activities, in order to build layered competitive advantages.

- In Nokia's business, the most spectacular industry failures involve companies that have engaged in technology development but ignored market creation. Conversely, unsuccessful companies have sought to dominate the markets but ignored technology development. In technology- and marketing-intensive environments, technology innovation is necessary, but it's not sufficient for success. It must be accompanied by complementary market creation.

- Innovation does not occur in isolation. National innovation systems can support or constrain innovative activities of multinationals. It is thus vital that companies seek to participate with and network in critical innovation systems worldwide through international R&D cooperation, as well as with universities and research institutes.

- At Nokia, sustained innovation is predicated on rapid expansion of long-term research by the Nokia Research Center, short-term unit-based R&D, and globally networked university cooperation, open innovation, and venture funds. New business development requires innovation internally and externally.

- Despite Nokia's extensive research activities, it avoids research for research's sake. Success is predicated on increasing industrial innovation with universities, optimizing research potential across technologies and markets, and corporate innovation through internal and extended venturing activities to ensure participation in new technologies and new markets.

6

DEVELOPING STRATEGIC CAPABILITIES ACROSS THE WORLD

Many companies excel in one or another competitive dimension, but few excel in several dimensions. "Nokia developed its capabilities over time," says Matti Alahuhta, a former senior executive. The company has turned potentially fateful moments of adversity into a learning experience, which have been built into powerful strategic capabilities that are difficult to imitate.[1]

In addition to innovation (including technology and architecture, as well as intellectual property described in Chapter Five), these global strategic capabilities include areas such as a demand and supply network, sourcing, distribution, the powerful brand, strategic marketing, and global consumer insight. Hoping to maintain its advantages, Nokia invests in these strategic capabilities. Let's look at these capabilities in greater detail.

Nokia's Demand and Supply Network

"The market is no longer falling in an uncontrolled manner," said CEO Kallasvuo during a conference call. "I am encouraged by the signs of stabilization seen at the end of the first quarter." These words sparked great interest amid the global economic crisis. In April 2009, the company reported a 90 percent drop in first-quarter profit, but it also saw signs of stabilizing demand in the slumping handset market. From Wall Street's analysts to the White House's economic advisors, this was perceived as still another sign that the crisis was stabilizing, even if it was too early to say whether the fall in consumer demand had reached bottom. The assumption was that Nokia's demand and supply network was so efficient that it signaled the fluctuations of demand globally, prior to many other indicators.

With the global economic crisis of 2008–2009, what companies needed was the ability to deal with changing conditions by making production processes more flexible and engaging in more effective collaboration with key suppliers.[2] Unlike many other companies, Nokia had begun to build this capability after the mid-1990s and globalized it by the early 2000s.[3]

Modularity Supports Global Scale Economies and Local Responsiveness

Around 1992–1993 Nokia made an important decision in mobile phones, which has greatly benefited networks as well. In the technology architecture, Nokia's senior executives opted for developing products in a modular way. The basic idea was to seek for 60–80 percent homogeneity; that provided the global basis for success. Conversely, it would always have 20–30 percent for local adaptation, which provided the local basis for success.

With modularity Nokia has enjoyed economies of scale in product development, production, and sourcing. That has also resulted in huge purchasing benefits. This modular combination of global and local was incorporated into the Nokia way of doing things very early on. It provides great economies of scale, while ensuring local responsiveness to those features that cannot be shared across markets.

Power of Scale Economies

During 2008, Nokia made more than 1.25 million devices per day in its device manufacturing facilities globally. It has a world-class logistics and distribution system, and it is a world leader in supply chain management. As scale increases, average cost per unit falls. Indeed, Nokia's substantial scale contributes to its lower cost structure and ability to invest in innovation.

Still, even scale is not an inherited birthright at Nokia but a result of a struggle. After all, economies of scale evolve differently in large-country multinationals that benefit from a large home market and in small-country multinationals that have virtually no home market. In the former, economies of *scope* are achieved through economies of *scale*. Typically, volume advantages in the home market are leveraged in foreign markets, and scale is thus a function of the ability to take advantage of the home market. In brief, international operations are an extension of the domestic market.

In the small-country multinationals, the situation is reversed; that is, economies of *scale* are achieved through economies of *scope*. Typically, volume advantages are amassed in many core country markets, and scale is thus a function of the ability to take advantage of many markets worldwide. In brief, global operations are the market.

Evolution of Nokia's Manufacturing and Logistics Success

Nokia achieved its strong positioning in manufacturing, logistics, and sourcing over time.[4] In the pre-1992 era when Nokia was still a diversified concern with ambitions to become a European electronics conglomerate, its units worked relatively independently. There was some level of cooperation in component sourcing, but none in manufacturing and logistics. When Nokia focused on mobile communications, it also acquired Technophone, the United Kingdom's only cellular phone manufacturer. This acquisition brought in Frank McGovern, the UK chief of operations, a passionate Scot who made a vital contribution to Nokia's manufacturing.[5] During this period, Nokia's mobile phone business grew very quickly for a couple of years—but without the right systems, competencies, skills, and processes to support that growth.

To many Nokians, the logistics crisis of 1995–1996 was the defining moment. Until that crisis, Nokia's manufacturing and logistics network was still relatively uncoordinated and without strategy for aligning internal activities. "We simply didn't know when the demand was shifting," acknowledges Robert Andersson, former head of Nokia's global demand and supply network.[6] "Without the logistics crisis, Nokia would not have become the world's best player in terms of demand-supply balancing and overall sourcing, logistics, manufacturing," he adds.

Nokia turned the situation around in Europe, Asia, and the United States by implementing new supply chain disciplines, which included improvements in manufacturing productivity and quality, supplier development, supply chain planning, and integration. The results were impressive.[7]

Flexibility and Scale via Centralized IT

Overall, Nokia's IT emulates the evolution of the organization, but it also anticipated the prevailing integrated business model by almost a decade. In 1992, Nokia still had a country-based IT structure in which every country and each business had its own IT system. If that structure had prevailed during the high-growth years of the late 1990s, "the result would have been a catastrophe," says Mikko Kosonen, former head of strategy and CIO, who joined Nokia in 1984.[8]

The logistics crisis allowed Nokia's leadership to see IT as a strategic asset that must be managed in a centralized way. It enabled the company to build worldwide systems and processes by putting in place a unified backbone of systems architecture. It was then that Nokia renewed successfully its internal management systems by employing a very robust SAP system coupled with a central IT philosophy, including bringing together financial information.[9] By 2002 Nokia had joint worldwide IT systems and unified processes that supported fast decision making and reallocation of resources.[10]

Even today, many companies still struggle with fragmented IT. They may have a CIO at the corporate level, but often with a relatively small staff. The real IT work takes place in the business groups, which have larger staffs. Instead, the production and logistics of Nokia's mobile devices is globally networked through its matrix organization. The centralized IT philosophy has gone hand in hand with Nokia's organizational capabilities.

A Centralized Hub Facilitates Global Manufacturing and Logistics

After its logistics crisis, Nokia changed from a decentralized hub to a global centralized hub. It used to have a regional demand-supply balancing system that was based on America, Europe, Africa, and Asia. Today everything is seen from a global perspective, as a centralized hub.

Since the early 2000s, the emerging economies have played a key role in Nokia's activities. Still, from a process point of view, Nokia is using the same equipment, the same processes, and the same training in India, China, Hungary, and other countries. The bottom line is that Nokia no longer gets an adequate price performance in advanced economies, but it has an abundance of that performance in emerging economies, which are also closer to its most important markets.[11]

Today, Nokia is among the half a dozen leading supply chain companies in the world, along with Apple, Dell, Procter & Gamble, IBM, Cisco, Wal-Mart, and Toyota. It operates some ten manufacturing factories in nine countries around the world for the production of mobile devices; Figure 6.1 provides an overview.

Here's how the hub works, in terms of products manufactured in each location:

- At three of these plants (in Salo, Finland; Beijing, China; and Masan, South Korea), production is geared toward high-value, low-to-medium-volume mobile devices.

- A fourth plant, located in the United Kingdom, serves Nokia's luxury mobile phone, the high-end Vertu business.

- Most production facilities (in Komárom in Hungary, Cluj in Romania, Dongguan in China, Chennai in India, Manaus in Brazil, and Reynosa in Mexico) concentrate on the production of high-volume, cost-sensitive mobile devices.

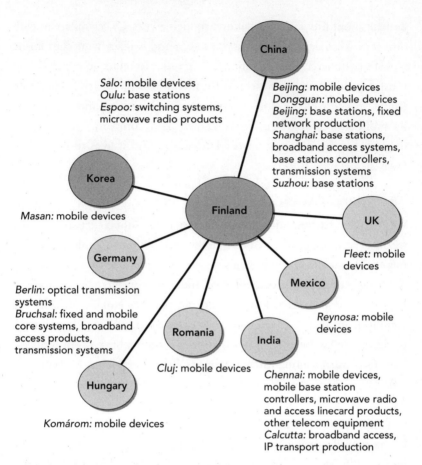

Salo: mobile devices
Oulu: base stations
Espoo: switching systems, microwave radio products

Beijing: mobile devices
Dongguan: mobile devices
Beijing: base stations, fixed network production
Shanghai: base stations, broadband access systems, base stations controllers, transmission systems
Suzhou: base stations

Masan: mobile devices

Berlin: optical transmission systems
Bruchsal: fixed and mobile core systems, broadband access products, transmission systems

Fleet: mobile devices

Reynosa: mobile devices

Cluj: mobile devices

Chennai: mobile devices, mobile base station controllers, microwave radio and access linecard products, other telecom equipment
Calcutta: broadband access, IP transport production

Komárom: mobile devices

FIGURE 6.1   Nokia's Manufacturing Facilities

Outsourcing Aligned with Culture

The manufacturing facilities form an integrated global production network, ensuring flexibility to adjust production volumes to fluctuations in market demand in different regions. Nokia's mobile device manufacturing and logistics is complex, requires advanced and costly equipment, and involves outsourcing to third parties.[12] It is Nokia's culture that provides the foundation even to outsourcing. Take, for instance, Nokia's multisourcing, commercial chipset strategy.[13] Nokia designs about fifty different handset models a year. Once you are in with one of Nokia's design projects, you are in and will see your chip inside Nokia's commercial handset model.[14] In order to retain your status, you must stay close to the productivity frontier. In fact, comparison shopping would violate Nokia's trust-driven, integrated business model. Despite its multi-sourcing strategy, it is known as a company "really tough to get into." It likes long-term relationships, and it likes to work with the best.

The Future of Nokia's Demand and Supply Network

Will Nokia maintain its current demand and supply network in the medium to long term? The bottom line: not without significant adjustments. Today, the early decisions to establish manufacturing operations in China, Korea, and subsequently in India are considered wise strategic moves in the company. Most of the components Nokia is buying are coming from Asia. Labor quality has been considered good, and price performance has been close to superior at a reasonable cost. In contrast, Nokia's competitors are neither as diversified nor as global. Most important, these rivals do not have the kind of supply base that Nokia has developed.

Still, some Nokians may be tempted to ask themselves: "Are we in the manufacturing business? Or are we in a design and integration business?"[15] They might argue that, in the medium to long term, it is not that certain that Nokia will be as involved in the manufacturing of its products. For instance, even Dell is no longer really manufacturing but mainly outsourcing from a supply chain, particularly to companies like contract electronics manufacturer Flextronics International Ltd. (which is also working with Nokia). For now, Nokia does have an in-house advantage. In the medium to long term, this may be subject to intensifying competition.

On the other hand, Nokia currently has a dual business model. Historically, it has been strong in products; it is moving toward solutions in the future. Economies of scale are critical to Nokia's strengths in manufacturing, which, in turn, drives its emerging strengths in solutions. Some outsourcing can contribute to its flexibility, but excessive outsourcing would mean the erosion of its scale advantage. As the Nokians currently see it, that would be a strategic hara-kiri in a high-volume business. To them, Nokia without its carefully developed scale advantage is a bit like Hamlet without the Prince of Denmark.

Leadership in Global Distribution and Sales

Since 2000, Nokia has patiently built the industry's largest distribution network. It comprises more than 300,000 points of sale globally and a substantially larger distribution network, particularly in China, India and the Middle East, and North Africa than its rivals in these regions. Due to this substantial lead, distribution is seen as one of Nokia's vital strategic advantages. Yet not much is known about it.

Achieving Scale Efficiencies in Distribution

Although Nokia may still have a technology company image rather than that of a high-performing marketing organization, it has gone through a great and well-timed effort since the early 2000s to build Nokia's channel in the developing world. The center of gravity has been in the large emerging economies, particularly China and India, but also in Southeast Asia, as well as the Middle East and North Africa.

The effort has been largely successful, as evidenced by Nokia's strong brand position in these markets. In addition to its demand and supply network efficiencies that contribute to lower costs of goods sold, Nokia is able to enjoy scale efficiencies in operating costs. For example, its distribution and marketing efforts can be spread across a broad portfolio of offerings, in contrast to smaller competitors that focus on a specific geographical market or product segment.

Today, mobile device market participants compete with each other on the basis of their product, services and solutions portfolio, user experience, design, price, operational and manufacturing efficiency, technical performance, distribution strategy, quality, customer support, brand, and marketing. Typically, the drivers of the success of a product or service vary by geographical market and product and services segment. For instance, price, brand, and distribution are often critical factors in entry-level markets. By the same token, distribution has played a vital role in the large emerging economies.

Transformation to Solutions Sales

Until November 2009 Timo Ihamuotila, currently CFO, was responsible for Nokia's global sales within the new Markets unit.[16] "It is a big change," he says about Nokia's transformation to a global solutions company. Now the entire sales process of the total Nokia offering will go through just a single organization. "But it's more than just a major transformation for the sales force," adds the soft-spoken Finn. "Now we must become a solutions sales force. The days of the traditional box moving mobile sales force are history."

However, it is not enough to get the sales force aboard; you must also change their mindset. Nokia's transformation to solutions is about new kinds of offerings—which require a new mindset.

Understanding the Sales Process

From the mid- to late 1990s, the market was growing so fast that the sales process was—as Ihamuotila exaggerates to make a point—"more of how we'd allocate the product between different markets." When markets started to saturate and slow down a little bit around the year 2000, the challenge became to build the right channel structure and reach. Until the recent organizational transformation, the point was to ensure the right channel structure around the world and the capacity to achieve optimal reach. Nokia also had to build optimal operator accounts and, in the open markets, it built distribution where it understood not just sell-through but also sellout; in other words, what actually happened at different points of sales.

Today, the challenge is to take the service components into the sales process, structuring the sales organization into solutions sales, which is a new and different strategic task. With solutions, it is now more important than ever before that the basics are in place. From the consumer's standpoint, these basics include four components:

- Easy discoverability of the solutions

- Usability

- The right channel economics that allows both the company and its channel partner (say, an operator) to make money

- The right points of sales and retail execution

As long as competition in mobile communications was only about the devices, sales had to get the device to as many points of sales as possible. It was the reach that defined how many consumers will find access to the product. Now that's not enough. At the point of sales, you must also get that consumer to activate the service. That's the main difference. In the old model, you basically sold the product and let the market take care of the rest. The distribution system ensured that the product found its way to as many points of sales as possible. Today the company must understand those points of sales and what kind of communication the salesclerks have with the consumer.

Different Sales Channels in Different Markets

In sales, the key challenge is to take into account different sales channels in different markets. In practice, there are three basic variations.

- In the U.S. market operators *are* the channel. Until recently, they controlled the marketplace.

- In Europe and Latin America the picture is more mixed. Although operators dominate in certain products, there is also a large open market.

- In developing markets the channel tends to be relatively open and the product is sold to the distributors.

In the past Nokia took its global product to the United States, but this leverage model has not performed adequately, as evidenced by the decline of Nokia's market share. Today, Nokia is making more original models for and seeks to also strengthen its distribution and sales in the U.S. market.

As an industry leader, Nokia has a sales strategy, which is somewhat different for each market. In addition to these channel differences, Nokia's sales and marketing in the BRIC economies takes into account consumer segmentation and consumer preferences. Some markets are seen as very rational; some other markets are very aspirational.

The Smartphone Opportunity

The rise of smartphones has not changed the basic equation but only highlights its importance. Since most services will first work on the smartphone, the latter has a critical role in the new offerings. It does not change the basics, but makes it even more important for the company to educate the consumers so that they find it easy to use not just voice or texting, but also other features of their devices. "Ultimately, the competition is really about the consumer segment preferences and the channel structure," says Ihamuotila. "If you understand these both right, you're going to be successful in sales."

As mobile device markets are becoming more segmented and diversified, Nokia faces increasing competition from different mobile device manufacturers in different user segments, price points, and geographic markets. The most important lesson of Nokia's sales is that no company that is going through such a thorough transformation should underestimate the great value of a good sales function that can support the transformation.

The Power of Nokia's Global Brand

In addition to its demand and supply network capabilities, Nokia's brand is another strong strategic capability. The power of the brand is evidenced by a story told by Yrjö Neuvo, Nokia's legendary former CTO. A while back, he was in Stockholm, making an outdoor phone call in the dark of the night, when a tall, large man in a leather jacket approached him. The biker was not a Hell's Angel, but he could have been. He asked to see the Nokian's mobile handset. As Neuvo gave his handset to the man, he prepared to run away, thinking he would be robbed. But the giant took the mobile device, turned it around in his big hand, and then compared it with his own Nokia mobile. "Oh well, I guess it's time to get a new Nokia phone," he said and gently gave the handset back to Dr. Neuvo. Now, *that's* a powerful brand!

Learning from Global Brand Leaders

In the United States, the *BusinessWeek/Interbrand* annual rating of *2009 Best Global Brands* positioned Nokia as the fifth most valued brand in the world, right behind Coca-Cola, IBM, Microsoft, and GE. Its value is estimated at $34.9 billion. Only two decades ago, such a position would have been inconceivable. In the early 1990s, Nokia was nonexistent as a global brand. Yet only a decade later, it is synonymous with mobile devices. Although Nokia has trailed behind Apple's iPhone and RIM's BlackBerry in smartphones in the United States, the brand value of the latter two is only 44 percent and 15 percent, respectively, of Nokia's. Among other things, these valuations reflect the *global* brand advantage.

In a consumer business such as these devices, brand is a major differentiating factor, with broad effects on market share and pricing. Through most of the 1980s, however, Nokia was known as an original equipment manufacturer (OEM). "Like its homeland, Nokia has an image problem," noted the *Wall Street Journal* in 1987. "Outside of Finland, it barely has one."[17]

Nokia's brand strength originates from 1991, when Jorma Ollila's executive team decided that Nokia would be marketed as a single brand and gave a young 3M marketing executive, Anssi Vanjoki, the mandate to make Nokia a household name. As an OEM, Nokia's products were then sold under such brands as Bosch, Alcatel, AT&T, Tandy, and others. Vanjoki was hired to reshape the organization and to develop the strategy for branding.

While researching companies that had developed successful brands, Vanjoki discovered a common denominator among such leaders as Nike, Daimler-Benz, and Philip Morris. These companies thought about the brand in *every aspect of the value chain,* including design, production, and distribution. Their brand strategy was holistic, which became Nokia's goal as well.

153

In an internal memo, Vanjoki defined branding as "an act of consistency and continuity along predetermined dimensions to achieve customer satisfaction." He scrapped previous slogan proposals, opted for "High technology with human touch," and presented his brand strategy in summer 1991. "Brand management is a necessity in the class of technological leadership and low-cost manufacturing for us," Vanjoki thought. "It is an element of survival, and prosperity in our business."

A Single, Unified Approach to Branding

The brand launch peaked in January 1992, with the release of the Nokia 101, the first consumer-designed hand portable mobile phone. A few months later, Nokia's executive team made the vital decision to increase brand investment. Soon thereafter, the company adopted the new English-language slogan, "Connecting People" (as described in Chapter Three).

Typically, Finnish brands had been largely domestic. Many brands were localized; foreign products were brought to the country with little modification and introduced as local brands. The small economy could not support many original brands. However, Nokia built on the success of its early cell phone campaigns (Cityman, Freedom, and Talkman models) and, initially, developed its brand on five basic dimensions: high technology, Nordic design, individualism, freedom, and enduring quality. Most dimensions emphasized lifestyle values, including ecological themes, which resonated particularly well with the critical early-adopter segment.

By September 1996—less than half a decade after the brand launch—Nokia had the strongest cellular brand awareness and image in Europe. Like Sony, Nokia branded the entire company and made sure that the look and feel of its mobile phones created a "single, unified approach" across the world.

"Strictly speaking, it's not globalization of the brand, but the globalization of the business," specifies Vanjoki. He believes strongly that Nokia brands and other historical brands have not become global without innovation. As a result, it would be very difficult to challenge incumbent brand leaders without creating something new and novel. "As you rapidly jump into that wave and surf it, you really are like a surfer on a wave that's bigger than you are," says Vanjoki, who has been working on the wave theory of branding for a long time. After the initial choices, it is consistency and continuity that will sustain branding. The point is to stay on the tip of the wave and just follow where it's going.

For all practical purposes, Nokia's branding has happened in stages:

- At first, Nokia worked on getting attention.

- Then, it focused efforts more on building its image and creating trust.

- A few years ago, the company reached a point where most people were aware of the brand and the image was very clear.

- That led to an orientation decision about whether the company would be diversifying the brand or keeping it fairly simple functionally. "Since the functionality that we have been offering is not constant but evolving, you have to create new meaning to the brand," says Vanjoki.

Today, Nokia is one of the leading brands in the world.

Sustaining Brand Value and Brand Leadership

But how does the company seek to *sustain* the brand and its brand leadership? Let's go back to the iceberg theory on sustaining the brand and brand leadership (Figure 6.2 shows the simplicity of this concept). Here's what the iceberg theory of branding means to Nokia: If you have a young brand, the iceberg is all visible. There is nothing beneath the water; it is all there. As a result, it is vital to keep the young brand constantly vivid and alive. As your brand grows older and attracts more following, the iceberg remains there, but much of it is not visible. Yet it provides trust and loyalty that will take you through some tough and difficult times. So even amid a downturn, your brand may not go down at all because of the trust that you have built over time.

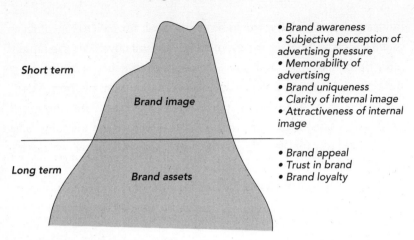

FIGURE 6.2 The Brand Iceberg

According to this model, brand strength—that is, brand value—is derived from brand image and brand assets:

- *Brand image* constitutes the components of a brand that are "visible" to consumers, that is, the short-term measures in the marketing mix (such as product and packaging design, advertising, promotions, events) that are perceived by buyers. It is shaped by brand awareness, the clarity and appeal of internal brand image, the distinctiveness of brand identity, the lasting impact of advertising, and advertising pressure as subjectively perceived.

- The *brand assets* make up the portion of the iceberg that is "underwater." They represent longer-term changes in consumer attitudes and also include earlier investments in the brand that exist beneath the surface more or less as assets. These assets encompass brand appeal and trust in the brand (in other words, brand loyalty).

Internal brand value can thus be understood as the sum of internal brand image and brand assets.[18]

At Nokia, the iceberg model has been consciously built, almost from the beginning. More recently, the company has reinforced the balance "under the water." As a result, the Nokia brand is stable. Vanjoki believes that Nokia is well positioned for the next stage. After all, there are well over one billion people who have a Nokia in their hand. That's a position that nobody else has. It represents the world's largest distribution of branded consumer durables. "Consumer disposables disappear just like that, whereas durables are there all the time, you know," Vanjoki says. "So if you have designed a coffee cup, or a car, or a mobile device, they're there all the time, they won't disappear, even if they are considered cheap, due to subsidized business models."

Although Nokia's great position in the *BusinessWeek/Interbrand* ranking of global brands is flattering, Vanjoki keeps his eyes focused on the wave theory and considers relative brand comparisons "hocus pocus." Certainly, the top-ten global brands are important, but it would be very difficult to identify a rank order. Shareholder value plays a vital role in the ranking, but it means very little in consumer behavior. Share prices can go up and down and be very volatile within a single day of trading, but it does not follow that the consumer will embrace or abandon a popular consumer durable within the same day. Consumer behavior moves slowly. If you don't keep a young brand consistent and steady, it will capsize and disappear. In contrast, an established old brand, most of which is under sea level, is more stable and can hold the balance far better.

Nokia's Small Home Market Forced to Build Brand Value Globally

The difference between large- and small-country multinationals applies to branding as well. From the standpoint of brand leverage, the U.S. economy provides a wonderful unified platform of more than 300 million relatively wealthy people. During the past two decades, more than 70 percent of the U.S. GDP has been driven by consumption, which translates to a great springboard for global brands in a tough competitive environment. With such a platform, a successful company can generate a huge volume of business.

As a result, the incentive for a large U.S.-based company, for example, to internationalize early and globalize its business is substantially *lower* than, say, in Finland, Sweden, or Switzerland. "Our home market does not serve as a springboard for volume and it cannot address the global marketplace," says Vanjoki. The moment you cross the border, things get more complicated. In branding, too, the fragmented worldwide marketplace is a tough issue. In the future, large emerging economies, such as China and India, will be in a very different position because if they can develop a unified economy, they will offer an even larger springboard for a global brand business.

When Vanjoki prepared his original brand slides, back in the early 1990s, he did not lack ambition. He had a twenty-five-year plan for Nokia, an internationally unknown company that had just escaped bankruptcy. "Now the job is to define the meaning of the new Nokia in the *converged* world," says Vanjoki.

In the new era, a mobile phone is no longer just a mobile phone. As we shall see in Chapter Seven, Nokia is diversifying its brand with Ovi (Finnish for "door"), the brand for Nokia's Internet services. To Vanjoki, Ovi is a way to diversify and extend the original Nokia brand.

Strategic Approach to Marketing

Instead of durable goods or major appliances (such as kitchen appliances), which are generally replaced less than once a year, Nokia has a distinctive marketing take on *fast-moving consumer goods* (FMCG)—that is, products that are sold quickly at relatively low cost, from cosmetics to detergents.[19]

Nokia Offerings as Fast-Moving Consumer Goods

Although the *absolute profit* made on FMCG products is relatively small, they generally sell in large quantities, so the *cumulative profit* on such products can be large.[20] The Nokians believe that it's very different to be in consumer *durable* brands than in *disposable* brands. "The brown sugar water is very different from this consumer durable, multimedia computer," says Vanjoki. "Cola-Cola is the same as it was more than a century ago when the so-called secret formula was born. The way you keep it alive is by creating stuff around it." In effect, Coca-Cola has failed almost every time it has tried to diversify, except with Coca-Cola Light, or

Diet Coke in the United States. This, however, has little to do with Coke and much with people's desire to be healthy.

In a fast-changing and technology-intensive environment, consumers *expect* progression and something new. In consumer durables, the core of the brand, which is the actual experience, does not remain stable; it's evolving. Like disposable products, consumer durables are characterized by repetitive use, but the users are not necessarily looking for something new. Rather, they expect the "same old" to be confirmed, which is validated by the imagery associated with the brand. All of this can be done with consumer durables as well, but if you fail to deliver the actual experience, whatever is new and novel, you're out, and your products or services will begin to decline. In other words, the role of innovation is very different in disposable products and consumer durables.[21]

PITA at Nokia

The realization that the mobile handset should be viewed not as a simple durable good, but as a complex fast-moving consumer good, evolved in Nokia during the 1990s. During those growth years, Nokians often put up slides showing the soaring penetration of the cell phone in different markets of the world, and how this penetration would surpass that of PCs. As mobile penetration hit 100 percent in the most advanced markets, Nokia's marketers asked the next question: "Now everybody has a cell phone in markets XYZ. How can we take advantage of this penetration while providing value-added to the consumer?"

Soon the Nokians realized that they might be able to unleash the potential of mobile devices by exploring the business models of the most successful FMCGs. For instance, Coca-Cola also measures penetration, but not penetration only. It has a more comprehensive measure called PITA, which stands for *population, incidents, times,* and *amounts.* When these four determinants are multiplied together, that is considered the basis of the revenue line. The PITA approach, however, is predicated on intimate knowledge of user behavior.

Only a few years ago, it was hard to find Nokians who were tracking the user base. Today, the task is pretty much a core part of Nokia's strategy and will continue to be so. Unlike most of its rivals, Nokia learns from its mistakes, and it learns and implements new processes relatively quickly. Says Keith Pardy, Nokia's former chief of strategic marketing, who joined Nokia in 2004 after working the better part of his career in FMCG leadership roles with Coca-Cola, "The good news is that when you start from the user base, marketing helps you to connect what you do to the business objectives."

Three Ways to Grow the Business

Nokia's strategic marketing is driven by its user base and the brand. With the user base, Nokia seeks to better understand well over one billion people who currently carry Nokia mobile phones. The idea is to expand and deepen the link between the user base and business strategy. There are at least three ways to do so:

- One way to grow the business is to try to *attract more* users, say, two billion rather than "only" one billion.

- Another way to grow the business is that Nokia seeks to *retain* its one billion existing users, which is far less expensive than attracting new users.

- A third way to grow is to *leverage* business with the current one billion users.

Nowadays, Nokia seeks to attract new users, improve retention rate and lifetime relationship management, and leverage business in new areas. At the same time, Nokia is trying to leverage the meaning of its brand. Today, it stands for the leading global mobile handset company in consumers' perception. In order to expand and deepen the link between the user base and business strategy, Nokia must shape the meaning of the company so that it is perceived not only as a company that sells phones but that also provides services and solutions while helping consumers access and navigate the Internet.

With its user base and brand, Nokia tries to leverage consumer insights and consumer research. It already employs some 150 people focusing on these marketing issues. Traditionally, Nokia has been a *technology* company. Now it seeks to move from a technology company to an *innovation* company. When you invent something that's wonderful, but also invent something that consumers really want, that's innovation.

In the 1990s, Nokia's objective was to create a global brand as quickly as possible. Today, the idea is to strengthen the link between brand strategy and consumer behavior. As exemplified by the success of Apple and Coke, the values of the business strategy and the brand strategy must be connected. At the end of the day, the brand strategy is a summation of your consumer insights and what you're trying to do with your user base, consumers, and the meaning of the brand. Nokia's objective is to tighten its business and brand strategies by the early 2010s, when the two streams are expected to come tighter together.

Over the past several years, brand has become a core strategic asset for Nokia, and it has been elevated to the corporate level. Nokia has a tight governance structure for the brand and the strategy; brand metrics are reviewed quarterly by the brand board and group executive board.[22] In effect, using brand metrics is not that different from financial analysis: If you to buy a stock, you wouldn't buy it only on the basis of its price-to-earnings ratio. Instead, you would (or at least you *should*) look at its margin, the management team, free cash flow, capital invested, competitive position, marketing, and other factors. Similarly, consumer purchases occur in a very dynamic environment in which many things matter. So the Nokians look at the awareness for the brand globally, by region, and by country.[23]

Nokia's Communication Strategy Reinforces the Nokia Brand

As in many other multinationals, branding and communications strategy go hand in hand at Nokia. "Overall, communications tends to enhance and reinforce our branding," says Arja Suominen, Nokia's chief of global communications. "When the company is doing very well, it helps the brand as well. People like to identify with successful brands. We're in a consumer industry."

As Nokia has changed, its communications strategy has evolved along with branding. In the 1990s, communications management was still relatively loose, and there was very little integration and coordination among units. This reflected the state of the evolution of the broader organization. It was only at the end of the decade that the new reporting structures brought more cohesion to communications. In 2004, when Nokia changed its entire organizational structure, communications was centralized as well. Both internal and external communications came under the same umbrella globally. In the past, regions did not report; now they report to the head of communications. "The current communications strategy is fully aligned with the overall strategy," says Suominen.

The changes also reflect in Nokia's image. In the early 1990s, the target was that every now and then there would be a story about Nokia somewhere. Then the goal became that there would be stories about Nokia abroad, and whenever telecom is mentioned, Nokia would be mentioned as one of the companies. Now the target is that Nokia would be featured as the leader of the industry.

American multinationals enjoy the inherited advantage of the U.S. market, which has the most powerful media in the world. As a small-country multinational, Nokia does not enjoy the communications benefits of its big-country counterparts, especially those in the United States. "We have had to create these relationships from scratch and it has taken years," says Suominen.

As information spreads from America to other places and not the other way around, the challenge is that U.S. media are not interested in Nokia globally but only primarily in the United States. The challenge is to gain visibility in America, to capture the "U.S. megaphone," as some Nokians like to call it. From the standpoint of a global company, Finnish media support is marginal, although foreign media follow Finnish media to track significant developments at Nokia.

The communications team tries to have a very proactive posture. Like their counterparts in other multinationals, they would like to know in advance what will be written about their company and how it will be written. But unlike their counterparts, they also worry about how the stories are translated because the news agencies in Finland practically live on Nokia, particularly those that cover items of interest to the investors. "The reality is that if you are not present all the time," says Suominen, "you just don't exist."

Even though Nokia is one of the most heavily traded stocks in the NYSE, it has had a smaller U.S. share in the 2000s, which poses a challenge to Nokia's communications. Large-country multinationals operate in a large domestic marketplace, with few consolidated news outlets. Small-country multinationals operate globally, with numerous and different news outlets.

Take, for instance, financial reports and analysts' reactions, which come out almost instantly. The relative importance of "one big story" is fading away, it is the constant flow of a wide array of news outlets that matters now; not the individual story per se, but the general tone of the overall flow of information. From the standpoint of companies, first impressions count because analysts subsequently tend to react to them. Along with trained journalists, bloggers and citizen journalists also play a role in the news flow, particularly in online media, which companies can take advantage of as well. Most recently, many debates have been initiated in social media, offering new issues for discussion in the traditional print world.

As Nokia is changing, so is the contemporary media world. "How do you address all these channels?" asks Suominen. "You don't; you can't. In the past, you had a whole day to follow up the stories. Today any story can become global in a matter of seconds and it is impossible to correct anything."

Seeking Insights from Customers Around the World

Since the 1990s, Nokia has excelled in sensing and responding to market shifts flexibly and swiftly. The Nokians understand that the key to their success lies in understanding consumer needs and responding with relevant mobile solutions. The precursors of the Global Consumer & Customer Insights (GC&CI) unit were created in the mid-1990s. A few years later, these activities were consolidated in tracking, theme, trend, and segmentation activities. The role of the unit was elevated in the early 2000s, when global consumer segmentation was adopted throughout the organization.

Armed with their exceptional research on trends and segmentation globally, the GC&CI provides consumer, market, and channel understanding and insights across Nokia's strategy, devices plus design and product development, services development, and marketing and sales. By the 2010s, the consumer insights activities have accelerated. In barely a decade and a half, a Finnish engineering company with some international activities seeks to transform into a global marketing specialist with worldwide operations.

Enabling Sustainable, Consumer-Led Value Growth

Today the bold vision of GC&CI is that Nokia is recognized externally as the "most consumer-focused, customer-centric organization on the planet." Its strategic intent is to enable sustainable, consumer-led value growth. Ultimately, Nokia is on a journey to truly embed the consumer at the heart of its corporate culture. "We have a fairly good holistic view of the consumer," says Björn Ulfberg, head of Nokia's GC&CI since January 2008. The team used to work closely with Nokia's marketing function and design. Through reorganization, GC&CI became a companywide process.

For most practical purposes, the GC&CI teams reflect Nokia's activities in development and planning, identifying and shaping opportunities, generating consumer solutions, as well as providing tracking and segmentation of longitudinal consumer data. GC&CI's insight generation is based on a five-step journey: from objectives to audit to analysis to options to allocations.

Unlike other consumer research organizations and marketers, Nokia has hundreds of millions of mobile devices that are closest to the consumer's heart and thus provide a unique distribution platform worldwide. As a result, the Consumer Insights can increasingly use digital touch points to capture consumer behavior while learning about consumers. In turn, this information can be combined with the knowledge gained through the GC&CI functions that explains *why* consumers behave in certain ways.

Because mobility appeals differently to different people, Nokia undertook the industry's largest and most comprehensive research when it polled 74,000 people, covering a total of twenty-six countries, to understand the needs and drivers for mobility for different segments of the market. In the Nokia Devices subunit, the operations are aligned with major business categories, which represent target segments for Nokia's portfolio of mobile phones, smartphones, and mobile computers.

Through GC&CI, Nokia seeks to ensure that billions of consumers' voices across the world are injected into Nokia's decision making. In the process, Nokia itself has had to embrace a new mindset. People can purchase a mobile device, be somewhat dismayed but keep the device. With services, however, a low degree of satisfaction means that consumers will leave immediately, and it takes on average eighteen months for them to return. "That's why services are kept at the beta stage for a long, long time," says Ulfberg.

Listening to Technology and Market Signals

Nowadays, many technology companies are doing consumer research. But this research barely differs from that conducted in research centers. In one way or another, it tends to focus on technology, or technology as an enabler of behavior. That's a part of what Nokia does, but that's not all Nokia does. What makes Nokia's consumer research different is that it studies *all kinds* of signals. In the shorter term, it tries to create solutions with technology as an enabler, but it is also building on fundamentals in behavior. Nokia also differs from other companies, which typically will cover ten major markets, if even that many. "We have a lot broader and deeper research," says Ulfberg, "and our global value covers 85 percent, not just 50 percent of the total."

Several companies—including Intel, Motorola, and Microsoft—employ trained anthropologists to study potential customers, whereas Nokia's researchers more often have degrees in design. Rather than sending someone to Vietnam or India as an emissary for the company—loaded with products and pitch lines, as a marketer might be—the idea is to reverse it, to have a patently good listener enlighten the company on how they live and what they're likely to need from a cell phone, allowing that to inform its design. "I specialize in taking teams of concept/industrial designers, psychologists, usability experts, sociologists, and ethnographers into the field and, after a fair bit of work, getting them home safely," says Jan Chipcase who conducts research for Nokia Design. "I split my time between running user studies and developing new applications, services, and products that, if I do my job right, you'll be using three to fifteen years from now."

This sort of on-the-ground intelligence gathering is central to what's known as human-centered design that has become vital to high-tech companies trying to figure out how to write software, design laptops, or build cell phones that people find useful and unintimidating and will thus spend money on.

First Observe, Then Design

The Nokians believe that no matter what makes us different, we share the desire to connect. That is the foundation of Nokia's human approach to technology: *first, to observe, and then to design* (more on Nokia's design principles in the next chapter). It is this principle that, among other things, accounts for the success of Nokia Life Tools, for example. After a successful pilot in the state of Maharashtra, India, Nokia launched its pioneering service in India. Designed specifically for emerging markets, Nokia Life Tools is a range of agricultural, educational, and entertainment services addressing the information gaps of target consumers. The service expanded to select countries across Asia and Africa later in 2009 and will continue its expansion. Customer Insights played a vital role in the development of the service.

Also, unlike technology firms, such as IBM or Microsoft, Nokia cannot be content with just technology-intensive research. In many segments, technology segmentation poorly differentiates different consumers. Nokia operates in technology- *and* marketing-intensive business areas. As a result, it offers lessons to both types of companies. With the transition of growth from the West to the East, the world of consumer-led companies will become more diverse. "The world is becoming more complex, and the world of consumer behavior more complicated," says Ulfberg. "We need to better understand it all."

Nokia's Lessons

- Many companies excel in one or another competitive dimension, but only a few excel in several dimensions. At Nokia, these global strategic capabilities include not just innovation, but economies of scale, demand and supply network, distribution, and a powerful brand, including a strategic approach to marketing and global consumer insight.

- Learn from your mistakes and vulnerabilities. Nokia has systematically turned potentially fateful moments of adversity into a learning experience, which can then be built into powerful strategic capabilities that are difficult to imitate.

- Nokia has a world-class logistics and distribution system, and it is a world leader in supply chain management. As scale increases, average cost per unit falls. Nokia's huge scale economies contribute to low-cost structure and ability to invest in innovation.

- Nokia's centralized demand and supply network is so efficient and global that amid the global economic crisis it was used as an indicator of stabilizing demand worldwide.

- The most successful companies achieve adequate price performance in large emerging economies, which are often also the most important markets.

- In order to be successful globally, it is vital to spread distribution and marketing efforts across a broad portfolio of offerings, in contrast to smaller competitors that focus on a specific geographical market or product segment.

- In the early 1990s, Nokia was nonexistent as a global brand. Today it is one of the top brands in the world. Nokia's brand is supported by a strategic approach to marketing in fast-moving consumer goods and global consumer segmentation. In a consumer business (such as mobile devices and solutions), brand is a major differentiating factor, with broad effects on market share and pricing.

7

HOW NOKIA IS
GROWING AND
TRANSFORMING ITS
BUSINESS AREAS

We have seen how Nokia's success builds on its legacy and globalization, strategy, culture, and strategic capabilities (Chapters One through Six). When everything is said and done, all of these create necessary preconditions for success, but they do not account for actually achieving it. In order to win, a company needs to create strategic advantage. In this chapter, we shall take a closer look at how Nokia develops business strategies, which generate these advantages.

Nokia's Winning Business Strategies

Augmenting its devices and networks with solutions, Nokia engages in four basic strategies in its business areas:[1]

1. To lead and win in mobile devices

2. To grow consumer Internet services

3. To accelerate adoption of business solutions

4. To leverage scale and transform solutions in network infrastructure

These strategies are driven by four business groups: Devices, Services, Solutions, and Markets. Led by Dr. Kai Öistämö, the Devices unit is responsible for developing and managing Nokia's mobile device portfolio, including the sourcing of components. The Services unit is headed by Niklas Savander; it operates in consumer Internet services: music, maps, media, and messaging. The Solutions unit is led by Alberto Torres. Today, it is solutions that drive the roadmap of what kind of portfolio will be developed and what kind of devices and services will be aligned with that portfolio. Led by Anssi Vanjoki, the Markets division is responsible for the management of the supply chains, sales channels, the brand, and marketing functions of the company. Until November 2009, NSN was steered by Simon Beresford-Wylie; today, it is led by Rajeev Suri.

In its most dramatic transition to date, Nokia seeks to grow and transform its business areas globally.

Leadership in Mobile Devices

Since the late 1990s, the mobile device has been morphing into something more emotional and intimate. Like Madonna's "Express Yourself," it has become a reflection of one's identity. And like Nike's sneakers, mobile devices draw from innovation in technology and fashion.

Generic Form Factors

The three generic form factors of the most popular mobile phones—block phones, flip phones, folder and slide phones—have been around for years. *Block phones* (candy bars) provided Nokia the base for its segmentation. Historically, this form has been typical of Europe's GSM markets. Along with U.S. firms (Motorola, AT&T), Asian producers (Samsung, LG, Kyocera, Panasonic) have had a substantial presence in *flip phones*. More recently, *folder phones* (clamshells) have gained popularity in China and other markets. Finally, slide phones combine many of the advantages of a flip-open clamshell design with the traditional one-piece candy bar mobile phone.

In the 1980s, Motorola was the dominant equipment manufacturer. Nokia overthrew Motorola by segmenting the cell phone markets. In the 1990s, the customer base exploded. Declining prices made high volumes possible. Penetration accelerated dramatically in the most developed markets, and differentiation took off. By 1998, Nokia was pumping out new models every thirty-five days. Just as Procter & Gamble fills up the supermarket shelves, Nokia has multiplied segments to dominate categories.

Four Waves of Segmentation

Historically, *technology* was the basis for segmentation until the early 1990s, when the penetration was still very low; even in the cutting-edge markets only every tenth person had a cell phone. The cell phone had not become ubiquitous as it is today. Technology and price drove the business, and function ruled over style: what mattered was what the phone could do. But that emphasis changed with the rapid growth and saturation of the digital transition later in the decade. *Lifestyle* segmentation became more important. By the turn of the millennium, style reigned over function. What mattered was not just what the phone could do, but what it represented.

By the early 2000s, segmentation by *functionality* concentrated on single-purpose phones, with one dominant function, such as games, data, messaging, music, and so forth. Augmenting technology and lifestyle segmentation, it was complementary and driven by optimization. What mattered was not just what the phone could do, but how well it could do whatever it did (e.g., imagining, messaging, gaming, music).

In one way or another, all three principles of segmentation can be identified in Nokia's product category matrix, which evolved in the early 2000s. It can be illustrated by style categories (basic, expression, active, classic, fashion, and premium) and application categories (voice, entertainment, media, imaging, and business).

Currently, a fourth layer of segmentation—*service experience*—is emerging with services and solutions. Again, with features, it is what the product can do that matters. With image, it is what the product represents that counts. With functionality, optimal performance is the prime objective. With experience, it is what the consumers feel, think, and do in relation to the product that counts.

New Markets, Competencies, and Devices

Amid the burst of the dotcom bubble, Nokia was the only industry player that managed to retain profitability. As speculation escalated on whether the market could grow any longer, Nokia made a critical strategic choice that was barely noticed at the time. At Nokia Mobile Phones (NMP; today, Nokia Devices and Services), Nokia decided to start creating new markets, new competencies, and new devices. NMP was segmented into *value domains*, each of which had their value drivers, including low-cost, basic phones, high-end, multimedia, corporate, and others.[2]

Many analysts said that Nokia was moving ahead too early, but the Nokians thought that the time was right. "We felt then that Microsoft was breathing [down] our neck and might become our most serious competitor," says Matti Alahuhta, Nokia's former senior executive. As a result, Nokia created a mobile software unit, where it accelerated to build the smartphone software capability. This software was used for the multimedia and corporate value domain devices, the precursors of Nokia Nseries and Eseries. These mobile devices were supported by digital multimedia services, such as music playback, video capture, photography, mobile gaming, and Internet services. With this early approach, Nokia developed a very strong position in the emerging smartphone market.

Nokia leaned into the future; in hindsight, perhaps too much. It took a few more years before even Apple developed its smartphone in the mass markets. While Nokia created the foundation of the category, Apple pioneered user-friendly solutions. In the past, products drove the business, and services were limited to texting; today, solutions are driving the business and can make or break companies.

Everybody's Gadget: From West to East

Today a person's choice of mobile device is influenced by a number of factors, including their purchasing power, brand awareness, technological skills, fashion consciousness, and lifestyle. The global market for mobile devices comprises many different consumer groups and markets with different characteristics, dynamics, and stages of development.[3]

At first, the growth momentum was in the advanced economies. In the 2000s, it shifted to emerging economies. This transition did not change Nokia's basic strategy, which sees the mobile device as "everybody's gadget."

The growth momentum in the emerging economies has also guided Nokia's views on manufacturing capability and cost paradigm, although initially the idea of a mobile device below $100 was seen as a very radical idea. "We were always strong in the low-end, and internally, our dogma was always cost, cost, and cost," says Chairman Jorma Ollila about Nokia's scaling up in the large emerging economies.

In November 2009, Nokia unveiled the 1280, a mobile phone for emerging markets that is 20 percent cheaper than its predecessor, the 1202. The unsubsidized cost of the 1280 was $30, which made it Nokia's cheapest mobile phone yet. But the quest for cost-efficiency may not end there. According to the Nokians, the concept of a $7.50 mobile phone is no longer that far out. Indeed, Nokia seeks to be the lowest-cost manufacturer, which is fully in line with its quest for scale economies.

Nokia's Devices

Nokia's Devices unit is responsible for developing and managing the broadest device portfolio in the marketplace, including sourcing of components.[4] Nokia shipped a total of 468 million mobile devices in 2008. Based on projected global market volume of 1.2 billion units, Nokia's estimated full-year global market share in mobile devices increased to 39 percent. It has held a leading position in the global market since 1998.

Nokia also shipped a total of 61 million converged devices, while the company and industry partners took the first steps to develop Symbian, the operating system for mobile devices, into an open and unified platform, which will eventually move toward "open source."[5] The higher-end converged devices, such as Nokia Nseries and Nokia Eseries smartphones, typically offer the functionalities of many portable single-purpose devices—such as megapixel cameras, music players, computers, gaming consoles, and navigation devices—in a single, converged device.

Nokia's Devices unit seeks to create winning devices while developing, maintaining and sustaining the "best, most loved device portfolio in the marketplace." At Nokia, "best product" is understood as the best fit for the needs of consumers, trade customers, and the target market. "Best portfolio" means that the entire market is covered with the appropriate number of very competitive products complementing each other.

Mobile Phones, Smartphones, and Mobile Computers

Driven by consumer and customer insights, the Devices unit is also responsible for creating compelling platforms to truly enable Nokia's services and solutions. The unit consists of R&D, Sourcing, Devices North-America,[6] and Nokia Gear.[7] The Devices unit comprises two subunits: Mobile Phones and Smartphones.

Led by Rick Simonson, Mobile Phones is responsible for the portfolio, product, and life cycle management of all S30 and S40 devices, which account for more than half of Devices and Services sales and thus represent a substantial part of Nokia's business. Mobile Phones drives a media-rich mobile platform in devices that are already used by hundreds of millions of people and growing, thereby also helping to build the solutions business.[8]

Led by Jo Harlow, Smartphones is leading the portfolio, product, and life cycle management of all Symbian-based devices. It is working closely with the Solutions unit to bring a wide range of services, as well as advanced smartphone technologies, to an even wider group of consumers.[9] Harlow, a former captain of Duke University women's basketball team, joined Nokia's marketing unit in 2003, after a long career at Reebok and Procter and Gamble. She faces the big challenge of responding to fierce competition from Apple, HTC, RIM and others.[10]

In November 2009, John Martin, former vice president of iPhone and Mac Internet Services at Apple, joined Nokia to head Nokia's Mobile Computers business. He will lead the group working on Maemo and Maemo-based devices. Prior to Nokia and Apple, Martin worked in a variety of companies, including Starbucks, Loudeye, Microsoft, and NASA.[11]

Competition in Mobile Devices

Nokia is operating in an industry that is really a combination of several industries, including mobile devices, the Internet, content and media, PCs, converging hardware, and others. "Our competitors used to be traditional hardware competitors like Samsung; now they're often new Internet players and new entrants," acknowledges CEO Olli-Pekka Kallasvuo. Overall, mobile device markets are becoming more segmented and diversified. As a result, Nokia faces competition from different mobile device manufacturers in different user segments, price points, and geographic markets. Some competitors use more aggressive pricing strategies, different design approaches, and alternative technologies. Others focus on building products based on commercially available components, which may enable them to introduce these products faster and with lower levels of R&D expenditures than Nokia.

Direct Competitors Historically, Nokia's principal competitors in mobile devices have been other mobile device manufacturers such as LG, Motorola, Samsung, and Sony-Ericsson. When Motorola dominated the competition, the U.S. marketplace was still the center of gravity for the industry, but it has been weaker in building strong linkages globally. Conversely, as Nokia didn't have a large home market of its own, the company was forced to engage in cross-border competition from the very beginning.[12]

More recently, these traditional market participants have been joined by mobile network operators, which are increasingly offering mobile devices under their own brand, and other new market participants, such as manufacturers traditionally active in other segments of the consumer electronics industry. These competitors include Apple's iPhone, Palm's Pre and mobile products, RIM (think of BlackBerry), Google's Android software and phones based on that software (including Google's own phone, Nexus One, manufactured by HTC), Hewlett Packard's cell phones, and mobile devices by HTC, a Taiwan-based manufacturer of primarily Windows-based mobile portable devices. At Motorola, co-CEO Sanjay K. Jha is betting on new mobile devices that run on the Android software, hoping to position the old player for a rebound. However, Android had a long way to go. By the end of 2009, barely one percent of mobile phones run Android.[13] Further, MediaTek Inc., a leading fabless semiconductor company, has developed and dominates a new ecosystem. Due to its strong position among off-brand Chinese cell phone makers, the chip giant actually showed double-digit growth in 2009. Meanwhile, focused players, such as GP3 producers (e.g., Garmin, TomTom) were suffering from free navigation software by mass producers, such as Google.

Chinese Rivals The competitors also include emerging Chinese players, such as Huawei and ZTE, which has become the world's number 6 maker of cell phones but hopes to become number 3 in half a decade. Like Nokia in the past, ZTE is focusing on building business organically, starting with handset sales in China and then moving to developing markets across Asia and Africa.[14]

Horizontal Competitors In addition, Nokia faces competition at the level of horizontal layers rather than solely at the level of complete products and solutions. For instance, in operating system software, its competitors include Apple, Google, Microsoft, Palm, and RIM. The competition also includes open source software initiatives, such as the Open Handset Alliance, which is developing the Android mobile device software platform and operating system, and LiMo (Linux Mobile) Foundation, which is developing still another mobile device operating system.

At the same time, attractive but expensive designs have become more accessible and affordable—or as the Nokians put it, design is being democratized.

Nokia Design Philosophy

As a personal trusted device, the handset has become a life management tool for business, work, and leisure. During the early 1990s, the design challenge was much about color. In the beginning, there was only one category: the brand product, but even in those early days, Frank Nuovo, Nokia's former chief designer, argued that one could appeal to certain segments with the same product just by changing the color. "We gave the business professionals the form they wanted: the black classic, or the 'serious black suit.' Yet, people want all kind of colors, patterns, and textures, which broadens the product appeal."

As entry barriers grow higher and escalating R&D costs are leveraged across markets worldwide, original demand has given way to replacement phones, with increasing price erosion. Yesterday's high-end devices—for instance, color displays and digital cameras—turn into today's low-end products. As technology, lifestyle, and functionality become generic elements of the game, service-led experiences differentiate. In this task, design in vital.

Beautiful Devices That People Will Love to Use

"My greatest concern is creative leadership, we can't live in an ivory tower," says Alastair Curtis, Nokia's former design chief who worked in Nokia from 1993 to 2009 and was in charge of creative strategy and creative direction after Frank Nuovo. Part of the device design is very executional and means working closely with R&D teams and programs to deliver the latest devices, headsets, or packaging. Another part of the team is working with a two- to three-year time horizon on next-generation devices, driving technology decisions with R&D in new technologies and new architectures. Still another part of the team is working with a four-year time horizon on corporate strategy, business development, and also with NRC and a longer-term agenda.

Curtis believes in maintaining creative excellence at everything Nokia does. His personal philosophy translates to Nokia's design philosophy: "Beautiful to use". The Nokia N97 mobile computer, the benchmark device launched at the turn of 2008–2009, offers an example of global design. Typically, the team that created the Nokia N97 is global, with a shared vision: the project was based in Tokyo, the industrial designer was in Finland, the mechanics team was in Tokyo, and software teams worked around the globe in Boston, Dallas, India, China, and Singapore.

Alastair Curtis has worked with Nokia since 1993. In April 2006, he replaced Frank Nuovo as design chief. Critics argued that Nokia was losing some of its touch, because some of the recent popular designs of mobile devices—including the clamshell and ultra-thin models—were introduced by competitors. Also, the entire design process was reorganized into a new companywide design organization, led from Finland by Curtis. Despite its broadest product portfolio, all Nokia devices reflect the brand in one way or another. They carry, as Curtis puts it, Nokia's distinctive legacy, the Nokia DNA, which has to do with the brand values (described in Chapter Six).

Nokia has a human approach to designing mobile devices. Using its understanding of the way people live and their aspirations, Nokians seek to create designs that people will want and love to use. This ethos is central to the design work and brand. Nokia's design process is influenced by consumers and their behavior: how they want a mobile device to look, function, and fit into their lifestyle—through sleek design, ease of use, and relevance.[15] Today, Nokia's design and user experience activities are led by Marko Ahtisaari.

Understanding Consumer Needs

Nokia has a multidisciplinary design team of 340 designers, psychologists, researchers, anthropologists, and technology specialists representing more than thirty nationalities. They are based at Nokia's main design studios in Espoo, Finland; London; Beijing; and Calabasas, California. Understanding consumers' needs is the cornerstone of Nokia's product and service design.

The team conducts in-depth research and analysis of consumer trends and behavior and studies of new technologies, materials, shapes, and styles. The mobile device is seen as a very personal object—one you keep close at all times. It is more than just a piece of technology: you take it everywhere, and it can even reflect your mood and personality. In the past, mobile devices were mainly about phone calls and text messaging. Today, we use them increasingly to connect—with others online, to guide us around cities, manage e-mails, take and share photos, or to play music.

For most practical purposes, there is little difference in the design objectives and style of design chiefs Frank Nuovo and Alastair Curtis, but there is a subtle shift of emphasis. It involves the importance attached to

178

customer needs, usability, and the transition to smartphones. First, with respect to customer needs, Nokia design under Curtis's direction is driven by a strong effort in understanding the consumer. "The best way you can design is to understand your market," he says.

Second, in addition to Nokia's strong consumer-centric approach and the centrality of customer needs, Curtis tends to emphasize more usability. Designing great products is equally about how they look, how you use them, and how you interact with them. The idea is to ensure that the physical and digital worlds as well as the user interface are aligned.

And third, with smartphones, mobile devices have changed dramatically. "Today, the devices are much less about making a phone call, much more about having a big screen," acknowledges Curtis. The market is now also more aggressive with new rivals. Concurrently, the services and solution dimension is coming in with different dimensions of differentiation. Still, Nokia designers strongly believe that when they get the basic elements right—if they succeed in creating things that are beautiful and easy to use—then the rest will follow.

Ultimately, Nuovo established the brand identity in the physical space of the product, while Curtis managed the incremental development of the brand. At the same time, Nokia is pushing the edge of the envelope to stretch the brand. This is no longer as simple as it was in the mid-1990s. Now Nokia is a big player with the largest market share. Everything is relative. If parents happen to like Nokia, it can be a challenge to be cool among their kids.

Mobility appeals differently to different people. In the Nokia Devices subunit, R&D, design, and category management subunits are each aligned with five product categories, which represent target segments for Nokia's mobile device portfolio:

- Market *Entry* provides mobile phones in cooperation with the local mobile phone operators.

- *Connect* (for the mainstream market) focuses on mobile devices in which the balance among price, functionality, and style is key.

Devices in this category typically have mainstream features, including megapixel cameras, music players, and navigation functionality.

- *Achieve* (for business users) is focused on mobile devices targeted at business users; the flagship range is the Nokia Eseries of devices.

- *Explore* (via advanced devices) focuses on advanced devices optimized for creating, accessing, experiencing, and sharing multimedia; the starting point is the current Nseries range of multimedia computers.

- *Live* (with music-driven subsegments) concentrates on mobile devices with designs and features targeted at style and music-driven consumer segments, under the Xpress subcategory.

Unifying the Nokia Experience

Today, what Nokia is doing with devices is changing, and so are the ways users interact with them. Nokia is looking at making gestures—new ways of using your device—as natural and human as possible. The design team has been working on potential new ways to personalize your home screens, so that you can truly make them your own, by matching your device to your mood, location, time of day, or the context of what you are doing.

The Nokia design team is also exploring new ways to make Internet-driven communication as intuitive to use as voice has become. This means digital design for use in the hand or with the body and not just held to the ear, creating innovative new input methods, menus, and new interfaces that fit the new Internet experiences. Simple pictures or "icons" played a key role in how we learned to use the functions of mobile phones for the first time. Now, as mobile devices transform into truly personal computers, this language of icons—the familiarity of the new—needs to again guide us and make new services and features easy and instinctive to use.

After Frank Nuovo, Alastair reshaped Nokia Design into a truly global and multidisciplinary team and fully integrated it within the wider Nokia business. He established world-class design studios in London, Espoo, Beijing, and Calabasas and built an international design team representing thirty-four nationalities. His leadership of Design led Nokia to a strong position across all series.

In October 2009, Nokia Design was moved to the Solutions unit and it became part of the Design and Consumer Experience organization.[16] This team is driving excellence in user experience and aims to unify the "Nokia experience" across devices, services, and solutions. It is in a key role, as design and user experience are at the core of the consumer experience and at the heart of solutions. Accumulating and cross-pollinating the expertise of these teams provides Nokia with an excellent basis to move consumer experience to a new level. The Design and Consumer Experience organization is led by Marko Ahtisaari.[17] "At Nokia, we believe that people are increasingly looking for simple and sensorial products," he says. "And so, the challenge is: how do you make an elegant simplicity that hides the complexity in the overall interface and experience of the product? This is a real design challenge and opportunity so we spend a lot of time at that."[18]

Growth of Consumer Services

In addition to its goal of being the leader in mobile devices, Nokia has been creating and developing services since the late 1990s. Years before Apple launched the iTunes and iPhone, Nokia created a Web portal called Club Nokia to let owners of its mobile devices download snippets of music known as ring tones.[19] When CEO Kallasvuo unveiled plans to launch a slate of services for mobile users through Ovi, he revived a new and more powerful reincarnation of Club Nokia.

Today all players are embracing services. The traditional, stand-alone handset manufacturing business has matured, and the global financial crisis has intensified the maturation process. Nokia's Services unit seeks to develop and grow consumer Internet services and enterprise solutions and software. These include NAVTEQ, a Chicago, Illinois–based provider of Geographic Information Systems (GIS) data, which is a dominant company in providing the base electronic navigable maps. It is a wholly-owned unit of Nokia but operates independently.

As far as Nokia is concerned, success in its core business requires excellence with both devices and service:

Devices + Services = Solutions

Nokia's Services unit consists of operational subunits—Music, Social Location, Media, Messaging—each of which is focused on the development of services in their respective areas that the company regards as having the greatest appeal to consumers and being the most financially viable. These subunits are supported by horizontal teams providing necessary technology enablers and service infrastructure.[20]

Goal to Become Global Leader in Mobile Services

Nokia estimates that the total market value of these targeted segments will be over $55 billion in 2011. In this market, Nokia seeks to support the average selling price of devices,[21] extend and enhance the Nokia brand, generate incremental net sales and profit streams, and create value and choice for consumers. It is growing its customer base and building customer loyalty in each of these focus areas. By combining value and choice for consumers with scale in mobile device deliveries, the goal is to become the global leader in "Internet on mobile."

From Nokia's standpoint, service evolution began with Alexander Graham Bell and the invention of the telephone: calling somebody was the first service. Narrowing the perspective to mobile communications, the predigital era (1G, analog) featured no real innovation in the service space. Rather, a new technology was applied to an old service paradigm. With mobility, the consumer was not asked to learn anything new, or to behave differently. The old paradigm—calling somebody—was simply extended. In this predigital era, the competitors were known, and they simply took an established business model based on one application, applied new technologies, and the business took off.

With digitalization, the players have been adding technologies that allow the service portfolio to expand. Obviously the Internet has changed how we work, live, and play. As technology enables richer consumer behavior potential, the user behavior is changing, too, particularly with younger demographics. Generation Y was born with the Internet, which has been swept by social networking. "Now the Internet and mobility are feeding each other," says Niklas Savander, Nokia's chief of services. "I know where my friends are; they know where I am. We live our real lives and online lives, virtually simultaneously."[22]

Ovi as Nokia's Windows to Services

Mobile devices are becoming the most popular platform—the "fourth screen"—for people to enjoy digital content and share their experiences. An important part of Nokia's services strategy is Ovi, the Internet services brand it introduced in 2007. In Finnish, *ovi* means a door. One opens the door to enter another space. In that sense, Ovi is a bit like windows and could be seen as Nokia's counterpart for Microsoft Windows. The Ovi services can be used from a mobile device, computer (through Nokia Ovi Suite), or via the Web (Ovi.com). Nokia focuses on five key service areas: games, maps, media, messaging, and music.

In February 2009, Nokia launched the Ovi Store site, a one-stop shop. By integrating its individual services under the Ovi brand, Nokia aims to simplify user experience of services and differentiate itself from competitors.

Ovi Mail, Nokia's mobile e-mail service, signed up over 5 million accounts in its first year, exceeding the first-year user totals for Gmail, Yahoo Mail, and Hotmail.

Through Ovi, Nokia is taking on device manufacturers such as Samsung and LG, and smartphone leaders such as Apple and RIM, as well as social networking sites such as Facebook and Twitter.

Success in devices business depends increasingly on developing unique and winning services to complement the hardware and usability of the handset. Unlike most of its rivals, Nokia seeks to make the *locational* context the very foundation of its services. Ovi Lifecasting and partnership with Facebook are an example of how Ovi combines messaging with location information. With Ovi, Facebook shows also where the status update was made on the map.

Toward Solutions

Historically, Nokia has had a very strong product architecture discipline. When the company was building its software capability at the turn of the 2000s, the learning curve came with pain.[23] Whereas the stock market is driven by quarterly pressures, Nokia has remained loyal to its strategic vision. Many of its rivals have enjoyed wins that have proved short term over time.[24] However, the long-term strategic vision has been strained with the service model. In February 2009 Nokia's management initiated a "transformation project" to move faster ahead and to improve execution. "We needed a tighter coupling of devices and services," says Mary McDowell, Nokia's chief development officer.

Service Model Differs from the Device Model

When a Nokia service is developed, it goes to the market as fast as possible with minimal features. Starting from that point, the modelers learn through service adoptions and feedback from users how to develop the next set of features. In a service business, taking the idea to the launch of the first version may require only 24 *weeks*, whereas in the handset business taking it to the floor may take 24 *months*. "You can't put half of the phone out into the market, you've got to develop the whole thing," says Nokia's services chief Niklas Savander.[25]

At the turn of the 2010s, the bulk of Nokia's services business is in the United States. In order to expand its portfolio, it has been acquiring new and innovative service providers since 2005. In its mainstream business, Nokia has offered the complete product *at once*. As the business model is diversifying, so is the revenue model. In the services management team, the managers typically start every new product review with the basic question: *"Please explain to me, who pays to whom and why?"* From the standpoint of Nokia, service users can be segmented to different groups by the business model.[26]

Nokia's service investments have been focused on maps, music, messaging, media, and games because these are the areas where the biggest opportunities lie. In 2008, Nokia refocused its device portfolio by realigning different product categories with consumer segments, price

184

points, and form factors. Its estimated consumer retention rate is 55 percent, almost twice that of its global competitors. This rate has increased 1 percent per quarter since early 2007, which highlights the significant impact of services on devices and vice versa.

Creation of Solutions Unit

Nokia's Devices unit remains responsible for developing mobile devices, while the Services unit develops services, and both continue to offer these offerings to consumers on a stand-alone basis. However, value is migrating toward more integrated bundles, which comprise a mobile device, services, and content. At Nokia, these bundled offerings are called solutions.

In its effort to become a leading provider of mobile solutions, Nokia launched its Solutions unit in October 2009. Under the leadership of Alberto Torres and his team, the unit reports to the heads of both Services (Savander) and Devices (Öistämö). It seeks to create solutions providing people a richer, seamless user experience. As Nokia seeks to accelerate its pace of change and innovation, it hopes the new unit creates solutions better and faster by

- Driving innovation through cross-functional concepts
- Planning, deciding, and delivering according to one portfolio
- Ensuring alignment between units to create these solutions
- Bringing together all design and user-experience activities in Nokia to drive excellence in consumer experience

At the same time, two new subunits were set up to manage portfolio, product, and life-cycle management in the Devices unit: Smartphones for Symbian devices and Mobile Phones for S40/S30 devices. Also, Design was moved to Solutions. In addition to the current devices and services products, three types of solutions will be developed in Nokia, as illustrated by Figure 7.1.

- Computer solutions, showcasing the ultimate high-end consumer experience (based on the Maemo software platform)

185

- Solutions relying on smartphones based on Symbian (e.g., social location, entertainment)

- Embedded solutions building on S30 and S40 devices led by the Phones entity, driving to execute the Entry strategy

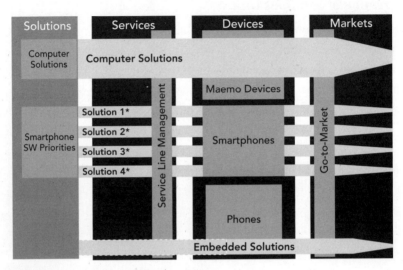

FIGURE 7.1 Nokia's Solutions Creation
*For example, "Connected Entertainment."

When products still reigned in the business, they defined the relatively rudimentary services. Today, it is the full package of sophisticated solutions based on real needs and wants that define the products and services. Nokia's early solutions successes include new X6 being sold in combination with Comes With Music, its "all-you-can-eat" music offer, as well as the 5800 Navigation Edition being sold with a lifetime of drive and walk navigation licenses. The Nokians, however, consider these solutions embryonic, the tip of the iceberg in the early stages of the learning curve.

In the past, Nokians developed an individual service and then tried to find a suitable device on which to load it. Today, they are developing the device, service, and content together from the outset, seeking to ensure that the different elements are fully aligned.[27]

Consumer Needs and Total Solutions

Nokia's experience is that basically the needs are not that different in the worldwide markets, but the level of expendable income is. The dilemma is similar to the paradigm that the company dealt with when it started business in these markets. If a handset's true cost is $1,000 and, creating the required volume, it should be $100, how can you make the impossible possible? Today, the challenge is how to build an effective service business with an absolutely lower cost of service.[28] Nokia's target is 300 million active users of services and some $2.8 billion by the end of 2011. "We're targeting pretty substantial numbers relatively soon," says Nokia's President and CEO Olli-Pekka Kallasvuo. "These goals are driven by solutions."

As far as Nokia is concerned, the Internet, PC, and mobile convergence is occurring faster than anyone anticipated. Concurrently, what consumers want is changing. The value proposition is no longer only about devices but also about total solutions, seamlessly integrating devices, services, content, and anything else that might complete the consumer experience.

In the near future, Nokia expects the volume growth in mobile devices to come from irresistible, seamlessly integrated solutions, as well as more sophisticated devices (read: smartphones and mobile computers). In this merged industry, "consumer relationships" are king. Since Nokia is wired for growth, it seeks to morph into a mobile solutions–led company in order to capture that growth. In other words, transformation means value creation through solutions.

"Whose Side Are You On?" asked *Fortune* in November 2009. The cover story featured BlackBerry versus iPhone. Nokia was barely mentioned. It was as if only the U.S. marketplace existed; the globe was an afterthought. Only two months later, iPhones debuted in China, the world's largest mobile marketplace, where Apple's partner, China Unicom, had predicted sales of $5 million in the first few years. The reality is that, at least in the entry stage, Apple and iPhone flopped in China. "In today's world, companies can no longer be strongly Americentric, starting product launches in the U.S. alone and only gradually reaching other markets as supply chains catch up," notes one perceptive critic. "You can't marginalize developing markets anymore."[29]

The competition for mobile phones, smartphones, and mobile computers will be intense. The only thing that's certain is that this rivalry and the winners will be global.

The Future of Services Is Sustainable

Nokia sees a future in which, linked to the Internet and aware of the user's location and preferences, the mobile device constantly adapts to the user's surroundings. As mobile device subscriptions pass the 4 billion mark, an increasing number of distributed and pervasive built-in sensors can capture, classify, and transmit many types of data. Nokia is also exploring nanotechnology. For example, Morph is a wearable device that changes shape, detects toxins on your food, and draws power from the sun.[30]

Network Infrastructure: Leveraging Scale and Transforming Solutions

In addition to leading and winning in mobile devices, growing and transforming consumer Internet services, and accelerating the adoption of business solutions, Nokia seeks to leverage its scale and transform solutions in network infrastructure. At Nokia, infrastructure and related services business is conducted through Nokia Siemens Networks (NSN), a separate company jointly owned by Nokia and Siemens and consolidated by Nokia.[31]

Why Nokia Networks Merged with Siemens Unit

By 2005, Simon Beresford-Wylie, then head of Nokia's Network business group, and his colleagues understood that they simply did not have the scale to justify the R&D investment in a new and critical technology platform (Long-Term Evolution, LTE). "It dawned on me and my colleagues that if we didn't have an investment case in LTE, we were going to die," acknowledges the British Australian Beresford-Wylie. In order to avoid being subscale, Nokia needed to have a bigger business case.

After a review of all alternatives, they understood that Siemens made sense in terms of the complementarity, footprint, product portfolio, and customer base, but also because of the lack of cultural complexity.[32]

Starting operations in April 2007, NSN combined Nokia Networks business with Siemens' carrier-related operations for fixed and mobile networks. At the time, intensified M&A activities, including the Alcatel-Lucent merger, were substantially changing the competitive environment for mobile and fixed networks infrastructure and related services. In fact, services today account for more than 40 percent of NSN's revenues.

How the Merger Grew NSN's Market Presence

Through the NSN merger, Nokia Networks turned itself from a $7–8 billion business unit in Nokia with an uncertain LTE business case into a $15–16 billion company. Today, it has a customer base second to none, and an opportunity to invest into LTE while protecting and leveraging the customer base that the two entities have built up over time. Now NSN sees itself as one of the three winners in business in terms of scale. "If we had not done this, the risk is that there would have been only one that would have a business case," says Beresford-Wylie.

Together with Ericsson and Huawei, there are now four major global players leading the network infrastructure market that offer a portfolio covering both equipment and services. Here's a quick overview of NSN:

- Its operational headquarters are in Espoo, Finland, along with two of its five business units.

- It has a strong regional presence in Munich, Germany, where two other business units are based; the Services unit is in New Delhi, India.

- At year-end 2008, NSN had 60,281 employees, more than 600 operator customers in over 150 countries, and systems serving in excess of 1.5 billion subscribers.

- By 2009, it had production facilities in nine major plants globally: three in China (Beijing, Shanghai, and Suzhou), two in Finland (Espoo and Oulu), two in Germany (Berlin and Bruchsal), and two in India (Calcutta and Chennai).[33]

In addition to cultural differences, the real problems in the integration did not only include a corruption case at the Siemens headquarters,[34] but also a very different organization. The structure of Siemens was based on countries and country clusters, whereas in Nokia business dominates worldwide, business units have a global responsibility, and the role of the country companies is primarily administrative. With consolidation and a global model, it was possible to establish a Nokia-like IT solution. Still, both companies wanted to participate actively in the consolidation, says Lauri Kivinen, NSN's chief of corporate relations. "Neither wanted to remain a wallflower as the music and courting began."[35]

Competition in Networks

Currently, NSN's principal competitors in network infrastructure include Alcatel-Lucent, Cisco, Ericsson, Huawei, Motorola, NEC, Nortel, and ZTE. Chinese competitors are no longer only cost players, and Nokia must compete with the quality of the product and innovation. Says Beresford-Wylie, "That's all happened in the past few years. In terms of the business model, Huawei may have a little cost base in terms of R&D, but when they come out of China, they lose their cost advantage."

Conditions in the market for mobile and fixed networks infrastructure and related services remain challenging, with equipment price erosion, maturing of technology, and intense price competition. The global economic turmoil has accelerated difficulties, and consolidation among network operators has increased the need for scale. Instead of operators like Vodafone, Telefónica, T-Mobile, or Orange, infrastructure players are running the largest mobile networks in the world. After the early 2000s, Ericsson and NSN became two of the largest mobile network operators in the world, managing the flow of voice, text, and data among the subscribers. With the global economic crisis, mobile operators have deepened the reliance on Ericsson and NSN to operate their networks. NSN alone helps manage 200 networks with 130 million customers.[36]

After the merger of Alcatel and Lucent, Nortel's bankruptcy, and Tellabs's economic difficulties, the North American marketplace remains in a state of flux. In June 2009, NSN initially won the stalking-horse auction for Nortel's wireless technology business, only to be eventually outbid by market leader Ericsson. "Eventually you have to get a return to the buck," said NSN's former COO Mika Vehviläinen who considered the price too high. By the end of the year, Ciena Corporation won an auction for the assets, which triggered NSN's offer of $810 million in cash. Right before Christmas Eve, Genband Inc. acquired Nortel's Internet gear, but there was no guarantee yet that it would end up with the assets. [37]

Competition is growing more intense in other regions as well, due to expanding technologies and technology choices, the transition from hardware to services and from equipment delivery to system integration, as well as new competitors. Industry players anticipate further consolidation in the short to medium term, which would eventually leave only a handful of infrastructure players, including one or two Chinese players.

Shakeouts and Consolidation

The launch and integration of NSN was a massive job. Typically, Nokia's senior executives may be on the road 200 days a year. As the story goes, NSN CEO Beresford-Wylie was traveling 250 days per year. In fall 2009, he left the company to serve as CEO of Elster Group and to spend more time with his family. He was succeeded by Rajeev Suri, head of NSN Services.[38]

In the aftermath of the NSN merger, those employees who stayed in Nokia sighed in relief, whereas those who became a part of NSN felt uneasy and more uncertain for their future. Most mergers mean rationalization and restructuring and, in difficult times, such moves tend to be more prominent. In October 2009, Nokia's shares fell 11 percent after a $1.3 billion write-down pushed the company to a third-quarter loss. Only two weeks later, NSN announced a companywide overhaul of business units, basically reducing five departments to three. The new business units are

- Business Solutions, which will focus on end user services, billing and charging, convergence, and subscriber data

- Network Systems, which will focus on both fixed and mobile infrastructure including optical transport systems and broadband access equipment

- Global Services, which will focus on outsourcing and network management

"NSN has good momentum within mobile broadband and managed services, and is confident it will outgrow a flat overall infrastructure market in 2010," said Rajeev Suri. Reviving sales is a key priority for NSN. As the company is trying to reduce procurement costs and operating expenses, it might cut 6-9 percent of its total 64,000 workers.

Cooperating Across Boundaries

Unlike most companies, Nokia excels not just in competitiveness but in cooperativeness. In the past, the strategic challenge for ambitious multinationals was seen primarily as one of competitive positioning. The idea was that companies would have to protect their profits from erosion, through bargaining or competition. In this perspective, competitors, customers, suppliers, and governments were all potential sources of threat. Today, strategy is seen differently. As companies must develop, build, and sustain multiple sources of competitive advantage simultaneously, collaborative relationships externally with other companies and organizations are vital.

This shift in strategic perspective has been driven by a wide array of forces, including escalating R&D expenditures, ever-shorter product life cycles, rising entry barriers, increasing needs for global economies of scale, and, particularly in technology-intensive industries, the growing importance of global standards. Unsurprisingly, Nokia seeks to build multiple sources of competitive advantage through worldwide competition *and* collaboration.[39] It is engaged in cross-border collaboration worldwide. Nokians pay attention to the customers and end users of their products, services, and solutions, and to their suppliers and collaborative partners.

Managing across corporate boundaries means different degrees of ownership and coordination.

- *Extended value networks.* Today, most firms can no longer create value autonomously; rather, many cooperate increasingly with their customers, suppliers, and partners. The focus of innovation is shifting from products and services to experience environments. These personalized cocreation experiences are the source of unique value for consumers and companies alike.[40] Along with other innovative pioneers, Nokia is developing unique ways to cocreate value with customers. Take, for instance, the launch of the new global music partnership—Nokia Play 2010—with the Island Def Jam Music Group and Universal Music Group International.

- *R&D collaboration.* The key objective of many strategic alliances is technology transfer or R&D cooperation. In the past, the boundaries between different industries and technologies were simpler and clearer. As innovations are increasingly driven by interindustry and interdisciplinary advances, the boundaries are now more blurry. As standardization reflects most challenges inherent in technology exchange, Nokia devotes substantial time and resources to creating standards and specifications for the industry.

- *Industry convergence.* Today, many technology-intensive industries are increasingly converging. In such circumstances, the preferred solution has been to create cross-industry alliances. Such alliances are often the viable way to develop the complex and interdisciplinary skills required in the time frame available. In June 2009, industry convergence led Intel and Nokia, for instance, to work together to create a type of mobile computing device beyond today's smartphones and netbooks.

- *Global competition.* With globalization, industry value chains are increasingly dispersed geographically and fragmented in terms of business. As a result, competitive rivalries are more often fought between teams of players aligned in strategic partnerships. In these rivalries of "global networks," the most successful multinationals are the ones that can garner the best set of allies. Take, for instance, Nokia's pioneering role behind Symbian, the mobile phone software maker, and other nascent ecosystems.

- *Joint ventures.* Nokia has entered into several joint ventures over time, particularly in manufacturing and R&D. Regional joint ventures have proven to be an effective way to combine Nokia's global technology leadership with strong local partners to accomplish faster and higher market penetration in new and emerging markets. This was particularly the case in China in the 1990s, when Nokia was still seeking access to new markets and engaged in penetration strategies.

- *Alliances as alternatives to merger.* Despite global competition, many industry sectors remain constrained by political, regulatory, and legal restrictions that limit cross-border M&As. In such case, allies may be preferred because they represent the best available alternative to merger, at least initially. Such considerations drove, for instance, the Nokia Siemens Networks merger.

- *Acquisitions.* Over the past few years Nokia has also increased R&D in services and supporting software and made a number of strategic acquisitions to bring the company the knowledge and technology that it believes is needed to compete effectively in consumer Internet services.[41]

In this chapter, we have taken a close look at how Nokia develops business strategies that generate strategic advantages. In the next chapter, we focus on the geographic markets in which Nokia has been most successful in executing these strategies.

Nokia's Lessons

- Nokia's success builds on its strategic capabilities, which create necessary preconditions for success but do not account for it.

Augmenting its devices and networks with solutions, Nokia is engaging in four basic strategies in its business areas: to lead and win in mobile devices; to grow consumer Internet services; to accelerate adoption of business solutions; and to leverage scale and transform solutions in network infrastructure. In order to win, a company needs to create strategic advantage.

- Today, mobile devices are a global consumer business, which is both technology- and marketing-intensive. Consequently, focus on one or the other is not enough. Nokia's success is illustrated by its product category matrix, which combines style and function (application). Along with service experience, style, function, and affordable pricing are all needed for success.

- In the global consumer business, design is increasingly vital for creative leadership. Nokia's success derives from designing beautiful devices that people will love to use.

- In addition to its goal of being the leader in mobile devices, Nokia has been creating and developing services since the late 1990s. As far as Nokia is concerned, success requires excellence with both devices and service. The formula of success is *Devices + Services = Solutions.*

- Infrastructure and related services is today a global business, driven by the needs of operators. In this business, Nokia's success derives from efforts to leverage scale and transform solutions in network infrastructure.

- Until recently, mobile devices offered primarily texting services. Now they are becoming powerful multimedia computers, despite the small size. Nokia's success in solutions is driven by the needs of the business, which are global and local by nature.

8

COMPETING IN
GLOBAL MARKETS

The Rise of Large Emerging Economies

Chapter Seven showed how Nokia is working to compete successfully in its various business areas. It detailed *what* Nokia is doing to win, whereas this chapter shows *where* it is winning. The key to Nokia's strategy is its broad global presence, which it is constantly seeking to expand and deepen. The quest of "Connecting People" includes all people—not just those in the developed nations, such as the United States, Western Europe, and Japan.

Today, global growth is also driven by the large emerging economies, especially China and India (which are often lumped together with Brazil and Russia as the "BRIC" countries).

There are some 4.6 billion mobile subscriptions among the planet's 6.8 billion people today. "For the majority of the world's people, their first and only access to the Internet will be through a mobile device, not a PC," says Nokia's CEO Kallasvuo. "And this access is spreading very, very fast."

In the 2000s, Nokia, among the pioneers, extended its global footprint from the advanced countries to the large emerging economies. Nokia saw an opportunity to make money and history—and not necessarily in that order, which this chapter explores in detail.

Winning Across Global Markets

For decades, technology has contributed to the emergence of global markets for standardized consumer products on a previously unimagined scale. Corporations geared to this new reality have benefited from enormous economies of scale in production, distribution, marketing, and management.[1] Until recently, it was taken for granted that these markets were primarily in the advanced economies. In reality, since the 1980s, global economic integration has drastically accelerated and many developing countries—the "new globalizers" (see Chapter One)—have broken into world markets for manufactured goods and services. With this new wave of global market integration, world trade and investment have grown massively. At the same time, the momentum of growth has shifted from advanced economies to large emerging economies; for all practical purposes, from the West to the East.

In the aftermath of the 1973 energy crisis, the combined gross national product (GNP) of Japan, the United States, and the four largest economies of the European Community (the United Kingdom, West Germany, France, Italy) accounted for some 45 percent of the global national product. Until recently, global competition was driven by these advanced economies. Augmented with Canada, the leading industrial economies—the G7 nations—dominated major markets, accounted for the competitive threats, and generated new technologies. Leading multinationals sought presence in all three regions, in order to take advantage of their "markets and forthcoming technologies and to prepare for new competitors."[2]

Over the next few decades, the growth generated by large emerging economies, especially the BRICs (Brazil, Russia, India, and China), is expected to become a much larger force in the world economy. And in the aftermath of the global economic crisis, this shift has only gained further momentum.

Mobile communications is not an exception. From the creation of the cellular concept in the late 1940s to the end of the 1980s, it was dominated by U.S. companies. In the 1990s, the transition to digital mobile communications allowed European players to capture industry leadership. Since the turn of the 2000s, the momentum of growth has shifted from the West to large emerging economies.

How Nokia Competes in Advanced and Emerging Economies

Today, both advanced economies and large emerging economies play a vital role in the world economy and global growth. Together, these dozen nations account for 76 percent of the world GDP and 72 percent of the world population, although much of the potential remains unrealized. Most emerging markets have promising outlooks for investment and future growth.

In 2000, the key *advanced* economies still accounted for 45 percent of Nokia's net sales. By 2008, the largest *emerging* economies had doubled their share to more than 30 percent of net sales, while the share of the key advanced economies had been more than halved to 20 percent. The balance of economic power has been reversed (see Figure 8.1).

Large Emerging Economies

In the early 2000s, the BRICs were worth barely 15 percent of the G7 GDP. Yet by 2025, the GDP of the G7 nations is expected to increase to $39 trillion, whereas the comparable figure for the BRICs will *quadruple* to $20 trillion. Only the United States and Japan are expected to remain among the six largest economies in U.S. dollar terms in 2050.[3] And these projections were made before the global economic crisis of 2008–2009, which has highlighted the vulnerability of the most advanced economies and the long-term growth momentum of China, India, and Brazil.

And there is more. In the past few years, other emerging economies have begun to follow in the footprints of the BRICs. In particular, another group of countries—Bangladesh, Egypt, Indonesia, Iran, Mexico, Nigeria, Pakistan, Philippines, South Africa, Turkey, and Vietnam have been

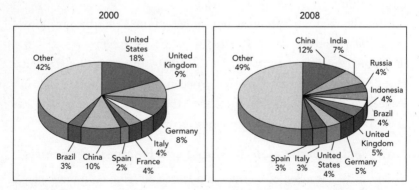

FIGURE 8.1 How Nokia's Major Markets by Net Sales Have Changed from 2000 to 2008

identified as having a high potential of augmenting the power of the large emerging economies over time.

The growth momentum is shifting from the advanced and wealthy metropolises of the West to the emerging and massive megapolises of the East. Among other things, this will bring about extraordinary dislocations of prosperity, competition, and innovation.[4] But it also intensifies lifestyle and design trends that Nokia has explored, among other things, in the shanty towns of Mumbai, Rio de Janeiro, and Accra in Ghana.

At Nokia, being a global company does not mean neglect of local context. In contrast, Nokia seeks to be a local company almost everywhere in the world, especially in its major country markets. As the old phrase goes, "When in Rome, do as the Romans do." For example, in China, Nokia is manufacturing, sourcing, employing, investing in R&D, paying taxes, engaging in responsibility programs, and so on. The company seeks to integrate itself well with countries where it has its key business units. "The idea is not to come from Finland and say that 'you should do as we do,' but to serve in a way that is in the interest of the [host] country," says Esko Aho, Nokia's chief of corporate relations.

As mobile demand has exploded worldwide, cultural differences may have grown smaller. Designers are closest to the user interface and sense the shift. "Over time, these emerging economies, particularly China and India, are bound to have a significant impact on the design, and even more so in services and solutions," says Nokia's former design chief Alastair Curtis.

Connecting *All* People

As described in Chapter Three, Nokia's mission of "Connecting People" is not for some people some of the time, but for all the people all of the time. The mission is as much about Nokia's business strategies and brand as it is about the Nokians' shared purpose.

Cost Is Critical in Emerging Economies

In emerging markets, too, it's extremely important to understand what people want, and what their lives are really like. After all, an innovation that may be very attractive in an advanced economy may not make much sense in an emerging economy. "In China, India, and other emerging markets, people are not necessarily driven by the lowest unit price," says Dr. Kai Öistämö, Nokia's head of Devices. "The key problem is the cost as such. Many people don't necessarily have salaries; with little cash at hand, it's not easy to plan ahead, and you have to feed your family."

Say that you need toilet paper, you're not going to pay for it for a month ahead but only a few days perhaps. In contrast, if you're buying prepaid services in an advanced economy, you may pay $10. In an emerging market, that's a lot of money and thus an entry barrier. So the producer must sell in 50-cent or 20-cent increments. In that sense, mobile services can be reminiscent of toilet paper in emerging markets. Despite the seemingly odd parallel, the insight is the foundation for the business model.

If there is one thing that all Nokians are proud of, it is their mission to make mobile communications available to everybody, not just in the wealthy metropolises of prosperous advanced economies, but also in the poorest megapolises and rural regions of the least developed nations. In the early 1990s, the Nokians saw that the day when half of the people on the globe would have a mobile phone was not that far away. "We thought that the actual day was twenty to twenty-five years away, but it happened in just fifteen years," acknowledges Jorma Ollila, Nokia's then-CEO. "Clearly, the Internet is the next step, due to the huge cost advantage of mobile access in China, India, or Africa."

Nokians are driven by their mission, "Connecting People," which gives a shared purpose to their lives. They are making a difference. They are changing the world. And that's what makes them passionate about their work.

Emerging Economies Require Different Business Models

As Nokia scaled up its operations in the large emerging economies, particularly in China and India, this was not exactly a cause of celebration among analysts. Many saw the move to the low-income markets as a disastrous strategic mistake. "You will destroy your share," they said, "and you will destroy your margins." At Nokia, however, this decision originated from and resonated with values, culture, and people.

From Nokia's standpoint, perhaps their most important innovation—the globally leveraged business model—is seldom understood, often misunderstood, and has occasionally penalized the company itself for all the wrong reasons. At one point, analysts focused on operating profit, net sales, or cash flow; now it's market share that drives the estimates. In emerging economies, however, the decline of the total cost of the ownership can be healthy when it supports long-term strategy and sustainable strategic advantage. "Market development has accelerated because of the efforts of Nokia that our competitors have followed," says Arja Suominen, Nokia's chief of corporate communications.

In worldwide terms, there are still an estimated 4 billion people who live on less than $2 per day. The phrase "bottom of the pyramid" refers to business models that deliberately target this demographic—also called the "base of the pyramid" or the "BoP."[5] It's important to keep in mind that this term is not just about "them," but also about "us." Initially, it was coined by Franklin D. Roosevelt to acknowledge the lot of forgotten Americans amid the Great Depression.[6]

Perhaps more than other multinationals, Nokia has been driving the opening of the low-income emerging economies for booming communications markets. For example:

- On the infrastructure side, it has deployed technology to lower the cost of rolling out operating networks while working with all the key operating partners.

- On the mobile device side, it has been designing and manufacturing phones at a very low price but still leaving room for some profit.

This has given rise to new business models in the "BoP" markets—from mobile devices and solutions to infrastructure solutions—that most companies thought were not economically viable. As Nokia has been able to reduce the total cost of ownership in communications, people are now prioritizing it among the top items that they will spend their money on. Indeed, there is strong correlation between increasing penetration of mobile communications and consumer welfare, particularly in portions of Africa and many areas of Asia and Latin America.[7]

Based on their mission, the Nokians have been developing business models that allow them to get a return on investment and make a sustainable profit, although the price levels are lower than what many people in developed markets pay for the leather case that goes around their device. "Now we can sell in developing markets a communication device for $35 which can change their life," says Richard A. Simonson, Nokia's head of mobile phones. "That's tremendous innovation!"[8]

Nokia's Geographies

At the end of 2008, there were 3.9 billion mobile subscriptions globally, representing 58 percent global penetration. According to Nokia's estimates, its global device market volume grew by 7 percent to 1,213,000 units. This growth was driven primarily by strong growth in both replacement sales and sales from new subscribers in emerging markets, particularly the Middle East, Africa, and Asia-Pacific. Developed market device volumes were driven primarily by replacement sales. Emerging markets accounted for the majority of industry device volumes (63 percent).[9] Nokia is the market leader in Europe, Asia-Pacific, China, and Latin America. It is also the market leader in the fastest-growing markets of the world, including the Middle East, Africa, Southeast Asia-Pacific, and India, as well as in critical technologies.[10]

Nokia Siemens Networks' net sales in 2008 increased 14 percent to $21.3 billion. Globally, the volume growth in the networks infrastructure equipment was significantly offset by the price erosion of the equipment, largely as a result of maturing technologies and intense price competition. Like Nokia, NSN has a balanced business in terms of the market position. In most key regions and nations, NSN is number one or two. It has achieved a great positioning in China, India, and Indonesia. It also has good positioning in Brazil and Russia. North America is challenging but NSN sees some possibilities of strengthening its position there. "Overall, we're similarly positioned to Ericsson where we are strong and we're far stronger than Alcatel-Lucent in many of these markets," says NSN's former CEO Simon Beresford-Wylie. "Huawei is coming strong as a top-three player."

Nokia's Major Country Markets Worldwide

For 2008, Finland contributed less than 1 percent of Nokia's revenues, but almost 19 percent of total personnel. The ten markets in which Nokia generated the greatest net sales in 2008 are shown in Figure 8.2b. Together, these top-ten markets represented about 50 percent of the company's total net sales in 2008.

(a) Net Sales

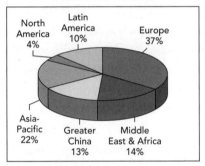

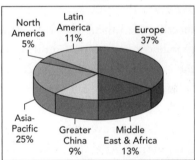

(b) Major Markets

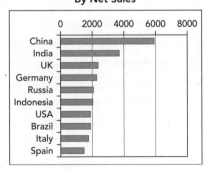

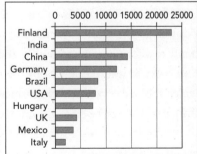

FIGURE 8.2   Nokia's Major Markets

Until the early 1990s, the United States was the center of mobile innovation worldwide. It had the most competitive markets; the most sophisticated vendors, operators, and customers; and the most advanced products, processes, and services. This era peaked after the mid-1990s, when Motorola and other industry players still enjoyed record profits. Due to the delay in the digital transition, both equipment manufacturers and operators fell behind their counterparts in Europe.

The United States remained the most populous mobile market until mid-August 2001, when China overtook the leadership in terms of the number of mobile subscribers. Indeed, the past few years have witnessed the dramatic rise of China and India as great powers of information and communication technologies.[11]

Quest for the U.S. Market

"You are the only ones who have a chance in the U.S. markets, go there!" urged then-CEO Kari H. Kairamo to the executives of Nokia's mobile communications unit in the 1980s. As Nokia prepared to enter the U.S. market, it opted for cooperation with Radio Shack, which also collaborated with operators.[12]

In most technology-intensive sectors, industry leaders make the most revenues and have the most people in the United States. Nokia is an exception. In 2008, the United States was Nokia's seventh-largest market in net sales and sixth largest in terms of personnel. Yet Nokia had almost as many people in Brazil and made more money in Russia and Indonesia than in the United States.

From the late 1990s to early 2004, Nokia enjoyed the number one position in the United States. Then the operators began to differentiate handset offerings with Motorola and Korean players.[13] Such customization has not traditionally been the modus operandi of Nokia's success, which is based on a global platform and the associated scale economies. In the United States, operators dominate, whereas Nokia has sought to build its own brand. "If you compete in the U.S. bulk markets, you are to some extent a cargo manufacturer," says a Nokia board director. "Nokia cannot make a 20 percent profit as a cargo producer."

What makes the U.S. business unique is that it is very much driven by carriers. In other markets, distributors and retailers also play a role. "It's not like we have 300 million+ customers in the U.S.," says Nokia's chairman Jorma Ollila. "There are four to five customers who control access."

As smartphones have become the future of mobility, Nokia has sought to reassert its market leadership. In early 2002, Nokia still led the American market with a 35 percent share. In 2008, it slipped to 10 percent; and in summer 2009, only 7 percent. Yet, the United States is now more central to the industry future than ever before. Nokia's objective is to expand its presence in smartphones, which is considered vital for volume sales, but also to gain the attention of U.S. communities of software developers that make games and applications for mobile devices.[14] Wooing application developers to its mobile platform through offices in Silicon Valley and Boston, Nokia hopes to take on Apple and RIM on their home turf.

Simply put, Nokia initially sought to adapt America to its models rather than adapting its offerings to the U.S. market. "In the past, we had a one-size-fits-all mentality that worked well on a global basis but did not help us in the U.S. market," acknowledges Mark Louison, president of Nokia's North American unit. Today, Nokians are adjusting their model in the United States; the idea is to be more responsive locally.[15] The company revamped its U.S. operations to cooperate more closely with the leading operators—AT&T Mobility, Verizon, T-Mobile USA, and Sprint Nextel—which together dominate 96 percent of U.S. sales of mobile devices.

In the past few years, Nokia's rivals have been successful, but at a price. Until recently, Motorola leveraged its success in the home market with similar product offerings in Latin America. In theory, it may be possible to maintain different approaches in many different markets; in a globalizing industry, it is a way to destroy one's bottom line, as evidenced by Motorola's decline. Simply put, global competition requires global business models.[16]

Historically, Nokia Siemens Networks has been less established in the United States than in the rest of the world. The global financial crisis has changed the rules of the game. NSN's competitors are in intensified consolidation. In July 2009, NSN's rival Ericsson snapped up Nortel's CDMA assets. Four months later, Ciena Corp agreed to buy some of Nortel's core properties after trumping a bid from NSN. It is vital for NSN to improve its market share in the United States, one of its top growth targets. An acquisition would be the fastest solution. In December 2009, Nokia said it will close its flagship stores in New York and Chicago and another two in London. That leaves twelve flagship stores worldwide after the first store was opened in Moscow in 2005. The store closings were part of Nokia's global retail strategy and a realignment to focus more on cooperation with operators and other retailers.

Sustaining Leadership in Western Europe

Building on indigenous industry developments and increasing diffusion of knowledge, Japanese and Nordic operators and vendors were able to catch up with U.S. developments by the late 1970s. In Western Europe, the early movers were countries that first implemented new telecom policies (liberalization, privatization, and deregulation) in the late 1980s and early 1990s. These players were primarily in the United Kingdom and the Nordic countries. The rise of the digital cellular coincided with the European Commission decision to promote competition while making GSM mandatory in Europe.

With the digital transition, the initial momentum in the mobile markets was in Western Europe's large countries (Germany, the United Kingdom, France, Italy), emerging markets (Spain), and several small markets. Today, few large countries reign over the European marketplace.[17] In terms of personnel, 20 percent of Nokia's workforce (23,300) remains in Finland; and after the launch of the Nokia Siemens Networks, half of this number are in Germany (12,300). With $3.2 billion in sales, Germany is Nokia's fourth-largest market worldwide and fifth-largest market in terms of personnel.[18] Since the 1990s, the United Kingdom has been a strategic nodal point in Nokia's global strategy and in sales, but no longer so in terms of personnel.[19]

Reducing Presence in Japan

In the 1980s, the Asian market *was* Japan. But at the end of 2000, China overtook Japan as the leading country market in Asia-Pacific, while Japan's NTT DoCoMo pioneered the first content services and 3G markets.

Nokia Japan was founded in April 1989 for technology sourcing and developing partnerships with Japanese high-tech companies. By the mid-1990s, Nokia was the first European manufacturer in Japan to begin cellular phone sales; it established a product creation R&D center for the mobile phones group and began to ship models to NTT DoCoMo. By 2008, Nokia employed nearly 500 people and had an office in Tokyo and Osaka. Japan was the world's fourth-largest mobile phone market.

Nokia had originally aimed to increase its market share in Japan to a double-digit figure. In 2008, it had only around 0.3 percent of the Japanese market and decided to discontinue mobile device sales, R&D, and marketing activities in Japan.

Sustaining Leadership in China

Today, China and India are the largest mobile markets worldwide.[20] "If you draw up the curve of the number of units sold in these two nations," says Nokia's chairman Jorma Ollila, "the curves are almost identical, but there is a five-year time difference." Whereas Nokia initiated its push in the large emerging economies in the mid-1990s, China took off earlier. In India, import tariffs constrained the mobile revolution until the early 2000s. The differences of the political systems also posed various challenges.[21]

Nokia's Early Competition in China

With more than $8.2 billion in net sales, China is Nokia's largest market worldwide. In terms of personnel, it ranks third, right after Finland and India. Nokia is the most loved mobile brand in China, and its popularity in China stretches across all demographic groups and all market segments.

Since the 1980s, the leading foreign multinationals in China have moved gradually from cautious market tests to substantial direct investment, while employing domestic suppliers and management. In the mobile industry, this "localization" approach was pioneered by Motorola in Europe in the 1980s. A decade later, it was emulated by most major rivals in China, including Ericsson, Motorola, Nokia, Samsung, and certain second-tier suppliers.

Two years after Nokia opted for its global focus strategy, it made a strategic decision on how to approach China. "If you want to win in this business globally," says Nokia's then-CEO Jorma Ollila, "you need to win in the major emerging economies."

Nokia had identified opportunities in China already in the early 1980s, but digital cellular really took off in the 1990s. To Nokians, China has had a great capability to absorb new production mechanisms. "We were able to create both efficiencies and quality very rapidly in China," says Matti Alahuhta, Nokia's former senior executive. With China's strong GDP growth, Nokia initiated a major investment drive, including a plan for a manufacturing factory in Beijing, and another in Dongguan, Guangdong. It had a regional organization with the best distributors, which it could pick since it was the first in the region.

Showdown with Chinese Rivals

In the early 2000s, many observers expected Nokia to be beaten in the high-end category by the likes of Microsoft and in the low-end category by Chinese low-cost producers. In the first case, the assumption was that Nokia would not be able to develop the requisite capabilities in software and operating systems. In the second case, the assumption was that Nokia is a European high-cost manufacturer. Both assumptions proved flawed. In reality, Nokia is the cost leader. "We're the world's low-cost manufacturer, we're more Chinese than many of the Chinese companies," says Nokia's chief of Mobile Phones Richard A. Simonson.

Despite its cost advantage, Nokia discovered soon that competition would be intense. And it was—as evidenced by the dramatic growth figures:

- In the 1990s, Chinese equipment manufacturers had no market share in China's mobile marketplace.

- In 2001, their aggregate share was less than 10 percent.

- In 2003, that share soared to 55 percent!

These extraordinary gains occurred because local handset brands—including Ningbo Bird, Amoi, Panda, and TCL—focused on building distribution networks that took them into smaller cities where foreign rivals seldom ventured. Also, Chinese vendors pushed clever ad campaigns and developed product designs, including "clamshell" handsets that appealed to local consumers.

After the rise of the indigenous challengers, however, the foreign multinationals mounted their counterattack.[22] The market share of Chinese vendors declined to 38 percent at year-end 2004. At the time, Nokia's HQ in Helsinki was coping with great challenges in software development.[23] But unlike Motorola, Nokia recognized and overcame the challenges faster. "We knew we had to change," says Colin Giles, Nokia's then-chief of Greater China. "Nokia's success is not just about the capability to change, but also about openness."

Nokia's Activities in China

Today, Nokia operates two major device manufacturing plants in Beijing and Dongguan. In Beijing, it has worked in partnership with some twenty suppliers to build Xingwang Industrial Park into one of the world's most efficient and environmentally friendly supply chains. This may well be the world's largest mobile phone industry chain. Nokia has combined all its operations, including R&D, production, logistics distribution, marketing, services, and the regional headquarters, to within one kilometer.

Nokia has also rapidly expanded its contribution in corporate social responsibility.[24] In Greater China and Asia-Pacific, it has used the global portfolio of devices, which has been received well. There has not been much customization, but the services story is different altogether. "While we need to try to drive a global services platform, there will need to be localization," says Colin Giles.[25]

Many foreign multinationals do not fully understand the Chinese market, or have been trying to drive a purely global or American business model into China. "We are well positioned in the service space, and we are willing to localize," says Giles. In order to deliver solutions, device makers and service providers must partner with operators, which is one of Nokia's strengths. The Chinese marketplace is dominated by China Mobile, China Unicom, and China Telecom. Nokia has good relations with each. At the end of 2009, the company established a joint venture alliance designed to offer a range of mobile services in China and support the local developer ecosystem.

Nokia's investments are not limited to manufacturing plants. China is no longer important only as the "world's factory," but also as an arena for innovation. Nokia's research center in China was established in 1998. A year later, the Nokia Beijing Product Creation Center (PCC) was launched to develop mobile devices catering to the needs of emerging markets around the world.[26] Nokia has also adopted an open innovation model with top-tier Chinese universities, as exemplified by the Nokia-Tsinghua joint research facility. Forum Nokia is the largest mobile community in the China area, connecting over 300,000 developers.

In addition to Devices and Services, Nokia Siemens Networks operates six R&D centers in China, located in Beijing, Shanghai, Suzhou, Hangzhou, Chengdu, and Shenzhen. In the infrastructure, China's marketplace is challenging. As 3G networks are being rolled out, most huge contracts have gone to domestic players such as ZTE, Datang, and Huawei.

"Trying Harder"

In January 2010, Colin Giles became the global head of sales, which led to Chris Leong taking over as head of Nokia Greater China, Japan, and Korea SU, reporting to Giles. As senior vice president of marketing GTM, Leong was responsible for the overall alignment of Nokia's go-to-market marketing across all local markets globally. She is also one of Nokia's new and rising Asian female executives.[27]

When interviewed by CEO Kallasvuo, then-head of the mobile phone business, she was asked for her opinion of Nokia's marketing. "You look at all the IBM advertising and then you look at Apple. In our industry we don't differentiate enough," she said. "We have a comfort zone where we all play. But I think that's an excuse. We can try harder."

The agencies that have been assigned to "try harder" are JWT and Wieden & Kennedy. Nokia chose the duo following a lengthy global pitch that culminated in the end of its twelve-year relationship with Asian incumbent Bates, an agency where Leong spent the bulk of her career. Indeed, she is said to know agencies better than they know themselves. "One of the key reasons we hired Wieden & Kennedy is because it came across as a genuine partner that can build our business—not as a wonk creative hotshop," she points out. "Today, the brand is transparent. I don't think anyone has ever found a way to respect that relationship with consumers and work with it."

Sustaining Leadership in India

In India, the seeds of the mobile revolution stem from Rajiv Gandhi's reforms in the 1980s, whereas the new era was initiated by the reforms of the Rarasimha Rao Congress government in the early 1990s. Through these years, the macroeconomic policies of Dr. Manmohan Singh supported the change. In 1995, the government issued eight licenses to eight companies for mobile services in the four major metropolitan cities of Mumbai, Delhi, Chennai, and Kolkatta. Along with China, India is a rising mobile communications power today.

There are only three countries in the world where Nokia has a full range of activities, from R&D to manufacturing to software and services, even retailing: Finland, China, and India. But in India, Nokia's presence did not evolve quite as smoothly as it did initially in China.

Nokia's Early Steps in India

In the aftermath of the mobile takeoff of China, Nokia began to look more at developments in India. By 1997, senior executives felt that the company should replicate its strategic decisions in India. Nokia invested up front, but things did not happen as they initially expected. Until 2001, the Indian marketplace was still extremely small, and the import tariff on firms was still 47 percent. It took several years of lobbying until it was cut to 7 percent. That is when the market exploded.

In 1995, Nokia's board met in India and decided to invest there. Some argued that Nokia would have to choose to focus on China or India, whereas Nokia decided it wanted to win in both. Nokia is now one of few multinationals that has a large market share in both China and India. Unlike many of its rivals in India, Nokia focuses on mobile communications, whereas Motorola has also pushed pagers, Siemens has consumer electronics and lighting, and LG and Samsung offer consumer durables.

Competing to Win

When the market finally opened up in India in the early 2000s, Nokia competed to *win*, whereas others were still building a presence. "You must have the strategic intent to win in a country," says D. "Shiv" Shivakumar, head of Nokia India. "Nokia had that, others didn't." Also, one must have an appetite for growth, and one must be able to manage growth. Finally, values are vital. Many multinationals have changed their values in the last one to two decades, that doesn't help.[28] "We're not offering Indian values," says Shivakumar. "We represent Nokia values as they are presented in Helsinki."

In India, Nokia's values are seen as Nordic and very egalitarian. Overall, Indian companies tend to be more hierarchical. Shivakumar describes Nokia's culture as "supportive, handholding, constructive, challenging, flat organizationally, results focused, and appreciated. It is not a culture where you'd say I'm a lone star and you'll do it my way. That's not the way things work in a Nordic culture. You have to understand how to influence the decision making rather than say, 'I'll make the decision.'"

With more than $5.1 billion in net sales, India was Nokia's second-largest market in 2008. In terms of personnel, it came second, even before China. As regulation struggles and licensing disputes are fading away, sales of mobile phones have soared, from 1 million in 1998 to 32 million in 2005.[29] In India, as in many other nations, voice still generates almost 90 percent of revenue, but value-added services (VAS) are emerging. Market players must find ways to offer a wider range of value-added services, starting with cricket-related content, latest news, Bollywood sound tracks, and video clips.

Price wars in mobile services and drastic falls in the price of handsets have boosted the growth rate and volume of penetration, while contributing to the rapid consolidation of the operators and equipment manufacturers. In the past, a mobile handset was a luxury of the wealthy; today, it is a utility of all people. With saturation in the urban centers, operators can sustain their growth strategies only by extending penetration strategies into the vast rural market.

Nokia's Activities in India

Nokia has played a pioneering role in the growth of cellular technology in India, starting with the first cellular call made on a Nokia mobile phone over a Nokia-deployed network. It dominates the GSM handsets, whereas Samsung and LG have secured a foothold via CDMA.

Today, Nokia operates out of offices in New Delhi, Mumbai, Kolkata, Bangalore, Hyderabad, and Ahmadabad. The Indian operations include the handsets business, R&D facilities in Bangalore, Hyderabad, and Mumbai, a manufacturing plant in Chennai, and a Design Studio in Bangalore.[30]

In infrastructure, NSN has made significant progress in realizing business opportunities and increasing its market share. It is a key supplier to the top five GSM operators including Bharti, BSNL, Hutchison, IDEA, and BPL. Nokia has also set up its Global Networks Solutions Center in Chennai, India. The Solutions Center performs network operation tasks for selected operator customers in Asia-Pacific as well as Europe, the Middle East, and Africa.

Nokia has three R&D centers in India, based in Hyderabad, Bangalore, and Mumbai. These hubs are staffed by engineers who are working on next-generation packet-switched mobile technologies and communications solutions to enhance corporate productivity.[31]

Nokia has set up its tenth mobile device manufacturing facility in Chennai, India, to meet the burgeoning demand for mobile devices and network infrastructure in the country.[32] Chennai was selected as the location for the Nokia Telecom Industry Park.[33] Nokia has positioned itself as the only telecom company to manufacture both mobile devices and network infrastructure in India. It is ranked as India's leading multinational, India's leading telecom equipment vendor, and leading brand.

Expanding Presence in Russia

Nokia has been operating in the Soviet Union since the 1960s. In the late 1990s, it established ZAO Nokia in Russia with the headquarters in Moscow. By 2008, Russia was Nokia's fifth-largest market in terms of net sales. There were almost 190 million subscribers in Russia (at the rate of active SIM-cards). Among them, 32 million were registered.

In Russia, mobile phone usage has come a long way since the mid-1990s, when it was still associated with illicit wealth. After the August 1998 Russian crash, when the ruble lost more than 75 percent of its value in a day, all that changed dramatically. With the loss of their elite subscriber base, the main mobile operators, Vimpelcom and Mobile Telesystems, rushed to turn mobile phones into a mass-market product. The takeoff was followed by explosive growth.

Today, major operators seek growth through continued consolidation and by expanding services outside the great metropolitan clusters. At the same time, they have been expanding to CIS countries, including the Ukraine and Belarus.

In order to raise the decreasing ARPU (average revenue per user), Russian operators will move from traditional mobile voice toward data communications. The mobile handset market was dominated by four equipment manufacturers (Nokia, Samsung, Motorola, Siemens), which had almost 80 percent of the market. Nokia continued to intensify its market presence and managed to take the lead.

Winning in Brazil

When Nokia moved its Latin America business unit from Dallas to Miami in 2006, it aimed to leverage the city's access to the region in its bid to gain market share. Concurrently, it was expanding its presence in the fourth major BRIC, Brazil.

In the mid-1980s, Mexico enjoyed regional leadership (60 percent) in Latin America. By 2000, only two country markets—Brazil and Mexico—accounted for 58 percent of Latin America's share. Nokia started distributing products directly to Brazil in 1994. Three years later, it began production in Brazil through a joint venture in the Manaus Duty Free Zone. Soon it was the national leader.

In 2007, Nokia commemorated ten years of operations in Brazil and reached the historical milestone of 100 million cellular phones produced in Manaus. The factory produces low-end and mid-range cellular telephones sold in Brazil and exports to the United States, Latin America, and Europe. Between 2000 and 2008, Nokia's net sales in Brazil almost doubled to more than $2.6 billion. The importance of the market is highlighted by the fact that, during the same period, Nokia's personnel in Brazil soared from less than 1,300 people to almost 9,000 people.

As in China and India, Nokia has been expanding its role in corporate social responsibility in Brazil.[34]

Winning the Next Big Emerging Economies

In the course of the past decade, Nokia has begun to leverage its success in infrastructure, devices, and services from the advanced economies to emerging economies. It is this emerging multipolar world that some incumbents have seen as a threat but that Nokia sees as an opportunity—the greatest opportunity of the twenty-first century.

What makes the BRICs unique is that they have the scale and the trajectory to challenge the major economies in terms of influence on the world economy. In the coming decades, there will also be other important growth stories outside of the BRICs, but these will not have the scale to match the large emerging economies, and only time will tell whether these will also be success stories. For example, despite its growth potential, South Africa will have a much smaller GDP by 2050 than the smallest BRIC. Without a substantial population, even a successful growth story is unlikely to have a global impact. For this reason, the "growth miracle" of the East Asian tigers (Hong Kong, Singapore, South Korea, Taipei/China) served as an important model, but with limited impact on global power.

The group of countries that have a "BRIC-like potential" includes Bangladesh, Egypt, Indonesia, Iran, Nigeria, Pakistan, Philippines, and Vietnam. In 2008, their population size ranged from 82 million (Egypt) to 240 million (Indonesia), while their GDP per capita ranged from $1,800 (Nigeria) to $5,400 (Egypt). The list could be augmented with other countries, such as Mexico, Turkey, and Iran. These nations have relatively large populations (66 million to 110 million), but their GDP per capita amounts to $10,800 to $12,600; they represent a different level of development. Among these nations, only the economies of Indonesia and Nigeria could overtake Italy and Canada by 2050. Although potentially significant in absolute terms, the rise of the rest is expected to contribute quite modestly on a global basis. By 2050, the BRICs and a few of the rest (Egypt, Philippines, and Vietnam) are anticipated to cross the high-income $15,000 threshold. At the end of the period, Bangladesh's income remains by far the lowest of the entire group at $4,500.[35]

Growth projections indicate that Vietnam (and to a lesser extent Iran, Egypt, and Philippines) also scores relatively well currently in terms of growth conditions. At the other end of the spectrum, Nigeria, Bangladesh, and Pakistan all score poorly. Africa is heavily represented in the worst-ranked economies, while Asia's developing economies fair relatively well. Among the developing economies, as well as Asian economies (Malaysia, Thailand), several Latin American and central European economies score well (Chile, Costa Rica, Bulgaria, Romania). The richer oil producers are also at the very top of the developing country list.

None of the emerging economies possess the kind of growth potential that the largest BRICs—China and India—currently represent. They are vital to Nokia as well. In the 2000s, these two vast nations have been creating some 5–7 million new mobile subscriptions *per month* (Finland's entire population is barely 5.3 million). Today, most people connecting to the Internet for the first time are doing so with mobile devices, not PCs. In December 2008 alone—even amid the global crisis—there were some 10 million new mobile subscriptions in India, which, as Nokia's CEO Kallasvuo once put it, is like connecting the entire population of Barcelona—every five days!

The rise of China and India will not only change Nokia from within, but the world itself. Among other things, their impact on value systems will grow. "This translates to an opportunity to a company like Nokia, which is less likely to have a 'we know how to take care of business' approach," says Sari Baldauf, Nokia's former senior executive. Unlike many American companies, Nokia operates in a more distributed way, closer to the customer interface, and is more sensitive about cultural differences.

In order to be able to create economies of scope, small-country multinationals like Nokia must be responsive in their markets globally. "Each of these markets is uniquely different and complex," says CEO Kallasvuo. "A one-size-fits-all approach just doesn't work." That requires extraordinary flexibility in terms of organizational capabilities and accounts for Nokia's insistence on a flat, globally networked organization. "You need both flexibility and scale, simultaneously," adds Kallasvuo. With scale, you can exploit and leverage the market, but that requires flexibility and responsiveness, especially if you come from a small country.

In open, global competition, the real question is not scale or flexibility, but the right balance between the two. Such leadership is extremely challenging, as we shall see in the next and last chapter.

Nokia's Lessons

- Until recently, it was the advanced economies (i.e., the United States, Western Europe, and Japan) that drove global growth. Today the countries that are driving growth worldwide are the large emerging economies—particularly China and India (which are often lumped together with Brazil and Russia as "BRIC" countries). Nokia's global success derives from extending its global footprint from the advanced countries to the large emerging economies.

- Nokia's mission of "Connecting People" does not apply to some people some of the time, but to all people all of the time. In emerging markets, too, it is extremely important to understand what people want and what their lives are really like. After all, an innovation that may be very attractive in an advanced economy may not make much sense in an emerging economy.

- As Nokia has been able to reduce the total cost of ownership in communications, people are now prioritizing it among the top items that they will spend their money on. Global success requires new business models in the "bottom of the pyramid" markets—from mobile devices and solutions to infrastructure solutions—that most companies thought were not economically viable.

- If you really want to compete across geographies, reject the idea that you can export your way to success or that you can replicate your home market elsewhere, especially if you want to compete in emerging economies. There's no shortcut to success. Small-country multinationals must adapt to the world, rather than the other way around.

- As growth is declining in the advanced markets and over time will decline in the BRICs, sustained success also requires strengths in a group of countries that have a "BRIC-like potential" including Bangladesh, Egypt, Indonesia, Iran, Nigeria, Pakistan, Philippines, and Vietnam.

9

HOW NOKIA SEEKS TO SUSTAIN LEADERSHIP

Nokia's successful leadership has been built on legacy and globalization. At the corporate level, strategy is developed and implemented by the group executive board. Values, culture, and people drive this company and facilitate the workings of Nokia's unique globally networked organization. Nokia's success rests on its strategic capabilities, especially global innovation, scale, demand and supply network, distribution, and the powerful brand, including strategic marketing and global consumer insights. In turn, these capabilities provide the foundation for Nokia's business strategies in mobile devices and solutions in consumer and infrastructure services. Unlike all its rivals, Nokia's footprint is truly global. It has been the quickest and most successful in expanding globally, particularly in the large emerging economies. Yet the question remains: how will Nokia sustain leadership in its technology- and marketing-intensive environment?

In the early 1990s, Nokia was barely known outside northern Europe. According to *Interbrand*, only Coca-Cola, IBM, Microsoft, and GE are better known worldwide than Nokia. It is better known than Toyota, McDonald's, or Disney. But can Nokia maintain its leadership?

Three Scenarios for Future Communications

At Nokia's R&D, the realization that the phone is more than just a phone certainly did not emerge from the footprints of Apple's iPhone in the early 2000s but was already in play in the mid-1990s. At the same time, the

219

Nokians were becoming aware of the potential of the mobile device and were engaging in scenario projects to forecast the future. In particular, three scenarios facilitated the thinking of the executives; these were called Autumn Harvest, Speech Cosmos, and Multimedia Jungle. The three scenarios can be updated and upgraded to illustrate Nokia's prospects in the present and tomorrow.

Scenario #1: "Autumn Harvest" — Toward Decline?

In the mid-1990s, Autumn Harvest was the most gruesome scenario because it suggested that, like so many other industries, the mobile communications business would grow, mature, and ultimately decline. After all, penetration figures would saturate in the advanced economies of North America, Western Europe, and Japan in the next half a decade. There was nothing much one could do, except to cash out and retire.

Still, the great potential of mobile devices and emerging usage patterns indicated that Nokia's story was far from over. As it decided to globalize and aggressively democratized communications from the advanced economies to emerging economies, worldwide penetration soared. In 1996, when these scenarios were first crafted, there were 141 million mobile subscribers worldwide and no—that is, *zero*—mobile Internet users. In 2001–2002, when the Nokians decided to penetrate emerging economies, there were already 1.2 billion mobile subscribers worldwide (and, of course, the pessimists lamented that now the end was near, *really*). Yet the number of subscribers soared to more than 4 billion subscribers by the beginning of 2009.

As the world population exceeds 6.8 billion, there is still substantial potential demand left in the emerging world—not to mention replacement demand worldwide. In this industry, scenario pessimists do not have a good track record.

Scenario #2: "Speech Cosmos" — Voice Will Rule?

The Speech Cosmos scenario presumed that it was the voice capability that would rule in the future. True, there were no mobile Internet users in the mid-1990s, but this scenario, too, conflicted with what the Nokians already knew about mobile usage. Younger demographics had embraced texting and were anticipating new services, including mobile chat, e-mails, location services, and TV.

Despite contrary evidence, this old scenario was revived amid the global financial crisis. It fit well with the doomsday mood of resignation and decline. "Cell phone sales are falling, manufacturers have announced thousands of layoffs, and wireless carriers are finding it harder to acquire and keep customers," reported the *New York Times* in spring 2009. "The cell phone industry's best days are behind it. Analysts and investors are beginning to ask whether the industry can continue growing."[1] Ironically, this lamentation in the advanced economies coincided with sales still soaring in the emerging world.

Certainly, the challenge may seem daunting: how to expand when 4 billion of the nearly 7 billion people on the planet already have phones? After all, even in the developing countries, where there are underserved markets, subscribers spend less on phones and services, due to the lower GDP per capita. Yet the simple reality is that, starting from scratch in 2000, the number of mobile Internet users soared to 405 million worldwide by the turn of 2009.

But what was even more intriguing, these users were no longer just talking on the phone. "According to our research, consumers nowadays use less than 20 percent of their time talking on the phone," says Dr. Kai Öistämö, chief of Nokia Devices. "They use 80 percent of their time to do something else with their phones." If only one-fifth of the time spent with mobile devices has been monetized so far, that's a great incentive to develop new business models to facilitate innovation.

It is interesting that the doomsday speculation may have been most pervasive in the United States, one of the few nations in which operators dominated the marketplace almost exclusively over distributors and retailers. Perhaps this concern for the future was predicated on the collapse of Motorola's sales and the U.S.-centered view of the business landscape? After all, Motorola stuck to an Americas-centered model at a time when the industry was swept by global forces, whereas Nokia took advantage of the new opportunities. Motorola did not adapt to the changing environment; Nokia did. Motorola's devastation reflects less industry fortunes than the inability to embrace globalization.[2]

Scenario #3: "Multimedia Jungle"—Different Mobiles All Over?

Finally, the Multimedia Jungle scenario suggested that penetration growth would be explosive, but mobile devices would leverage their data potential in new directions. Multiple standards would complicate roadmaps for the future. There would be no single path to the future, Instead, the digital convergence in technologies and the ensuing consolidation across industries would result in many different paths. "In our scenario work, we argued that the multimedia jungle was a significant trend," recalls Yrjö Neuvo, Nokia's former CTO.

The Potential of "Connecting People"

In the Autumn Harvest scenario, neither voice nor data would save from the inevitable decline. In the Speech Cosmos scenario, voice offered future prospects, data did not. In the Multimedia Jungle, voice and especially data provided the gateway to the future.

Well, now we know that we all live in the multimedia jungle. In retrospect, the Autumn Harvest scenario was just plain silly. It made sense only in the ivory tower of a few wealthy metropolises in the West; it was predicated on the neglect of most of humanity. As for Speech Cosmos, it was a tempting scenario, especially amid the dotcom crunch in the early 2000s. Yet the parallel rise of social media, from YouTube to Twitter, indicates that speech will always be just a part of the story.

Also, consumer usage of mobile communications suggests that there is actually a huge potential *need to connect* that has not been met yet. The glass is not half empty, it's half full; or to be precise, it's only a *tenth* full. If, at the turn of 2009, there were more than 4 billion mobile subscribers and more than 400 million mobile Internet users, this means that there were 3.6 billion subscribers who expect to use mobile Internet services in the coming years.

Further, even if the penetration would saturate the globe's 6.8 billion people, it should not be forgotten that in the most developed markets, a 100 percent penetration was exceeded in the early 2000s. For example, moving into 2008, Hong Kong's mobile penetration already exceeded 150 percent, and it soared to more than 190 percent in the United Arab Emirates (UAE). If people are able and willing to use one or more mobile devices, the role of demand will escalate accordingly. As long as globalization drives trade, investment, and ideas worldwide, there remains mobile potential in the emerging world, mobile Internet potential in the advanced and emerging economies, and replacement potential in all economies.

These three scenarios depict the emerging landscape of converging industries, but they say nothing about the fate of individual companies or Nokia's quest to sustain its leadership well into the 2000s. In order to understand how Nokia could sustain the competition for the future, it is necessary to identify the sources of its success in the first place.

Competition for the Future

Until recently, mobile devices offered primarily texting services. Now they are becoming powerful multimedia computers, despite the small size. Competition is accelerating leadership rivalries in mobile devices, the expansion of consumer Internet services, the adoption of business solutions, and efforts to leverage scale and transform solutions in network infrastructure. "It's a completely new value proposition that we're trying to make and requires new capabilities," says Dr. Öistämö.

Digital Convergence

Today, mobile devices are still used primarily for voice and text message communication, but people increasingly use them to take and send pictures, listen to music, record video, watch TV, play games, surf the Internet, check e-mail, navigate, manage their schedules, browse and create documents, and more. This trend—in which mobile devices increasingly support the features of single-purposed product categories—is often referred to as *digital convergence.*

For two decades, there has been increasing speculation over consolidation; now the barriers are falling rapidly between the Internet, the PC, and the mobile device.[3] In the past, U.S.-based firms dominated these M&A activities. In the 2010s, many expect U.S. consolidators to be augmented by those from China and other emerging economies.

How Computing Was Horizontalized

Before the 1980s, an old-style computer company, such as IBM, had its own semiconductor chip implementation, built its own computers around these chips according to its own design and factories, developed its own system software, and marketed its own applications software. This package—the company's own chips, computers, operating system, and software—was sold by its own sales force. So a company competed in this industry as one vertical proprietary block against other computer companies' vertical proprietary blocks.[4]

This world ended with the emergence of the microprocessor and the PC and the ensuing economics of cost-efficient mass production. As no single company could have its own vertical proprietary block, different horizontal layers of the industry grew to represent different kinds of competencies and competition. For instance, chips were led by Intel, and operating systems were dominated by Microsoft's DOS and Windows. Meanwhile, intense rivalry among PC producers reduced the margins among them. In this transformation, Microsoft and Intel captured the driving role, first through licensing rights and later through market power in microprocessors (Intel) and operating systems and application software (Microsoft). The "Wintel" duopoly contributed to the fall of IBM, the old vertical giant, and established a horizontal industry structure.

Will Mobiles Be Horizontalized?

Just as the PC changed the "rules of the game" in the computer industry, the new generation of mobile devices and solutions is about to change the rules in communications. With digitalization and the economics of cost-efficient mass production, a vertically aligned industry is being augmented by a new horizontally layered industry.[5] "In PCs, Wintel drove a strong growth environment, whereas communications is more fragmented," says Nokia's CEO Kallasvuo. New layers of added value have emerged. In operating systems, there is intense competition with more than half a dozen major players.

Until the 2010s, the only known success stories involved vertically integrated solutions in national environments, from NTT DoCoMo's iMode in Japan in the late 1990s to Apple's iPhone and RIM's BlackBerry in the United States in the early 2000s.[6] Despite some consolidation, vertical solutions and horizontal layers are likely to coexist in the foreseeable future. Unlike PCs, the mobile device remains a personal gadget. People don't show off their PCs, whereas cell phones are more intimate reflections of identity. "A mobile device is selected much on the basis of its look and feel," says Nokia's celebrated technologist Dr. Yrjö Neuvo.

Vertical Integration and Horizontal Layers

With the massive transformation, Nokia has moved into services and developing solutions. Even as it continues to compete with the traditional mobile device manufacturers, it is dealing with new competitors entering the market from the PC and Internet industries. But it is operating from a position of strength. It enjoys unmatched scale, one of the best brands in the world, and a highly efficient demand and supply network. Its financial position is good and it can make investments in technologies and services, whereas many of its rivals struggle to differentiate from competition.

The secret of success is in being able to seamlessly integrate vertically while the sector as a whole is generating horizontal layers. Nokia is hedging its bets by seeking success in both worlds. As a mobile device maker, it is contributing to *horizontal layers* with its popular mobile devices, promotion of operating systems, software, services, and, in cooperation with suppliers and partners, components. And as a service provider, it is boosting *vertical integration* in order to come up with sticky services that consumers cannot live without.

In this transformation, Nokia has the driving role in several horizontal layers, including network infrastructure (Nokia Siemens Networks), handsets (Devices), operating systems (Symbian, Series 60), and application software (Services).[7] One central element in Nokia's multipronged strategy is the Symbian platform, an open source operating system for mobile devices.[8] Until recently, Symbian has been little known in Silicon Valley, and only 5 percent of smartphones run Symbian in North America, but it enjoys global muscle. "It has reach and flexibility like no other platform," as CEO Kallasvuo puts it.

- Symbian's overall global market share is 49.3 percent.

- In Asia-Pacific, the comparable figure is 80 percent.

- In Europe, the Middle East, and Africa, its market share is 60 percent.

- Even in Latin America, it commands 40 percent of the market.[9]

Scaling Up Services, Facilitating Dialogue

"We can evolve into the world's largest entertainment media platform," says Tero Ojanperä, Nokia's chief of Services, focusing on entertainment and communities. Where Apple has tried to attract record labels to sign on iTunes or getting application makers to sell their work through the App Store, Nokia, loyal to its style, has sought to build relationships with individual artists, through the industry but also via Ojanperä's close friend, Dave Stewart, the Eurythmics founder and Nokia consultant.[10] Music is a very desirable element of Nokia's offering, which includes mobile video and TV, games, software distribution, and social networking services. "We have launched many of our services," says Ojanperä. "Now we are scaling them up and targeting some 300 million active users by the end of 2011."

Nokia's priority is to scale up the services, create compelling offerings, and facilitate this dialogue with the user as part of its overall solutions. Today, Nokia serves basically every demographic segment in the global marketplace, from urban New York City or Paris to rural India and Africa. It serves young and old, technology enthusiasts and agnostics. It seeks to create offerings that can pass through all markets and segments from the highest to the lowest.

A typical example is Nokia's launch of a groundbreaking new global music partnership—Nokia Play 2010—with the Island Def Jam Music

Group (IDJMG) and Universal Music Group International (UMGI). It coincided with the global availability of the Nokia X6, a powerful entertainment device in combination with Comes With Music, Nokia's "all-you-can-eat-music" offering. The partnership featured international superstar Rihanna's new album, Rated R, with Nokia via an exclusive live, streamed concert in multiple locations around the globe in November 2009.[11] "Too little, too late," said critical analysts who did not expect the service to be able to take on Apple's iPhone and iTunes.

Conceptually, the Rihanna partnership was no different from the legendary Muhammad Ali–George Foreman champion fight in Zaire. In both cases, a high-profile mass event serves to promote and familiarize a new media—HBO's pay-cable in 1974, Nokia's mobile music offering in 2009. And as far as Nokia is concerned, this was only the beginning. "The idea is to transform the relations Nokia has with the consumer," says Ojanperä. "Instead of shipping devices, we shall have active dialogue with the users on a daily basis, through our services."

Nokia Drives Transformation Globally and Locally

As half of the new mobile subscriptions are created in the BRIC economies, these figures underscore the point that Nokia is the only major player that is driving transformation with a global strategy that is sensitive to local conditions. In turn, other major players, including Apple and RIM, essentially seek to export their U.S. strategy worldwide. Ironically, current mobile services may be most sophisticated in Japan, which has failed in both global and export strategies. Starting with NTT DoCoMo's i-mode, Japanese mobile phones have long been ready for Internet and e-mail, and they double as credit cards, boarding passes, and even body-fat calculators. Yet despite great innovation, they have little presence beyond Japan. The architect of i-mode, Takeshi Natsuno, calls this the "Galapagos syndrome." Nokia was right to have a global mindset, he says. "Domestic strategies do not work globally."[12]

Nokia's challenge is that its foothold in the smartphone segment is rapidly rising in absolute terms but decreasing in relative terms, particularly in the United States, the home base of thousands of developers. If, on the other hand, Nokia can reverse its fortunes in the smartphone segment and in the United States, it is better positioned than its rival to dominate several layers globally.

- *The Apple Scenario.* In the emerging ecosystem, Apple seeks to dominate primarily through a vertical chain. In this scenario, iPhone is tied up with iTunes. In this sense, it is a déjà vu of the 1980s Macintosh strategy. It is based on a less open, vertical innovation environment that emphasizes services at the expense of devices.

- *The Google Scenario.* Smartphones will run on Android operating system whose market share was almost 4 percent in late 2009. In January 2010, Google launched the Nexus One, a handset made by HTC of Taiwan that the Internet giant will sell directly to consumers and that runs Android. Like in the Apple scenario, the home base of activities is the United States.

- *The Nokia Scenario.* In the Nokia scenario, Nokia devices work with an operating system that is either open (Symbian, Maemo) or more proprietary (Sseries) and application software (Ovi). The scenario is based on an open, horizontal environment that emphasizes both devices and services. In this case, the home base of activities is global but increasingly localized.

What makes the Nokia scenario both attractive and challenging is its enormous, escalating complexity. Already in summer 2009, Nokia's Ovi site—the counterpart of Apple's i-Tunes—had registered users in 180 countries, worked in five languages, and ran on more than seventy-five devices that used four different operating systems, with twenty-seven operators in nine countries offering the possibility of mobile billing. It also recognizes where users are located, which language they speak, and how they have used the store in the past, while recommending contents and applications accordingly. Unlike its rivals, it truly acknowledges the potential of mobile lifestyle and social networking.[13]

At the end of the day, the smartphone race is not a sprint, but a marathon. Although the race may have been initiated in the United States, it will be run and won globally. American giants are best positioned in their home base: the United States. But Nokia may be best positioned in its home base, which encompasses the entire globe.[14]

In order to assess Nokia's prospects in the changing mobile world, it is vital to understand the strengths that it can and will deploy.

What Are the Sources of Nokia's Success?

A decade ago, when MIT economist Bengt Holmström joined the board of Nokia, he asked Nokia's then-CEO Jorma Ollila, "What's your secret?" The two went on for an hour or two on what it could be. "There is no secret code," Ollila recalls his response. "But it's not a bad way of asking the question."

Since the 1990s, Nokia's explosive growth has intrigued industry practitioners, analysts, investors, and consultants worldwide. A cottage industry of "Nokiologists" and management gurus have struggled to offer an explanation to decipher the source of the success of this highly recognized but ultimately surprisingly little-known company.

Since the early 2000s, Michael E. Porter, the pioneer of strategy, has argued that the case of Nokia and Finland illustrates the interplay of the success of a nation, a cluster within a nation, and an individual firm.[15] This interplay has certainly been more pronounced in Finland and other small open economies than in the large European nations, the United States, or Japan. Still, the Finnish mobile communications cluster is today just a subcomponent of the rapidly globalizing industry; a strategic nodal point, but marginal in high volume production. Conversely, much of Finland's recent success in innovation stems from Nokia rather than the country or the cluster itself, as we saw in Chapter Five. In fact, today Nokia may need Finland less than Finland needs Nokia. The cluster theory, or the way it has been used so far, may thus describe a phase of Nokia's success rather than the sources of success itself.

More recently, Yves L. Doz, a pioneer of international business, and Mikko Kosonen, Nokia's former executive, have argued that Nokia illustrates how a firm can use strategic agility to transcend commitments and discontinuities.[16] Agility is certainly another vital part of the puzzle.

After all, Nokia is famous for its ability to change with the times and listen to the markets. But Nokia's strategic success is not only about organizational flexibility, and there have also been times when even Nokia has failed to respond to the markets. For example, take the clamshell debacle of the early 2000s, when Nokia suffered a temporary setback in Asia as it was offering mobile handset models that were not to the liking of the market, which preferred clamshells. So agility, too, is a vital part of the story, but it's not all there is to the story.

Stanford's John Roberts and Oxford's Katherine Doornik have a broader theoretical scope. In their observations they focus simultaneously on Nokia's need to innovate, maintain efficient operations, and deal with rapid growth and the challenges of globalization from a narrow national base. Yet unlike Nokia, there are many companies that originate from tiny national home markets, but most fail in the struggle against global giants.[17] Why did Nokia succeed where most have failed?

Still other authors have focused on certain specific aspects of Nokia's success, such as innovation. For instance, MIT's Rebecca Henderson and Harvard's David Yoffie used the cooperation of Nokia and MIT as an illustration of how an industry leader adapts to fundamental technological shifts.[18] And certainly it is true that, coming from a small country, Nokia has sought to take advantage of worldwide networks of science and technology, R&D, and innovation. But this is not to say that all of these efforts have been productive. Off the record, some of Nokia's senior executives have regarded the net benefit of such projects as generic or prohibitively expensive. Today they go through a lot of trouble to negotiate sophisticated framework agreements, in order to ensure that the results will be proportionate to the costs incurred.

Today there are also a wide array of Nokia cases, dissertations, theses, studies, estimates, and projections. Many seek to dissect the sources of Nokia's success. The accounts that have been made in Finland tend to ignore Nokia's global operations. The studies that have been conducted abroad tend to neglect the role of Nokia's activities in Finland, which remain strategic. Even more important, both tend to bypass the highly distributed relationships between the Nokia headquarters and the country units worldwide, which are the juice of the story. At best, some illuminate aspects of the secret that so intrigued Holmström. But if Ollila is right and Nokia's success has something to do with its culture—a notoriously soft, vacuous, and difficult notion—and if existing explanations of Nokia's success remain insufficient, what is it exactly that drives this widely admired but often misunderstood corporate giant?

Nokia's success may not be based on a single code, but it is possible to identify a wide array of sources that do seem to account for its triumphs. Most important, the lessons of Nokia's strategic success are not just limited to companies in mobile communications.

As we have seen in the previous chapters, Nokia has to excel in both technology- and marketing-intensive activities. As a result, the lessons are vital to most ambitious multinational companies that seek success in a global world that is increasingly multipolar, that is, in a globalized world which is characterized by several great powers that dominate different dimensions of economy, politics, and culture. These lessons are also vital to those small- and medium-size enterprises (SMEs) that seek to collaborate with large multinationals in a wide array of functions.

Building Layers of Strategic Advantage Across the World

How does Nokia build layers of strategic advantage? And what are these advantages? Strategic advantage is vital to Nokia, just as it is to most multinationals worldwide. But to call it just a *competitive* advantage is to ignore much of the story. With its market-making strategies, Nokia, along with many other multinationals, often operates in emerging industries, which may or may not materialize or where competitors may or may not exist yet. In other words, there is far more risk and uncertainty in this competition for the future than is habitually acknowledged.

Also, Nokia does not seek to build a single or a singular kind of advantage. Instead, ever since the early 1990s, it has sought to build layers of strategic advantage, that is, multiple and diverse drivers of strategic advantage. "We did talk about competitive advantage, and we did seek to build competitive advantages," acknowledges Sari Baldauf, Nokia's former senior executive.

Developing Cost Advantage Cost is a central layer of Nokia's strategic advantage. "We have always wanted to be the lowest-cost producer," says Nokia's chairman Jorma Ollila. And certainly Nokia seeks to introduce cost-efficient products with new or enhanced functionalities and services, and with higher prices in a timely manner. The products, services, and solutions that Nokia offers are subject to natural price erosion over their life cycle. In addition, the average selling price of Nokia's devices has declined during recent years and it is likely to continue to decline in the future, especially as some of its customers may trade down to lower-priced devices as a result of the challenging global economic conditions. As long as Nokia can maintain its leadership in both high-end and low-end products and services, it will benefit from both good times (when people trade up) and bad times (when people trade down). In order to be profitable, Nokia must be able to lower costs at the same rate or faster than the price erosion and declining average selling price of its devices. As Nokia's chairman Ollila likes to say, Nokia's leadership is about "cost, cost, and cost."

Differentiating Holistically Along with cost, differentiation is another layer. When Nokia opted for its winning strategy in the early 1990s, it also initiated global branding, which allows for the premium price. "We have thought of these advantages in a holistic manner," says Matti Alahuhta, Nokia's former globalization expert. "They can be associated with *any activity* associated with the extended value chain." In other words, don't think of strategic advantages on the basis of products alone. Some companies concentrate on products or services. Others concentrate on their processes. Nokia pays a lot of attention to the extended entire value chain; in other words, not just its own conduct but that of its partners, cooperators, and suppliers. It is continually seeking dimensions that allow it to differentiate systematically and through the extended chain. That makes it different from the rest. Many of its rivals have been great in this-or-that value activity, such as technology and

232

distribution, but none of its competitors has been strong through the entire chain. "Thank God, the cell phone and the network businesses are so complex," smiles Ala-Pietilä. "If the company made just a single mistake, no success in other areas would be adequate to compensate for that mistake. So our imperative has been to pay attention to the full chain of activities."

Innovating in Technology and Marketing   In the 1990s, Nokia excelled primarily in technology innovation. More recently, it has been preparing for marketing innovation. Both are necessary. Unlike global brand leaders such as Coca-Cola and Procter & Gamble (which are primarily marketing-intensive), Nokia operates in fast-changing business areas that are both technology-intensive and marketing-intensive. Accordingly, it offers lessons to leading marketers, technology concerns, and global companies worldwide: marketers, who struggle for brand premiums; technology leaders, who develop innovations; and global companies that seek for cost efficiencies. Nokia has done it all, simultaneously.

The Drivers of Nokia's Strategic Advantages

Although Nokia has managed to maintain its strategic advantages since the late 1990s, there is nothing automatically sustainable about this success. Unlike its rivals, Nokia has struggled for much that most multinational companies take for granted. The company has several layers of strategic advantage, but none of them are automatic and each requires ceaseless upgrading and innovation. Conversely, under adverse conditions, these layers, as drivers of Nokia's strategic advantages, could also dissipate. Here's a concise recap (see also Figure I.1).

Nokia's Legacy and Globalization   Founded in 1865, Nokia's legacy has evolved through several eras and reincarnations from a forestry company to a diversified conglomerate to a European technology concern and, ultimately, to the globally focused mobility and Internet giant. Nokia's success stems from its legacy and ability to take advantage of globalization, in particular since the 1990s. Unlike large-country multinationals it cannot rely on a large home market.

Team-Driven Strategy   Operating in a technology- and marketing-intensive environment, Nokia is a global company that seeks to be externally oriented but internally collaborative. Nokia's strategy is formulated by its executive team, which drives its transformation.

Values, Culture, and People   What truly animates Nokia are its values, culture, and people. Through perseverance and increasing diversity, Nokia builds a shared purpose through values, which also provide guidance for global human resource management.

A Globally Networked Matrix Organization   Historically, Nokia's executives have paid special attention to building organizational capabilities. At the same time, Nokia has moved from an area structure to a worldwide product structure, with its flat, team-driven, and globally networked matrix organization.

Innovating Globally via R&D Networks   Innovation is Nokia's most critical capability. Indeed, its emphasis on sustained innovation is reflected by the rapid expansion of the Nokia Research Center, unit-based R&D, and globally networked university cooperation, open innovation, and venture funds.

Strategic Capabilities   Many companies excel in one or another competitive dimension, but few excel in several dimensions. In addition to *innovation,* these global strategic capabilities include *economies of scale, demand and supply network, distribution,* and the powerful *brand,* including the *strategic approach to marketing* and *global consumer insight.*

Strategic Advantages   Nokia is a pioneer in mobile telecom and the world's leading maker of *mobile devices.* Today, it is connecting people in new and different ways—fusing advanced mobile technology with *personalized services* to enable people to stay close to what matters to them. It also provides comprehensive digital map information through NAVTEQ, and equipment, solutions, and services for *communications networks* through Nokia Siemens Networks. Nokia continually seeks to grow, transform, and build its business.

What Could Go Wrong?

What kind of conditions could indicate Nokia's loss of leadership? First of all, any competitive erosion would have to be reflected in Nokia's layers of strategic advantage. For instance, the company would have to lose its cost advantage, or fail in technology innovation or market development. Secondly, Nokia's strategic capabilities would have to weaken. For instance, its brand or scale economies might erode, or there might be substantial problems with its supply chain or distribution. Thirdly, Nokia's strategic advantages would have to soften in infrastructure, devices, or solutions. At the beginning of 2010, Nokia's primary losses have been in its market share for high-end smartphones. The success of Apple's iPhone and iTunes caught the leading mobile device makers by surprise. However, the rivalry is only about to begin in the global marketplace.

In December 2009, Nokia expected the global mobile phone market to grow by 10 percent in 2010 but cautioned that its market share, currently at some 38 percent, would be "flat." In the 1990s, competition for the mobile future was still about success in the leading advanced economies. Today, more is needed. Global leadership also requires triumph in the large emerging economies. Historically, Nokia has been at its best globally, while Apple has been more successful in exclusive high-end segments in advanced economies. The rivalry for the cell phones, smartphones, and mobile computers of the future is a marathon, not a sprint. Nokia remains an extraordinarily resilient competitor in almost every part of the world, but it is not invincible. And now it faces new challengers from Silicon Valley to emerging Asia.

Through the years of globalization, Nokia has thrived along with emerging economies. But globalization is neither automatic nor irreversible. Forces of friction, especially nationalism and protectionism, have a potential to harm both emerging economies and multinationals operating in them. For a quarter of a century, Nokia's CEO Olli-Pekka Kallasvuo has witnessed intimately Nokia's challenges and its success in overcoming such adversities. When he took his job in 2006, the company was at the peak of the most recent wave of globalization. Only two years later, the global economic crisis caused world trade to plunge for the first time since the early 1980s, and the world shifted close to a global financial meltdown for the first time since the Great Depression. These challenging conditions coincide with the transformation of Nokia's business areas. Yet Nokia is operating from a position of strength. Difficult environmental conditions are more harmful to many of its rivals.

When you ask Kallasvuo what are Nokia's most important lessons for new and ambitious multinationals, whether they originate from advanced or emerging economies, he is almost reluctant to say anything. The world is pretty complex, so it's hard to advise others, he suggests. When everything is said and done, it all comes down to the global mindset and people. Or as he puts it:

> We're probably the most global company there is. What is important is to be truly global, not just talking about it. It's extremely important to people that they feel they are working in a global organization and that they have the same opportunities to get ahead. Everybody must be respected. There must be no glass ceiling of any kind. It is this kind of globalization that I believe has helped us a lot. This relates to the fact that we don't really have a home market. We had no alternative but to think differently from the very beginning.

Nokia's Lessons

- As the Nokians became aware of the potential of the mobile device, they engaged in scenario projects to forecast the future. And as they moved from mobile devices to solutions, they began to stretch the meaning of the corporate slogan "Connecting People." In a future-driven business, scenarios support foresight to embrace change and adapt to the future.

- Nokia's success is not based on a "single code." Unlike many of its rivals, it has strategic capabilities along several dimensions (innovation, economies of scale, demand and supply network, distribution, brand, strategic approach to marketing, and global consumer insight). Nokia's success has several drivers (legacy and globalization, team-driven strategy, strong values and culture, social human capital, unique organizational capabilities, and global innovation). And these are supported by layers of strategic advantage (cost, extended value chain, and technology and marketing innovation).

- Despite its capabilities, drivers, and layers of strategic advantage, Nokia's global leadership is not automatic but must be sustained. In this quest, flexibility and execution are invaluable.

NOKIA'S KEY
EXECUTIVES

The key Nokians interviewed for *Winning Across Global Markets* were some thirty high-level executives. For a broader account of all Nokia interviews, see the Acknowledgments.

Esko Aho was appointed executive vice president of corporate relations and responsibility in late 2008 and has been a group executive board member since 2009; he is Finland's former prime minister, former president of Sitra, the Finnish Innovation Fund, and a veteran Center Party politician.

Marko Ahtisaari heads the Design and Consumer Experience organization, which brings together the Nokia Design, Nokia User Experience, and Consumer and User Experience team from Category Management. Ahtisaari's role focuses on design, content, and experience and is more strategic by nature. He rejoined Nokia in 2009.

Matti Alahuhta is a former member of Ollila's executive team, who served as president of Nokia Telecommunications 1993–1998, president of Nokia Mobile Phones 1990–2003, and Nokia's executive vice president in 2004. He wrote a dissertation on global growth strategies for high-technology challengers. Currently he is president and CEO of KONE.

Pekka Ala-Pietilä served as president of Nokia (1999–2005) and president of Nokia Mobile Phones (1992–1998); he was one of Ollila's right-hand men and today serves as CEO of Blyk, the first free mobile network in the United Kingdom funded by advertising.

Robert Andersson has been head of Nokia Corporate Alliances and Business Development since summer 2009; formerly head of Finance, Strategy, and Strategic Sourcing in the Devices unit, he left the group executive board in October 2009 and is responsible for companywide strategic partnerships, including cooperation with Microsoft. He joined Nokia in 1985.

Sari Baldauf is Nokia's former senior executive who spent twenty-two years at the company, including six and a half years as executive vice president and general manager of its networking business, prior to leaving the company in early 2005; a year later, she joined HP's board of directors.

Simon Beresford-Wylie joined Nokia in 1998; as CEO of NSN, he oversaw the creation of NSN and its integration phase and left the company in 2009 to become CEO of Elster Group, the world's largest provider of smart metering and smart grid systems and solutions to the gas, electricity, and water industries.

Alastair Curtis is Nokia's former chief designer in 2006–2009. He joined the company in 1993 and held a number of senior positions including design director of Nokia's Los Angeles Design Center and head of design for Mobile Phones, Nokia's largest business unit. He left the company in fall 2009.

Georg Ehrnrooth is a legendary Finnish industrialist who has been a Nokia board member since 2000.

Colin Giles has been global head of sales, reporting to Anssi Vanjoki, since January 2010. Giles is Nokia's former senior vice president of Sales, Greater China, Japan, and Korea, as well as president of Nokia China; he joined Nokia in 1992 and has played a critical role in the company's success in China and Asia-Pacific.

Jo Harlow heads Smartphones, which leads the portfolio, product, and life cycle management of all Symbian-based devices. Harlow joined Nokia's marketing unit in 2003 after a long career at Reebok and Procter & Gamble.

Bob Iannucci served as senior vice president and head of the Nokia Research Center, 2004–2008. Previously, he held high-level R&D positions at Compaq Computer and IBM Corporation.

Knut Fredrik Idestam (1838–1916) was a mining engineer and businessman, who founded Nokia in May 1865. The groundwood paper mill at Tampere, Finland, began operations a year later. In 1871, Idestam and Leo Mechelin, Finland's first parliamentarian, founded Nokia and moved the operations to the city of Nokia, Finland. Idestam retired from the management of the company in 1896.

Timo Ihamuotila has been Nokia's CFO as of November 2009. In addition to being Nokia corporate treasurer, he has held several other senior positions over the years in, for example, risk management and portfolio management. Formerly, he was global head of sales. He has been a member of the group executive board since 2007; he first joined the company in the early 1990s.

Kari H. Kairamo joined Nokia in the late 1960s; he served as Nokia's chief executive in 1977–1988 and, through bold M&A activities, transformed the company into a technology conglomerate.

Olli-Pekka "OPK" Kallasvuo, CEO of Nokia Corporation, group executive board member since 1990, has been group executive board chairman since 2006 and a member of the Nokia board of directors since 2007; he joined Nokia in the early 1980s and, along with Ollila, formulated Nokia's winning strategy.

Lauri Kivinen heads NSN's corporate affairs function and has a wide range of experience within the Nokia Group, which he joined in 1988; during Nokia's high-growth period, he served as the company's senior vice president of corporate communications.

Mikko Kosonen has held several senior executive positions at Nokia since joining the company in 1984, most recently being the head of strategy and CIO. He is current president of the Finnish Innovation Fund (Sitra).

Chris Leong is currently head of Nokia Greater China, Japan, and Korea SU. Formerly, senior vice president of Marketing GTM, Leong was responsible for the overall alignment of Nokia's go-to-market marketing across all local markets globally. She is one of Nokia's new and rising female Asian executives.

John Martin heads Nokia's Mobile Computers business. Formerly vice president of iPhone and Mac Internet Services at Apple (2005–2008), he leads the group working on Maemo and Maemo-based devices. Prior to Nokia and Apple, Martin worked in a variety of companies, including Starbucks, Loudeye, Microsoft, and NASA. He joined Nokia in 2009.

Mary T. McDowell is executive vice president and chief development officer leading the Corporate Development unit. She has been a group executive board member since 2004; the veteran HP executive joined Nokia in 2004.

Hallstein Moerk is Nokia's executive vice president of human resources and a member of the group executive board since 2004; the veteran HP executive joined Nokia in 1999 and has global responsibility for all human resources activity in Nokia.

Yrjö Neuvo served as Nokia's chief technology officer and a member of the group executive board in 1993–2005; he is the legendary visionary of Nokia's R&D and currently advises the Finnish government on issues of science and technology and innovation.

Frank Nuovo is the founder of the Nokia Design organization, which he headed from 1995 to 2006 defining Nokia's early styling and global industrial design innovations. Initiating the building of an international design group of over thirty nationalities, he was also very active in brand development and renewal.

Kai Öistämö is Nokia's executive vice president of Devices and group executive board member since 2005; he joined Nokia in 1991 and is seen as one of the key executives, along with other Nokians who have headed the company's most vital unit.

Tero Ojanperä is Nokia's executive vice president of Services unit, group executive board member since 2005; he joined Nokia in 1990, has held an array of high-level positions, plays a key role in the current transformation, and is seen as one of Nokia's young rising stars.

Jorma Ollila is chairman of Nokia's board of directors, and chairman of the board of directors of Royal Dutch Shell Plc; he joined Nokia after the mid-1980s and served as chief executive from 1992 to 2006.

Keith Pardy, former head of Nokia Strategic Marketing, has contributed to making Nokia the most loved and admired brand in the world; he spent the majority of his career in marketing leadership roles with the Coca-Cola Company.

Niklas Savander is Nokia's executive vice president of services and group executive board member as of 2006; he joined Nokia in 1997 and is in charge of the most vital unit in Nokia's current transformation.

D. "Shiv" Shivakumar is vice president and managing director of Nokia India; he joined Nokia in 2006 and has played a vital role in the company's success in India.

Richard A. Simonson is executive vice president and the first non-Finnish head of the Mobile Phones subunit within the Devices unit; he also heads strategic sourcing for Devices. He is Nokia's former CFO and has been a group executive board member since 2004; he joined Nokia in 2001 and is currently based in the United States.

Veli-Pekka Sundbäck was Nokia's executive vice president of corporate relations and responsibility until fall 2008 and retired in 2009; he joined Nokia in 1996, having served as Finland's secretary of state, Ministry for Foreign Affairs.

Arja Suominen is Nokia's senior vice president of communications; she joined Nokia after the mid-1980s and has been the company's highest-level spokesperson since 2004.

Rajeev Suri was appointed as chief executive officer of NSN in October 2009; the telecom veteran joined the company in 1995 and previously led the NSN Services business.

Henry Tirri is senior vice president and head of the Nokia Research Center and responsible for labs worldwide; he joined Nokia in 2004 as a research fellow in the Software and Applications Laboratory.

Alberto Torres was appointed head of Nokia's new Solutions unit in October 2009 and member of the group executive board. He joined the company in 2004 and previously headed the Devices category management.

Anssi Vanjoki is Nokia's executive vice president and general manager of the Markets unit. In this role, he is responsible for consumer insights, sales, marketing, manufacturing, and logistics across all Nokia products and services. He has been a member of the Nokia group executive board since 1998 and joined Nokia in 1991.

Björn Westerlund (1912–2009) was a Finnish businessman and the former and first chairman and CEO of Nokia Corp. after the 1967 merger of Nokia Company, Finnish Rubber Works, and Finnish Cable Works. CEO until his retirement in 1977, he remained chairman of the board until 1979.

Kurt Wikstedt built Nokia Electronics as its first head during the first two decades; he stuck to Moore's Law, digital vision, and portfolio management, even though it meant years of financial losses.

Kari-Pekka "KP" Wilska joined Nokia in 1973 and held various executive positions in the company, including as president of Nokia, Inc. (Nokia Americas) from 1999 to December 2004; joined Austin Ventures as a partner in 2005.

NOTES

CHAPTER ONE

1. On Nokia's transformation and mobile communications through history, see
   Steinbock, D. (2001), *The Nokia Revolution* (New York: Amacom); Steinbock,
   D. (2002), *Wireless Horizon* (New York: Amacom). On Nokia's history, see
   Bonsdorff, L. G. (1965), *Nokia Oy 1865–1965* [in Finnish] (Helsinki: Nokia Oy,
   1965); Ekman, K. (1928), *Nokia's Factory 1868–1928* [in Finnish] (Helsinki:
   Nokia Oy); Cronström, E., Ström, H., et al. (1965), *Half a Century of Cable
   Industry 1912–1962* [in Finnish] (Helsinki: Suomen kaapelitehdas osakeyhtiö);
   Hoving, V. (1948), *Suomen Gummitehdas Oy 1898–1948* [in Finnish] (Helsinki);
   Mäkinen, M. (1995), *Nokia Saga* [in Finnish] (Helsinki: Gummerus, 1995);
   Palo-Oja, R., and Willberg, L. (1998), *Rubber: The History of Rubber and the
   Finnish Rubber Industry* (Tampere: Tampere Museums); Haikio, M. (2002),
   Nokia Oy History [in Finnish], 3 volumes (Helsinki: Edita); Bruun, S., and
   Wallen, W. (1999), *Nokia's Highway* [in Finnish] (Jyväskylä: Gummerus).

2. The socialists, or the "Reds," wanted to create a socialist Finland, possibly in
   union with the Soviet Union, but the "White" government troops, led by General
   Mannerheim, Finland's legendary war hero (and Nokia's former board member),
   won the bloody civil war. For years, Renny Harlin, the Finnish-born director of
   Die Hard classics and an acquaintance, has tried to garner funds for a biopic on
   the Mannerheim story.

3. Finland fought three interconnected wars: the Winter War (1939–40) against
   the Soviet Union after its aggression; the Continuation War (1941–44) along-
   side Germany against the Soviets in an effort to recapture its eastern areas; and
   the Lapland War (1944–45) against Germany to drive its forces out of northern
   Finland.

4. See Ostry, S. (1997), *The Post-Cold War Trading System* (Chicago: University of
   Chicago Press).

5. As Nokia researched radio transmission technology, the French computer firm
   Machines Bull selected the company as its Finnish agent in 1962. At the same
   time, activities were divided into computing and electronics.

6. The phrase is by Harri Holkeri, Finland's veteran conservative leader and
   Kairomo's friend who played a critical role in telecom regulation. Steinbock, D.
   (2001), Interview with Harri Holkeri, United Nations, New York, May 10, 2001.

7. The Nokia Corporation was the result of the merger of three Finnish
   companies: Nokia AB, a wood-pulp mill (founded in 1865); Finnish Rubber
   Works, a manufacturer of rubber boots, tires, and other rubber products

(1898); and Finnish Cable Works, a manufacturer of telephone and power cables (1912).

8. After the consolidation of Finnish electronics, Nokia Mobira—the precursor of Nokia Mobile Phones—was launched. In the 1980s, Kairamo saw the mobile company's future potential and hoped to use it to raise awareness of the Nokia brand, in order to boost the stock on the New York Stock Exchange. See Steinbock, D. (2001), *The Nokia Revolution* (New York: Amacom), Chapter Two.

9. At Nokia, the idea of upgrading Nokia's sources of competitive advantage had been discussed since the 1973 oil crisis, which sent tremors across energy-intensive industries worldwide, including in Finland. As Kairamo later recalled, "We came to the conclusion that we couldn't grow in Finland with cables or tires anymore. . . . We decided to keep what we had but also to put all the new money we could scrape together into high tech." It was time for people to replace the trees. See Saari, M. (2000), *Kari Kairamo* [in Finnish] (Jyväskylä: Gummerus).

10. Oceaninc was a French TV manufacturer that Electrolux had bought from ITT (International Telephone & Telegraph) in 1980.

11. At the time, Vladimirov, a longtime official working at the Soviet embassy in Helsinki, was highly regarded in Finland and even published his memoirs later. According to the historian Kimmo Rentola's recent history of the Finnish Security Police, Vladimirov worked as the head of the KGB's sabotage and assassination section in the late 1960s. See Vladimirov V. (1993), *The Way It Was* [In Finnish] (Helsinki); Simola M. (ed.), *Ratakatu 12: The History of Finnish Security Police (SUPO) 1949–2009* (Helsinki).

12. In 1984, Richard N. Perle, the U.S. assistant secretary of defense for international security policy, visited Finland. In the past, Nokia had built cable factories in Russia; now Kairamo wanted to export Nokia's new DX 200 stations. As Perle's host, Kairamo talked about the U.S. export controls, which were threatening Nokia's technology exports to the Soviet Union. With Western technology, argued Perle, the Soviets saved at least $5 million and five years in product development. Eventually, the American guest did appreciate Kairamo's persuasive diplomacy, expressing his confidence that a solution could be found. Later that year, Nokia exported the first DX 200 stations to the Soviet Union.

13. "Sometimes when we entered new markets, we used consultants, but they were not much of a help," recalls Kari-Pekka ("KP") Wilska, Nokia's former chief of Americas. "When Sakari Salminen was the chief of Nokia telecoms, the problem was that he barely spoke English. All business activities were now the responsibility of those who reported to him."

14. On the Finnish national cluster strategy, see Steinbock, D. (2008), *Finnish Strengths, Global Opportunities* (Helsinki: SM); Steinbock, D. (2006), *Competitiveness of Finnish Cluster Leaders* (Helsinki: SM).

15. Steinbock, D. (2001), *The Nokia Revolution* (New York: Amacom), see ch. 2.

16. NMT (Nordic Mobile Telephony), the world's first mobile telephony standard that enabled international roaming, provided valuable experience for Nokia for its close participation in developing GSM, which was adopted in 1987 as the new European standard for digital mobile technology.

17. "In the past, we had been something amorphous in the gray zone between East and West, now we really became an integral part of the West and the Western markets," says a veteran Nokia insider. "That meant a new sense of hope and strength. As Finland was developing an international position, Nokia took advantage of it."

18. The way to global focus was first paved in 1987, when the company began to build the digital cellular infrastructure.

19. In particular, the collapse of bilateral trade with the Soviet Union required deep shifts in corporate strategies. Along with some other industrialists, Georg Ehrnrooth, one of Nokia's current board directors, argued that being good domestically was no longer enough, and that Finnish companies would have to focus in order to join global industry leaders.

20. Along with rapid technology development, increasing global competition resulted in shorter product life cycles, which forced companies to place more emphasis on R&D and to exploit new opportunities faster, Alahuhta argued. Because markets were growing uniform, the winners would be companies that operated in several markets simultaneously, timed new product development right, and achieved higher volume and faster learning. To stretch limited resources around the globe, they would have to concentrate on fewer businesses but expand those businesses into all relevant parts worldwide. See Alahuhta, M. (1990), *Global Growth Strategies for High Technology Challengers* (Espoo: Finnish Academy of Technology, 1990).

21. Martin Dickson's agenda-setting *Lex* column, "The Golden Era of Nokia Is Over," was released in the *Financial Times* in May 1996.

22. On the waves of globalization and multinational companies, see Collier, P., and Dollar, D. (2002), *Globalization, Growth, and Poverty* (New York: World Bank); Bartlett, C. A., and Ghoshal, S. (2002), *Managing Across Borders: The Transnational Solution*, 2nd ed. (Boston, MA: HBSP).

CHAPTER TWO

1. The same is true of Ericsson and its home market, Sweden. When it comes to globalization, these two Nordic multinationals are in a category of their own.

2. The home market of Korean electronics giants comprises some 48 million people. It is small in comparison to the two leaders of global electronics, the United States (with 305 million people) and Japan (with 127 million people), but it is still almost ten times larger than Finland (which has about 5.3 million people).

3. See Baker, S. (1998), "Q&A: Nokia's Ollila on CEO Profiles and the Company's Future," *BusinessWeek,* August 10.

4. "At Nokia, *Andy Grove's Only Paranoids Survive,* which outlined the principles of discontinuities, strategic inflections, and horizontal forces of change, has really struck a chord," says Kari-Pekka ("KP") Wilska, Nokia's former U.S. chief.

5. NSN was created as a result of a merger between Nokia's network group and Siemens AG's COM division (for more detail, see Chapter Seven). Nokia has de facto control over NSN and CEO Kallasvuo is its chairman.

6. The chairman and the members of the group executive board are appointed by the board of directors. Only the chairman of the group executive board can be a member of both the board of directors and the group executive board.

7. In 2009, the merger between the Helsinki School of Economics, the University of Art and Design Helsinki, and the Helsinki University of Technology resulted in Aalto University. Nokia played a vital role in the inspiration for a combined university for business, technology, and design.

8. At the time, Hamel visited Finland and was impressed by the Nokia executive team, which planned to beat Motorola but didn't have the arrogance often associated with senior executives.

9. J. Ollila, (1999) "Nokia's Strategic Intent," lecture at the Finnish Strategic Society in Helsinki, Finland, January 20. Compare Prahalad C. K., and Hamel, G. (1989), "Strategic Intent," *Harvard Business Review* (May–June).

10. On the resource theory of the firm, see for example Foss N. J., (ed.), (1997), *Resources, Firms and Strategies: A Reader in the Resource-Based Perspective* (New York: Oxford University Press). On market-based strategy, see Porter, M. E. (1980), *Competitive Strategy* (New York: The Free Press); Porter, M. E. (1985), *Competitive Advantage* (New York: The Free Press).

11. There is also an inherent balancing of tensions between current and future returns, or more broadly, between protecting current strategic advantages, while building new ones. "Many of our rivals have reaped short-term profit but missed the transition into the future," says Heikki Norta, Nokia's head of corporate strategy. The problem is that, in a highly dynamic environment, it is not always easy to identify the breaking point because it often involves markets in the making. Compare Dodd, D., and Favaro, K. (2007), *The Three Tensions: Winning the Struggle to Perform Without Compromise* (New York: Wiley).

12. Nokia has had the courage to focus and grow into a global player very rapidly. It has taken advantage of industry transitions several times, simultaneously (in the 1990s, the transition from analog to digital cellular and the deregulation of telecom operators) and subsequently (in the transition from digital cellular to multimedia and broadband cellular, and the rise of software and services).

13. Between the early 1990s and early 2000s, these were semi-independent, highly cross-functional teams—enterprises within enterprises. For decades, the basic design process was based on a sequential flow, or the "waterfall model," which proceeded in a linear fashion by starting with user requirements and moving sequentially to the finished product. Unlike this old model, concurrent engineering is based on parallel tasks.

14. In addition to Nokia's president and CEO Olli-Pekka Kallasvuo, Nokia's directors represent international corporations (nonexecutive chairman of ICICI Venture Funds Lalita D. Gupte; former co-CEO and chairman of SAP Henning Kagermann, Karlsson; CFO of PSA Peugeot Citroën Isabel Marey-Semper; chief executive and board member of Pearson Plc Dame Marjorie Scardino); Finnish corporations (Finnish industrialist Georg Ehrnrooth, former president and CEO of Finnair Keijo Suila; president and CEO of F-Secure Corp. Risto Siilasmaa); and Ivy League universities (Paul A. Samuelson professor of economics at MIT Bengt Holmström).

CHAPTER THREE

1. Kallasvuo, O.-P. (2007), "Humility," *Harvard Business Review,* January 2007, pp. 1–2.

2. In August 1939, the infamous Molotov-Ribbentrop Pact between the Bolshevik Soviet Union and Nazi Germany shook the world: instead of fighting the Nazis, Stalin invaded Poland. Soon thereafter came Finland's turn and worldwide moral protest. Yet the Finns found themselves alone at the eve of the Soviet invasion in the Winter War, which began on November 30, 1939. It was the Finnish spirit and national unity that saved the small country from breaking under the Soviet attack. Finland held out until March of 1940, and that resistance popularized internationally the notion of Finnish perseverance, or *sisu:* "the ability to keep fighting after most people would have quit, and to fight with the will to win." See "Northern Theater: *Sisu,*" *Time Magazine,* January 8, 1940.

3. See *Global Gender Gap Report 2009* by the World Economic Forum.

4. In 2008 some 14 percent of senior management positions within Nokia were held by women, and 47 percent were held by people of non-Finnish nationality. In Nokia and Nokia Siemens Networks, about 23 percent of senior management positions were held by women. Senior management positions are defined differently in Nokia and NSN, and accordingly their related data are not directly comparable. Data for both companies reflect year-end 2008.

5. "But through my work on the boards, I have discovered that there remains an attitude towards female executives in Finland, especially in the boards of more traditional industries and organizations," adds Baldauf. In 1998, *Fortune* selected her as the most influential female executive of the year. Half a decade later, the *Wall Street Journal* named her as the Europe's most successful female executive.

6. Seen in the context of Nokia's history in Finland, the slogan may seem simple but is actually complex. While the statement is universal, the colors of the logo reflect those of the Finnish flag (light blue on a white base). Through the Cold War, Finland had an uncertain status and could not easily connect with the world at large. Also, the Finns are not known for expressive conduct; to many, the handset provides a nice way to connect with people without really connecting. The slogan also has a missionary aspect that reflects Finland's historically active role in the UN and peacekeeping activities. And finally, one might add an unintended meaning. With the globalization of the company, the family-friendly but travel-weary Nokians came up with a slogan of their own: "Disconnecting Families."

7. "If in the 1980s and 1990s the PC was a society-changing tool, today the mobile device is the instrument of change," adds Thomas Jönsson, Nokia's regional communications chief, who came to the company via Intel. "Both companies are very focused on results. Both are very straightforward and reject internal politics. In the growth phase, both also had strong leaders. In large emerging economies, both have been active investors and participants in the broader society."

8. On such perpetual entrepreneurial startups, continuously changing their form, direction, even their identity," see Malone, M. S. (2009), *The Future Arrived Yesterday: The Rise of the Protean Corporation and What It Means for You* (New York: Crown Business).

9. In 2006, after twenty-two years at Nokia, Baldauf became a board member of Hewlett-Packard, a leading technology solutions provider with more than 320,000 employees and revenues of almost $120 billion.

10. Both India and China have profited handsomely from their young, able, and seemingly unlimited workforces over the past two decades. But according to research carried out by the McKinsey Global Institute in 2003, only 10–25 percent of potential job candidates in these two countries are suitable for work in a foreign company. Overall, multinationals that are pioneering industries and R&D networks worldwide seem to have a more optimistic view of the skills and capabilities of educated workforces in China, India, and other emerging economies. Nokia's R&D executives note that some of the best technologists now come from China and India.

11. In China, Nokia has been using Human Technology (科技 以人为本) as a key slogan. As Nokians explain it, these four characters 以人为本 are very ancient in Chinese and thus have a deep meaning that is understood at a very visceral level and it really resonates. It means "derived from people for people" or "everything is rooted (grounded and/or comes from) from the people to serve's the people's needs." These characters can be broken down into two elements, 科技, which mean "technology."

Notes

12. Led by Tero Ojanperä, chief of entertainment and communities, and Juha Äkräs, Nokia's head of global human resources, Nokia surveyed some one thousand employees, clients, and partners on Nokia's values and culture.

13. Nokia's inside innovation has been featured as a model for other companies as well. See Ewing, J. (2009), "Nokia: Bring on the Employee Rants," *BusinessWeek,* June 22.

14. In addition to nationalities, the emerging NSN had mobile and fixed-line people. However, both companies also had a strong legacy, fine engineering traditions, and long experience in the telecom sector.

15. Porter, M.E. (2002), "The Competitive Advantage of Corporate Philanthropy," *Harvard Business Review,* December 1.

16. The Gini index, that is, the distribution of family income, measures the degree of inequality in the distribution of family income in a country. The more nearly equal a country's income distribution, the lower its Gini index and vice versa. Worldwide, these ratios range widely from 23 percent or more in Nordic countries to more than 70 percent in certain African countries. See CIA country profiles.

17. The satellite data released by NASA and the National Snow and Ice Data Center show that the maximum extent of the 2008–2009 winter sea ice cover was the fifth lowest since researchers began collecting such information thirty years ago. See Eilperin, J., and Sheridan, M. B. (2009), "New Data Show Rapid Arctic Ice Decline," *Washington Post,* April 7, A03.

18. "Despite many green claims, major companies like Dell, Microsoft, Lenovo, LG, Samsung, and Apple are failing to support the necessary levels of global cuts in emissions and make the absolute cuts in their own emissions that are required to tackle climate change." See "Greener Electronics: Major Companies Fail to Show Climate Leadership," November 24, 2008. See *Guide to Greener Electronics,* Greenpeace International (annual).

19. This posture includes timing, multilevel lobbying through several venues, selection of the European Commission as the most important political institution for lobbying, reshaping rather than defiance, multilevel ad hoc alliances, and the importance of personal contacts in the policy-making process with the EU. See Kautto, P. (2009), "Nokia as an Environmental Policy Actor: Evolution of Collaborative Corporate Political Activity in a Multinational Company," *Journal of Common Market Studies,* 47(1), 103–125.

20. Nokia has dozens of capability development activities to help employees face new challenges, including recruitment practices to support service-specific resourcing needs, programs to increase retail- and solutions-selling competencies, modified incentive and target-setting guidelines for the Services unit, increased software engineering capabilities, a product-making excellence program to execute

solutions-based strategy with speed and scale, and so on. There are also several ongoing business transformation and change projects.

21. Kharif, O., and Reinhardt, A. (2009), "Nokia: Outsmarted on Smartphones," *BusinessWeek,* July 30.

22. For instance, performance management (Investing in People, IIP) is closely aligned to the company strategy and planning processes and involves biannual formalized discussions between employees and their managers.

23. Right after General Electric and Procter & Gamble, Nokia has ranked very high in *Fortune*'s global leadership ranking and as one of the best companies in Europe.

24. The idea is that individual Nokians possess the overall responsibility for their own careers. At the same time, they can rely on a manager, who will coach and support their professional development and career planning and will explore their interests, aspirations, career paths, and opportunities with them.

25. The transition solutions are for the first-time managers and are now compulsory. Every Nokian who hopes to become a first-time manager—some two thousand people in 2008—is expected to take these compulsory programs for six months. With complementary programs, there is more flexibility and greater depth. The program is called "Voyager" and it includes an estimated 600–800 people. The highest level is called "Compass," which targets some 250–500 people annually. At each level, the programs are designed not to intervene too much in the managers' daily activities. At transition 1 level, the program comprises a three-day workshop, plus three to four days for preparation. At the second level, the process requires two modules, free work, and program, altogether ten to twelve relatively heavy days. At the third level, four modules take about ten days.

26. "In this program, you may end up being a team leader, even if people around you don't report directly to you. Everybody needs to know what it takes to be a leader," says Rosanna Cella, an Italian who heads Nokia's southern European human resources team.

27. Born largely between the 1980s and early 1990s, contemporary young adults—often referred to as "Generation Y"—grew up with the digital revolution. They are far more comfortable with the Internet and social media than another large demographic cohort: the postwar baby boomers. In the workforce, these so-called Millennials tend to seek more feedback, responsibility, and involvement in decision making. To Nokia, it is a vital generation because it reflects and understands better the highly valued lead users. See Alsop, R. (2008), *The Trophy Kids Grow Up: How the Millennial Generation Is Shaking Up the Workplace* (San Francisco: Jossey-Bass).

CHAPTER FOUR

1. The core matrix reflects a balance of business and geography, but it also includes matrices of processes, projects, service platforms, and line organizations.

2. At the same time, the importance of the country market for Nokia's strategy is increasing because ultimately consumer tastes, regulation, and technology choices follow country-based markets.
3. Stopford, J. M., and Wells, L. T. (1972), *Managing the Multinational Enterprise* (New York: Basic Books).
4. "Better results can be achieved when there is a clear profit responsibility," argues a veteran Nokia senior executive, who suggests that the matrix may work better in Europe, where culture supports cooperation, than in the United States, where competitiveness reigns, or in emerging economies, where "command and control" structures require customization.
5. Coming from Hewlett-Packard and Compaq, Mary McDowell, Nokia's CDO, was familiar with strong matrix fields. "One day each year, we'd lock into a room to determine who'd pay for what level of a service. Nokia was the opposite. To some extent, the egalitarian background worked a little bit against us because nobody wanted to see themselves as acquired to another part of the organization."
6. Conversation with Jack Welch on May 22, 2007, as moderator of "Jack Welch on Winning and Leadership," KPMG Finland, Helsinki.
7. For instance, a number of multinational companies initially built their businesses country by country. When they launched global business units, there were no accounting systems to track the performance of a business across countries, and thus no way to coordinate the global units. See Galbraith, J. (2009), *Designing Matrix Organizations That Actually Work: How IBM, Procter & Gamble, and Others Plan for Success* (New York: Wiley), p. 12.
8. Further benefits include better management, compliance controls, and corporate governance, which are critical to the CEO and CFO. It is the complexity of the small-country multinational that accounts for Nokia's adoption of cutting-edge reporting systems. Unlike U.S. companies that are primarily subject to U.S. laws and regulations, Nokia has a dual regulation under Finland and the European Union, and in the United States. That regulation comprises Finnish law, as a Finnish-registered company and under EU, traded on the Helsinki Stock Exchange, as well as the Securities and Exchange Commission (SEC), primarily in the United States as a listed company on the New York Stock Exchange.
9. As Jönsson puts it, "We run the organization very much in a project mode in which people get together to solve problems through a wide array of program groups, project groups, or task forces."
10. The integrated unit is the result of years of purposeful development. In the early 2000s, the Nokians concluded that they would have to launch new and divergent initiatives to stretch the market. Since the future was murky, Nokia hedged bets. By 2004, the key activities were organized into three business groups (mobile phones, multimedia, entreprise). Just three years later they

were integrated into a single unit, and now the company is moving toward services and solutions. Although Nokia is a relative latecomer in consumer Internet services, it has unique advantages. "Our mobile devices serve half a billion consumers annually," says Heikki Norta, Nokia's head of corporate strategy. "We can use the mobile phone as a distribution platform for integrated services."

11. "With the common P&L, we're dealing with issues more openly and collaboratively," says Nokia's CDO Mary McDowell. "We want to do this because we think it's good for the business, and we want to model behavior because we think it's good for our team."

12. The varying needs of Nokia's devices, solutions, and networks differ in terms of cost-efficiencies globally (global integration) and differentiation on a country-by-country basis (national responsiveness). For instance, in mobile devices, the need for global integration is vital, whereas the need for national responsiveness is relatively low overall. These needs differ from those of NSN, which tends to be driven more by national differentiation, not to speak of services and solutions, which are even more localized.

13. A device maker is very different from a service or solutions provider. And as these services and solutions are extended across the world, organizational imperatives will grow increasingly complex. In the 1990s and 2000s, Nokia defined globalization with mobile infrastructure and devices. "In the 2010s, we must define localization with mobile services and solutions," says Giles.

14. Nokia's business focuses on independent channels and operators, whereas NSN's business is primarily with operators. As operators have globalized, the mindset of Vodafones and Verizons has shifted accordingly. "In the U.S., operators are markedly U.S. operators," says Beresford-Wylie, "but outside the U.S., we have global entities."

15. In September 2008, Nokia's ownership, excluding treasury shares, was estimated as follows: U.S. (46 percent), Finland (12 percent), UK (11 percent), Germany (6 percent), France (6 percent), and Switzerland (4 percent). The remaining share belonged to the rest of Europe (10 percent) and the rest of the world (5 percent).

16. If you have a culture of "command and control" and try to instill a matrix organization into that culture, it is almost bound to fail. With fast-changing companies, the tight processes, control points, and records might be particularly tricky to implement. On the other hand, if the organization is largely driven by a vision and strong values, there will be less need for processes, controls, and records. The matrix benefits are easier to achieve without hierarchical bureaucracies. "We don't necessarily have the typical conflicts associated with the dual reporting of matrix," says Moerk. "Maybe it has something to do with the fact that we have goals rather than trying to control every aspect all of the way."

17. Matrix here is seen not as a choice between a structure *or* a frame of mind but as a complementary use of structure *and* mindset. Compare Bartlett, C. A., and

Ghoshal, S. (1990), "Matrix Management: Not a Structure, a Frame of Mind," *Harvard Business Review,* July–August.

CHAPTER FIVE

1. Quoted in "Vuorineuvos valoo elektronikkaa," *Talouselämä* 33, 1984. In 1980, the electronics unit invested in product development some FIM 180 million—12 percent of all Finnish R&D. By the mid-1980s, these investments had increased to FIM 400 million.

2. Even in 1967, electronics still generated only 3 percent of the Nokia Group's net sales and provide work for only 460 people. In the early 1970s most telephone exchanges remained electromechanical analog switches, but Nokia's electronics unit began developing the digital switch that eventually became the famed Nokia 200 DX, a multifaceted platform that remains the basis for Nokia's network infrastructure.

3. Steinbock, D. (2005), *The Globalization of Finnish ICT* (Helsinki: SM).

4. Until the mid-1990s, Juhani Kuusi had been the chief of Tekes, the Finnish Funding Agency for Technology and Innovation, but he left for the NRC after Ollila's call. He was succeeded by Yrjö Neuvo, who played an important role in the 3G standardization talks and was in charge of product development in NMP. "I like to encourage and inspire people," Neuvo says. "I give substantial freedom to do things, but I also expect people to make difficult decisions."

5. In addition to different R&D allocations, comparisons are complicated by differences in size, R&D allocations, and integration and organization. Nokia and Qualcomm are focused on mobile communications, whereas Motorola and Ericsson are diversified electronics giants.

6. The growth was driven primarily by strong gains in replacement sales and sales from new subscribers in emerging markets, especially the Middle East and Africa and Asia-Pacific. Today, developed market device volumes are driven primarily by replacement sales.

7. In contrast to Apple and RIM, Nokia is more diversified geographically and deploys business models that make low prices possible in large emerging markets.

8. Typically, the most spectacular industry failures involve companies that have engaged in technology development but ignored market creation (e.g., the Europeans' rush to 3G, i.e., the new multimedia cellular technology generation in the 2000s). Conversely, companies have run into trouble as they have sought to dominate the markets but ignored technology development (e.g., the delayed transition of Motorola and AT&T into digital cellular in the 1990s). Or they have failed in both technology innovation and market creation. See Steinbock, D. (2005), *The Mobile Revolution: The Making of Mobile Services Worldwide* (London: Kogan Page).

9. As a leader in the development of the wireless technologies of GSM/EDGE, 3G/WCDMA, HSPA, OFDM, WiMAX, LTE, and TDSCDMA, Nokia has a robust patent portfolio in all of those technology areas, as well as for CDMA2000.

10. *Rich context modeling* seeks to meet user needs based upon user environment, including location, motion, weather, connectivity options, and proximity to others. *New user interface* allows users to interact intuitively through technology by incorporating a user's unique characteristics seamlessly. *High-performance mobile platform* seeks to offer devices that adapt to users and their environment. *Cognitive radio* seeks to liberate access to optimize the spectrum. Together these focus areas explore the experiences people will have in the future, the technology and interfaces they will use, and the infrastructure required to make it all happen.

11. The NRC representative currently also chairs the Wireless World Research Forum, a forum formulating visions on research strategies in the communications industry. In the European 6th Framework Program, Nokia leads the MobiLife research program on user-driven communications solutions for the future.

12. The ten patents in the suit related to technologies fundamental to making devices that are compatible with one or more of the GSM, UMPTS (3G WCDMA) and wireless data, speech coding, security, and encryption and are infringed by all Apple iPhone models shipped since the iPhone was introduced in 2007.

13. "Nokia Sues Apple in Delaware District Court for Infringement of Nokia GSM, UMPTS, and WLAN Patents," Nokia, PR/Newswire, Espoo, Finland, October 22, 2009. "Apple Countersues Nokia," Apple's Media, Cupertino California, December 11, 2009.

14. Nokia previously had a long-running dispute over wireless patents with U.S.-based Qualcomm, which the two companies finally settled in July 2008. In a turnaround in the companies' relationship, in February 2009 they said they would work together to develop advanced mobile devices, initially for North America.

15. While Apple promised to "vigorously" fight against Nokia's patent infringement suit, it also admitted that "because of technological changes . . . it is possible that certain components of the company's products and business methods may unknowingly infringe the patents or other intellectual property rights of third parties." As the filing notes, the company was defending more than forty-seven patent infringement cases, twenty-seven of which were filed during fiscal 2009. See Apple, SEC 10-K annual report, October 27, 2009.

16. Some argued that Nokia was pursuing claims for "essential patents" that it is required to share at reasonable cost, which gives less leverage at the bargaining table. Others considered the suit a negotiating tactic to gain access to Apple technologies via a settlement. Still others thought Nokia sought to head off a potential infringement lawsuit from Apple; after all, Nokia is planning to release handsets with multi-touch features for which Apple may own intellectual

property rights. Nonetheless, the potential return to Nokia could be substantial. The wholesale cost to wireless carriers of the iPhone is estimated to average about $600. A 2 percent royalty would represent $12 for each phone sold. In just the most recent quarter, Apple sold 7.4 million iPhones. It has sold more than 34 million total.

17. Nokia discontinued its own chipset development in 2007 and has since expanded its use of commercially available chipsets. The multivendor strategy is aimed at increasing the efficiency of R&D efforts.

18. In 2008, Nokia and industry partners took the first steps to develop Symbian OS, the market-leading operating system for mobile devices, into an open and unified mobile software platform, which will be licensed royalty free and eventually move toward "open source."

19. In India and China, the effort is to achieve more than only local innovation or local technology development. Nokia has not only R&D people but also people close to the government and standards bodies that understand how these requirements might emerge in the Indian or Chinese market, respectively.

20. Since its creation in 2001, Wikipedia has grown rapidly into one of the largest reference Web sites, so far attracting an average of more than 330 million monthly visitors this year. There are more than 75,000 active contributors working on more than 14 million articles in more than 260 languages. Wales is also the cofounder of Wikia.com, a project that expands the participatory editing model into new areas, allowing the global community to come together to build the "rest of the library."

21. Chesbrough, H. W. (2003), *Open Innovation: The New Imperative for Creating and Profiting from Technology* (Boston: Harvard Business School Press). See also Chesbrough, H. W. (2003), "The Era of Open Innovation," *MIT Sloan Management Review, 44*(3), 35–41.

22. In 2009, the key universities were the following: Helsinki University of Technology, Tampere University of Technology (Finland); Eidgenössische Technische Hochschule Zurich (Germany); Ecole Polytechnique Fédérale de Lausanne (Switzerland); MIT, Stanford University, University of California, Berkeley, University of Southern California (United States); Tsinghua University (China).

23. Launched in April 2007, it is linked to other Nokia beta applications, such as Wellness Diary and Sports Tracker. Wellness Diary makes it easy to monitor and track a range of elements of everyday well-being, including weight, eating habits, exercise, blood pressure, and others; it is essentially a health journal that resides on a mobile device. The response to Sports Tracker alone was extraordinary: more than 1 million people downloaded the program and used it for sports that the developers had not even thought of, including paragliding, hot-air ballooning, and motorcycle riding. Eventually, Nokia spun off Sports Tracker in 2009.

24. Having validated new opportunities with sound business cases, it develops them as new business programs within Nokia or collaborates with companies to establish licensing deals, joint ventures, acquisitions, or partnership agreements.

25. The development of new business and technology ideas comprises several stages: verification and development of technologies and value models; development of business case and business plan for optimal execution; development of technology strategy and its alignment with a corresponding business plan; creation of concepts, prototypes, designs, and architectures; testing and validation of user experience and user acceptance; setting up the R&D process, product/service creation, and production for business ramp up.

26. Nokia uses two scouting modes. In the nontargeted mode, it searches for any company or business ideas that might be relevant to it. Nokia also runs targeted searches for specific initiatives by senior management or based on an assignment from a Nokia business unit.

27. These channels include the following: industry networking via conferences, trade shows, and industry alliances; discussion forums, roundtables, and partner network events; cooperation with venture capitalists, investors, enterprises, and startups; cooperation with universities and other educational institutions; news services, publications, and business and market intelligence; business case and innovation competitions; and concept device launches, pilots, and commercial trials.

28. Nokia validates business cases, consumer/customer needs, and new technologies by taking business plans all the way to the marketplace. NCBD's new businesses range from mobile learning solutions to smart home solutions, including Mobiledu, Nokia Tej, Smart Home Solutions, and Nokia Point & Find.

29. Nokia Growth Partners has publicly announced investments in Bitboys (Finland), Coding Technologies, Global Locate, and Inside Contactless (France), Kyte (United States), Madhouse, Inc. (China), Morpho, Inc. (Tokyo), Sasken Communication Technologies Limited (India), Summit Microelectronics (United States), and Vivotech (United States).

30. Amid the global economic crisis, Nokia, along with other truly global companies, also had to cope with the most volatile credit and currency markets in a lifetime. Nokia has been developing into a global company since the 1990s and it was one of the first countries to adopt the International Financial Reporting Standards (IFRS). Large-country multinationals enjoy a large home market, but they often report in a single currency. Nokia is more dispersed geographically and uses several exchange rates. Despite greater diversification, it cannot escape exchange rate risk. "We are as equipped as anybody to deal with challenging volatility," says Nokia's former CFO Richard Simonson. Essentially Nokia deals with euro or euro-linked markets, or dollars or dollar-linked markets. For instance, China and India are dollar-linked markets. Nokia sets its selling price based on dollars;

Latin America and the Middle East are somewhat similar in this regard, whereas the countries in the Euro zone are euro linked.

CHAPTER SIX

1. For instance, the systematic development of the brand since the early 1990s and the development of distribution; since the mid-1990s the development of manufacturing and design capabilities; thereafter the logistics crisis followed by the development of logistics; since the late 1990s the development of sourcing and software-based platform; the development of multimedia capability and Symbian and software competition strategy in the early 2000s.

2. Glatzel, C., et al. (2009), "Building a Flexible Supply Chain for Uncertain Times," *The McKinsey Quarterly*, March.

3. Overall, Nokia aims to manage inventories to ensure that production meets demand for its products while minimizing inventory-carrying costs. The inventory level it maintains is a function of a number of factors, including estimates of demand for each product category, product price levels, the availability of raw materials, supply chain integration with suppliers, and the rate of technological change.

4. Over time, Nokia's organizational agility has increased and been optimized for the changing environmental conditions. Similarly, "strategic agility" has been seen as the result of three major capabilities of strategic sensitivity, leadership unity, and resource fluidity. In the study at hand, Nokia's roller-coaster experiences and successes are seen as results of many more partly dependent and partly interdependent drivers. Compare Doz, Y. L., and Kosonen, M. (2008), "The Dynamics of Strategic Agility: Nokia's Rollercoaster Experience," *California Review Management*, 50(3), 95–118.

5. In the 1990s, McGovern built factories all over the world, coached teams, hired thousands of people, and grew Nokia into a company that was able to take product from the R&D phase and bring it to market in the best possible way.

6. Until recently, Andersson managed Nokia's global demand and supply network, as the head of finance, strategy, and strategic sourcing in the Devices unit. Currently, he heads Nokia Corporate Alliances and Business Development and left the group executive board in October 2009 in connection with the new duties.

7. For example, on-hand inventory was reduced from 154 to 68 days in nine months, releasing EUR 450 million in cash. Taken together, these actions put the company back on track for profitable growth. See Cohen, S., and Roussel, J. (2005), *Strategic Supply Chain Management: The Five Disciplines for Top Performance* (New York: McGraw-Hill), p. 34.

8. "The IT transformation would not have succeeded without Ollila's strong support," acknowledges Kosonen. Change is never easy, and the IT transformation was especially complicated and difficult.

9. At the time, Nokia was one of the first major corporations going central. Today, centralized IT is accepted wisdom. "To us, the Sarbanes-Oxley Act was a piece of cake after we had already gone central in the late 1990s," says Jorma Ollila. "While even the *Wall Street Journal* wrote us off as a company, we were actually re-organizing ourselves, getting the management supporting systems right, and preparing to overtake Motorola in the summer of 1998. We were very strong during those high-growth years because we could handle our components flow, sales information, pricing information, and we managed globally."

10. Unlike many of its rivals, Nokia learned from its mistakes, which prepared it for the global success in the late 1990s. Still, Nokia continued to have a regional organization in terms of how it managed sales, global logistics, sourcing, sales and pricing information, and cash.

11. In early 2009, Nokia relocated its factory in Bochum, Germany, to Romania. Despite loud howls of protest, the company had few options. In Romania, labor costs were one-tenth those in Germany. Moreover, Nokia's generous compensation package amounted to $280 million and provided employees with average payoffs worth over $111,000, in addition to well-paid retraining opportunities for twelve months.

12. During 2008, outsourcing covered 17 percent of its manufacturing volume of mobile device engines, which includes hardware and software that enable the basic operation of a mobile device. Outsourcing has been utilized to adjust production to seasonal demand fluctuations.

13. Nokia gave up its internal custom-chip development program in 1987, parting ways with its longtime ASIC (Application Specific Integrated Circuit; a chip that is custom designed for a specific application rather than a general-purpose chip such as a microprocessor) partners, Texas Instruments and STMicroelectronics. Nokia, meanwhile, sold its ASIC team (some 200 designers) to ST. The change sparked lots of emotional responses from the industry.

14. Samsung, for instance, may welcome design teams with open arms, but it also prides itself on having multiple design teams working in parallel, pitting one against the other in a race to solve the same problem. Of seventy to ninety handset projects under way in parallel at Samsung at any given time, only 25 percent will reach the market. See "Deconstructing Nokia's Multi-Sourcing Strategy," *EE Times-India,* October 29, 2008.

15. In the medium to long term, it is not that certain that Nokia will be as involved in the manufacturing of its products. For instance, even Dell is no longer really manufacturing but is mainly outsourcing from a supply chain, particularly to companies like contract electronics manufacturer Flextronics International Ltd. (which is also working with Nokia). For now, Nokia does have an in-house advantage. In five to ten years it will no longer be as clear that it is sustainable.

16. In addition to being Nokia corporate treasurer, Ihamuotila has held several other senior positions over the years in, for example, risk management and portfolio management.
17. Moore S. D., (1987), "Nokia Has Vexing Problem with Image: Outside of Finland, It Doesn't Have One," *Wall Street Journal,* April 21.
18. On the brand iceberg, see e.g., BBDO, (2001), "Brand Equity Excellence," Vol. 1: *Brand Equity Review,* November 1.
19. The low cost is not identical with the real cost. With subsidization, the business model shifts cost elements away from the consumer to operators, retailers, resellers, vendors, and other participants, thus enabling the low cost.
20. Examples of FMCG generally include a wide range of frequently purchased consumer products such as toiletries, soap, and cosmetics. FMCG may also include pharmaceuticals, consumer electronics, packaged food products, and drinks. Best-known examples of FMCG companies include Miller, Coors, Cadbury's, Coca-Cola, Unilever, and Procter & Gamble.
21. "Absolutely," says Vanjoki. "I don't think that Coke will get a challenge from other brown sugar water with cola taste. But if somebody manages to convince people that, 'hey, you don't have to drink at all, but take this pill, it takes care of everything,' well, that would be a challenge to Coke."
22. The brand board has in one room a group of Nokians that represent devices, services, operational marketing, corporate strategy, and brand strategy.
23. How many people are aware of Nokia? Along with such questions, you have a battery of diagnostics. The idea is to understand the full context. In addition, there's a whole series of questions Nokia uses to look at the user base. Then there's the behavioral matrix. Since Nokia invests close to $2 billion a year in marketing, it looks at where it spends its money. Nokia also looks at the agencies and advertisers, market shares, and a whole battery of other things, which they call the "dashboard."

CHAPTER SEVEN

1. Instead of traditional business *units* or *groups,* Nokia sees itself operating in business *areas.* Consistent with its market-making strategy, these are not as clearly defined as business units, say, in mature markets. Nor are they loosely defined core competencies, which could be determined only ex post facto. Rather, they refer to changing businesses whose boundaries are fluid.
2. With value domains came additional investments into technology platforms. That way Nokia could strengthen competitiveness in low cost, multimedia, and other areas where it began to create value in a new way.
3. Nokia believes that in order to meet the customers' needs, a competitive product device portfolio needs to include leading flagship products and be innovative and ahead of the expectations. For services, it means offering value-added services

that are easy to access and use. Over time, economies of scale and scope allow brand leaders to employ high volume in order to cut costs.

4. The unit consists of four operational subunits: R&D, Design, Category Management, and Focused Businesses.

5. In December 2008, Nokia acquired full ownership of Symbian Limited, the company that develops and licenses Symbian OS, and, together with industry partners, initiated plans to establish the Symbian Foundation, an independent, nonprofit entity to lead this development.

6. Based on the CDMA and TD-SCDMA standards.

7. In another transfer, Timo Toikkanen, former head of Europe SU sales, moved to Devices to head the Strategic Business Operations subunit in January 2010. Strategic Business Operations comprises Vertu, Nokia Gear, Connected Computers, and Devices Strategy and Business Development. Toikkanen reports to Kai Öistämö.

8. In addition to heading the Mobile Phones subunit, Simonson will drive Nokia's product mode execution, working together with Services, Markets, and Devices R&D.

9. Smartphones will consist of the following entities: Portfolio Management, Nseries Smartphones, Consumer Smartphones, Business Smartphones, Product Management, Product Excellence, In-Market Portfolio Management, Strategy Development, and Execution Planning.

10. Harlow earned a reputation for developing and implementing successful marketing organizations and strategies to achieve volume growth and market share goals. At Nokia, she has served as senior vice president of global marketing and vice president for marketing for North America. It was Harlow who led Nokia's North America marketing organization through the successful launch of a series of Nokia Experience Centers and Nokia-branded theater venues.

11. Martin sued Apple back in February of 2008 for failing to compensate him for a patent he holds, U.S. Patent No. 6,926,609, "Method for operating an electronic machine using a pointing device."

12. At Ericsson, mobile handsets have been secondary to networks. There is always some tension between the two businesses, mobile devices and infrastructure. The two should be autonomous but interdependent.

13. In September 2009 Motorola unveiled the first model in its Android-powered line, a phone called Cliq. The company hoped to reverse its dwindling fortunes by targeting Twitter types.

14. Initially, ZTE is targeting Europe and North America with higher-end phones. These growth plans are facilitated by a five-year $15 billion credit line from China Development Bank to build business overseas.

15. Compare Lindholm, C., and Keinonen, T. (2003), *Mobile Usability: How Nokia Changed the Face of the Mobile Phone* (New York: McGraw-Hill).

Notes

16. Design and Consumer Experience also brought together Nokia User Experience, and Consumer and User Experience teams from Category Management.

17. As of October 2009, Design and Consumer Experience brought together the Nokia Design, Nokia User Experience and Consumer and User Experience team from Category Management.

18. Campion, S. (2005), "Hybrid: Interview with Marko Ahtisaari," Danish Design Centre, November 25. Born in Helsinki, Finland, Ahtisaari is the son of former President Martti Ahtisaari. Prior to joining Nokia, he built and led the mobile practice at startup design consultancy Satama Interactive. He also worked in the Insight and Foresight strategy unit at Nokia, where he was responsible for identifying and driving new growth opportunities based on user experience. Afterward, he was head of Brand and Design at Blyk, a free mobile operator for young people, funded by advertising, and cofounded Dopplr, an online service for smarter travel.

19. By 2000, the company saw Club Nokia as a logical extension of its business to sell content and services, along with mobile devices. The problem was that it created a channel conflict by irritating mobile operators. "We didn't like Nokia's Trojan horse," said a high-ranking operator executive. "In the United States, device makers sell devices and operators sell content and services, each has its proper place." Nokia backed down but did not give up.

20. People & Places builds and develops links between the five core services and acts as the primary interface between Services and NAVTEQ. Service Experience develops ways to improve the experience people have when using the services to ensure that there is a common look and feel across the portfolio. Service Platforms is tasked with developing the infrastructure to ensure that services can be deployed speedily and efficiently.

21. The average selling price (ASP) is the average price at which a particular product or service is sold across channels or markets. ASP is typically affected by the type of product and the product life cycle. In technology businesses, the commodification can happen very fast. The more mature the product, the lower will be the ASP.

22. The young adults in America are the leading users of the new mobile services. Nokia's service developers consider this so-called Generation Y—teenagers and young adults—mercurial and fluid. It is vital to touch the true needs of the consumer quickly enough before they move on.

23. Through the years, Nokia has consciously avoided the short-term temptation to ignore architectural issues at the expense of optimization. It saw that total competitiveness gained most from the completion of the platforms.

24. Few years ago, Motorola came up with the Razr phone, but it had nothing new and exciting in the pipeline thereafter, notes Matti Alahuhta, Nokia's former senior executive. "A few years before, Samsung challenged us but we saw pretty

soon that they would face a ceiling soon because they were continuously tailoring products, product by product by product." Despite short-term gains, the challengers lacked systematic platform thinking and could not scale up.

25. An example of this interactivity is MOSH, a Nokia service which provided a user-driven distribution channel. It took literally sixteen weeks from an idea to first version. "At best, we had a new version every eight weeks," says Savander. "On the other hand, Nokia Map is a much bigger and complicated service; we need a new version every six months."

26. There are those who are certain about what they want. If, for instance, you know you want navigation and travel a lot, you may want a work and life navigation license. Here a classic subscription or license is the appropriate model. But, say, that you do not know exactly what you want, but when you do, you are ready to pay for it. That's the classical transaction model. There are also a number of potential hybrid revenue models that can drive industry alliances.

27. By bringing together Nokia's products and solutions, the Solutions unit is, first of all, giving direction. Second, it is creating a single, aligned road map for solutions. Finally, it complements current processes with solution concept and road maps, while driving alignment across units, thereby ensuring execution and better prioritization. The Solutions unit will drive Nokia's solutions offering and align it with the company's Devices and Services portfolio, manage the end-to-end creation and delivery of solutions across the company together with the other Nokia units, and bring together all design and user-experience activities to drive excellence in consumer experience.

28. Successful examples include Nokia's entry phones, which have an FM radio. In many African markets you can store four songs from the radio station. That's the basics of a paradigm of "my phone equals my music storage."

29. iPhone's price (the 16-gigabyte 3GS model went for about $730 up front) was prohibitively high, but consumers have paid even more for cracked versions over the last two years. First, local consumer preferences were ignored. The phone is being sold packaged with monthly subscription plans, just as in the United States, but the vast majority of Chinese prefer to buy pay-as-you-go charge cards. Second, Apple did not choose the best partner, China Mobile, which has almost a 70 percent share of China's 702 million phone users. Chinese users do not want to change carriers, especially as consumers believe China Mobile has better signal stability than China Unicom. Third, Apple had a U.S.-centric approach, instead of launching globally at once. See Rein, S. (2009), "How Apple and iPhone Blew It in China," *Forbes,* November 6.

30. Newly enabled flexible and transparent materials blend more seamlessly with the way we live. Devices become self-cleaning and self-preserving. Transparent electronics offer an entirely new aesthetic dimension. Built-in solar absorption might charge a device, while batteries become smaller, longer lasting, and faster to

charge. Nokia believes that some of the device's imagined features could appear in high-end devices by 2015.

31. NSN's board has seven directors, four appointed by Nokia and three by Siemens, and Nokia appoints the CEO.

32. Nokia and Siemens each had an infrastructure unit with a significant presence in the world markets, with Siemens more focused on fixed infrastructure and Nokia on mobile infrastructure. Each was a group, not an independent company. Each provided offerings that would best complement the new portfolio. Owners were good, known, and stable. Over time they can decide whether the combined entity will thrive, whether each owner will continue to have interest in it, and whether it will be taken public.

33. Soon after the facility in Chennai was opened, NSN completed the sale of its manufacturing site in Durach, Germany.

34. In December 2008, Siemens agreed to pay a record $1.34 billion in fines after being investigated for serious bribery involving two former CFOs and an ex-chairman, and a former management board member.

35. Due to Siemens's dispersed IT units across countries, the integration process was complicated. Concurrently, the marketplace has changed faster than anticipated and is now more global.

36. For now, mobile operators in Europe, Asia, Africa, and the Middle East are doing most of the outsourcing, and U.S. players are expected eventually to outsource the management of their networks as well.

37. The initial auction drew three competitors: Ericsson, NSN, and distressed-debt investor MatlinPatterson Global Advisers LLC. NSN had set off the auction process with an unsolicited $650 million bid. The deal would have made North America the largest region within Ericsson.

38. The Indian born Suri has twenty years of industry experience and an intimate understanding of the vital Asia-Pacific region. At Nokia, he has a reputation as a dynamic and results-oriented leader and is known for relentlessly building strong and diverse teams.

39. Worldwide collaboration has not been a given at Nokia. In the mid-1980s, for instance, Finland struggled to join the European EUREKA research program. Many Western countries felt threatened by the Finns' participation, which—as the skeptics argued—might lead to technology secrets leaking to the Soviet Union and Eastern Europe. It was only with persistent diplomatic efforts that Finland was eventually able to participate in EUREKA. During the Cold War, U.S., European, and Japanese companies engaged in mergers and acquisitions. Nokia had to struggle for years to become a legitimate partner in the West.

40. Prahalad, C. K., and Ramaswamy, V. (2004), *The Future of Competition: Co-Creating Unique Value with Customers* (Perseus, 2004).

41. Nokia's recent acquisitions include Loudeye, a global leader in digital music platforms, and gate5, a leading supplier of mapping software and services (October 2006); Twango, a leading provider of comprehensive media-sharing solutions (July 2007); Enpocket, a global leader in mobile advertising (October 2007); Avvenu, a leading provider of secure remote access and private sharing technology (December 2007); Plazes, a major context-based services provider (July 2008); OZ Communications, a major consumer mobile messaging provider (July 2008); bitside, a major mobile map developer (February 2009).

CHAPTER EIGHT

1. On the globalization of markets thesis, see Levitt, A. (1983), "The Globalization of Markets," *Harvard Business Review* (May/June): 92–102.
2. Ohmae, K. (1985), *Triad Power: The Coming Shape of Global Competition* (New York: The Free Press), pp. 27, 121.
3. Wilson, D., and Purushothaman, R. (2003), "Dreaming with BRICs: The Path to 2050" (Goldman Sachs), October 1.
4. On the emergence of new global cities, see Steinbock, D. (2008), "The Wealth of Cities: Established Metropolises and Emerging Megapolises," *Report to the Commission for Future,* Finland's Parliament, August.
5. C. K. Prahalad has argued that businesses, governments, and donor agencies should stop thinking of the poor as victims and instead start seeing them as resilient and creative entrepreneurs as well as value-demanding consumers. Prahalad served as a Nokia consultant in the early 1990s. See Prahalad, C. K., and Hammond, A. (2002), "Serving the World's Poor, Profitably," *Harvard Business Review,* 2002.
6. "These unhappy times call for the building of plans that rest upon the forgotten," said Franklin D. Roosevelt amid the Great Depression. Those are plans that must "build from the bottom up and not from the top down and that put their faith once more in the forgotten man at the bottom of the economic pyramid." See Roosevelt, F. D. (1932), "The Forgotten Man," radio address.
7. The rapid growth in mobile phone use throughout the developing world is helping to transform national economies, according to economist Leonard Waverman. Funded by Vodafone, a series of studies on the socioeconomic impact of mobile communication has demonstrated that mobiles aid the process by which disadvantaged groups, including the low-skilled labor force, enjoy the fruits of economic growth.
8. Says Simonson, "Every euro matters in the cost chain, so you simply must have the efficiency of scale. That is why Motorola has been unsuccessful to break in these markets. Nor has Sony-Ericsson been able to make ultra-low-end devices and make money. Many other companies that were supposed to win these markets have failed to do so."

Notes

9. The entry-level device market (devices priced at $70 or under continued to be one of the fastest-growing segments for the market. In 2008 this part of the market represented an estimated 44 percent of the total industry volumes.

10. In regional volumes, Nokia had the greatest shares in the Middle East and Africa (54 percent), Asia-Pacific (47 percent), and the lowest in North America (9 percent).

11. On the rise of China as ICT and mobile power, see Steinbock, D. (2007), "China as ICT Superpower" *China Business Review,* U.S.-China Business Council, March.

12. This provided an initial growth momentum, but as operators began to launch retail outlets of their own and thereby influence sales of product categories, the Nokia/Radio Shack model no longer worked. Also, Nokia hoped to operate in the United States under its own brand name. "We knocked on the doors of all operators and some offered small opportunities, but Motorola dominated the markets," recalls Kari-Pekka "KP" Wilska, Nokia's chief of Americas in the late 1990s. Then Motorola made a strategic mistake. It launched MicroTAC: a superior product, but they tried to use it to control the market, including the distribution. "As that led to a defensive reaction by Southwest Bell [which is now AT&T], we were able to get our foot inside the operators' door and our sales took off in America," says Wilska. "And when AT&T came up with its One Rate plan, that gave a momentous push to mobile growth in the U.S., and our phones practically flew off the shelves."

13. According to operators, Nokia was not adequately flexible. Also, most of Nokia's phones are designed to operate on the global standard GSM, whereas the dominant standard in North America is CDMA.

14. In addition to the corporate office in New York, Nokia opened new offices in Atlanta to be close to AT&T Mobility and in Parsippany, New Jersey, to be near Verizon Wireless. It put several hundred product developers in its San Diego Design Center to collaborate with both operators on new products.

15. "We went to China with humility and we had strong local advisors," says Sari Baldauf. "We did not go to America with the willingness to modify our processes, such as R&D so that it would have allowed us to reach the customer interface already there."

16. Despite some success in the Americas, Motorola has lost out in Europe and Asia, whereas Nokia is strong in Europe and Asia, the Middle East and Africa, and Russia. In China, Motorola had more of an eastern China strategy, focusing on the prosperous coastal cities.

17. See Steinbock, D. (2003), "Globalization of Wireless Value System: From Geographic to Strategic Advantages," *Telecommunications Policy, 27,* 207–235.

18. Through the 1990s and early 2000s, Nokia expanded the activities of its device and infrastructure activities as well as R&D in Germany. In March 2009, it closed its German manufacturing plant.

19. Despite recent relative decline, the UK market remains Nokia's most lucrative market in Europe by net sales. After Hungary, it is Nokia's largest market by personnel in Europe.

20. See Steinbock, D. (2006), "The Mobile Revolution and China," *China Communications, 3*(2), April.

21. "In China, it could take a while before a decision was made in the central government, but thereafter things moved really fast," recalls Sari Baldauf, Nokia's former senior executive. "In India, a decision could lead to a complaint to the Supreme Court, which meant a loss of a year or two after which the process began from scratch."

22. The multinationals imitated their challengers, flooding the market with me-too products, engaging in aggressive marketing campaigns, capitalizing on extensive distribution channels, while slashing prices.

23. "In order to maintain our strong approach, we had to optimize certain changes before we began to push clamshell phones and new form factors," says Matti Alahuhta, Nokia's former senior executive.

24. Among other things, Nokia in 2007 donated 6.7 million CNY to set up the Nokia Young Entrepreneurs Education Fund at 150 universities across China. It joined the Yuanmeng Program to provide financial support to two hundred students. It donated 1 million CNY to the Youth Business China program.

25. "In China, we have a large team who are localizing our global services, while looking into the domestic business. With standards, we also need to localize technology and will use our R&D base for that purpose. As the largest market for Nokia and the world, there is a business case for localization in China."

26. In April 2008, for instance, Nokia launched the Nokia 5000, the Nokia 2680, the Nokia 7070 Prism, and the Nokia 1680 classic—all products created in Beijing.

27. Sudhaman, A. (2008), "Profile... A New Edge to Nokia's Global Marketing Plans," *Media Asia*, January 30. Leong was crowned Marketer of the Year at Media's Agency of the Year awards for 2007, twelve years after winning Suit of the Year at the same competition. Prior to joining Nokia, she had led Southeast Asia of WPP's Grey Global Group, one of the most profitable agency businesses. The former Singapore Airlines flight attendant began her career at Grey Group in Malaysia, before moving to senior roles as managing director of WPP's Bates Asia in Singapore and then Hong Kong. She spent eight of these twelve years working as Nokia's agency partner, with her Nokia experience dating back to 1994.

28. Steinbock, D. (2006), "India and Mobile Revolution," *Strategic Innovators* (IIPM/India), June.

29. Between 1996 and 2001, mobile service revenues grew tenfold in India, to $980 million. The same recurred by 2005, when these revenues soared to $9 billion. As in China, growth has been driven by prepaid cards, not by postpaid contracts.

Due to cost-efficiencies, Indian operators have shifted from deploying landline to deploying mobile. GSM services dominate. Most maturing mobile markets are replacement markets. In India, original demand is still driving the explosion of mobile growth.

30. Nokia has built a diverse product portfolio to meet the needs of different consumer segments. The company has also launched nine Nokia "concept stores" in Bangalore, Delhi, Jaipur, Hyderabad, Chandigarh, Ludhiana, Chennai, Indore, and Mumbai to provide customers a complete mobile experience.

31. India has also played a critical role in Nokia's efforts to reinforce its strengths in the CDMA technology. In 2004, Nokia launched a new CDMA R&D facility in Navi Mumbai hoping to leverage Nokia's global CDMA competencies. Nokia has recently also set up its first Design Studio in Bangalore in partnership with Srishti School of Art, Design, and Technology.

32. The manufacturing facility is operational with an investment of U.S. $210 million and currently employs 8,000 people. In addition to catering to the domestic market, it exports to more than fifty countries in Southeast Asia, the Middle East, Africa, Australia, and New Zealand. Nokia has announced fresh investments to the tune of $75 million toward its manufacturing plant in Sriperumbudur, Chennai, for the year 2008.

33. Chennai's selection was due to the availability of skilled labor, support from the state government, and the presence of good logistics connections. Developing the Nokia Telecom Industry Park in Chennai into a world-class, high-tech industrial zone is an important part of Nokia's global manufacturing and R&D network strategy. It also provides Nokia with the benefits of a pollution-free environment, in-house customs clearance, and an uninterrupted power supply.

34. Today, Nokia's activities in Brazil also include Tupiniquim' (Brazilian original) research. The first Nokia Institute of Technology unit in Manaus was founded in 2001. INdT, with units in Brasilia and Recife as well, is already working on research projects of international coverage. Nokia's investments in Manaus also include the Nokia Learning Foundation (Fundacao Nokia de Ensino), a second-level technical school.

35. For data, see O'Neill, J., et al. (2005), "How Solid Are the BRICs?," *Global Economics Paper* no. 134 (Goldman Sachs), December 1, 2005.

CHAPTER NINE

1. Richtel, M., (2009), "Can the Cellphone Industry Keep Growing," *New York Times*, February 3.

2. After lagging in the mobile communications business after the mid-1990s, the United States has been closing the mobile innovation gap since the early 2000s. Yet technology innovation alone is not enough to capture or sustain leadership. The strategic mindset of companies can no longer be domestic or even regional,

but global. Further, the emerging world of smartphones is driven by open innovation, which is constrained by the role of mobile operators in the United States. See Steinbock, D. (2005), *The Mobile Revolution: The Making of Mobile Services Worldwide* (London: Kogan Page).

3. In the past, Cisco and Hewlett-Packard, for example, did not compete; now they are rivals in data centers. Meanwhile, most technology-intensive companies have initiated transformation initiatives.

4. Grove, A. S. (1996), *Only the Paranoid Survive: How to Exploit the Crisis Points That Challenge Every Company* (New York: Random House). See particularly Chapter Three.

5. Until the 1990s, the mobile world was dominated by national telecom monopolies, typically the national mobile operator along with its closed club of equipment manufacturers. With deregulation, privatization, and liberalization, this order fell apart. See Steinbock, D. (2003), "Globalization of Wireless Value System: From Geographic to Strategic Advantages," *Telecommunications Policy, 27,* 207–235.

6. In June 2009, Apple said one hundred thousand developers had already created more than sixty-five thousand iPhone applications, and customers had downloaded those applications more than 1.5 billion times.

7. Symbian was launched in 1998 as a for-profit partnership among handset makers including Nokia, Sony-Ericsson, and Samsung. A decade later, Nokia bought out the other partners, released the code into the open source community, and created the Symbian Foundation to manage the operating system. "In a way, we have always been horizontal in Nokia in that we do not make our components," says Neuvo. "We have not been vertically integrated. With Series 60, the idea was initially to generate a horizontal layer through software."

8. Reportedly, Nokia is also about to extend its operating systems from Nseries and Eseries to new C and Xseries.

9. Canalys Smartphone Analysis for 2008 and the first quarter of 2009.

10. "The two make for an odd pairing: Stewart with his quintessential British rock-'n'-roll-ness and Ojanperä with his Finnish-savant, electrical-engineering-ness," as Mark Borden put it in "Nokia Rocks the World: The Phone King's Plan to Redefine Its Business," *Fast Company,* September 1, 2009.

11. In front of fans in London and an audience globally, the exclusive gig showcased Nokia and IDJMG's ability to bring fans closer to artists, and artists closer to fans, via its home on www.nokia.com/rihanna. IDJMG, UMGI, and Nokia took advantage of the latest technology solutions to promote and broadcast this unique event via Nokiamobile music, video, and communications services. Selected bloggers at the event could record, broadcast, and share elements of the exclusive live concert with fans around the globe, linking them all via Web-based social computing technologies. Fan participation in the groundbreaking live event

was free of charge from Nokia Music Stores. Plus Nokia Comes With Music customers were able to download an exclusive version of Rated R with a bonus track, remix, and other additional content free as part of their subscription. Nokia will also make available an exclusive Rihanna application and exclusive footage.

12. Steinbock, D. (2004), Interview with Takeshi Natsuno, managing director, i-mode Strategy, NTT DoCoMo, Inc., May 5. See also Tabuchi, H. (2009), "Why Japan's Cellphones Haven't Gone Global," *New York Times,* July 19.

13. Further, there is a wide array of other models, and even mobile operators are gearing up to challenge Apple and other players, eager to have a cut in the estimated sales of mobile applications that could hit $25 billion in 2014 (Juniper Research, August 2009). Among others, Verizon Wireless is crafting a strategy by teaming up with Vodafone, Japan's SoftBank, and China Mobile to create a common software foundation, which is expected to reach a potential of one billion customers.

14. Today, many technologists believe that the future belongs to "cloud computing." In this scenario, U.S.-based companies (e.g., Microsoft, Google) will dominate Internet services. The devices that provide these services are less important than the services themselves. If the Internet is primary and mobility has to be built on it, the question is as follows: Will devices rule over services (which is Apple's iPhone scenario), or will services rule over devices (which is Google's Android scenario) in the new era? If the latter is true, cloud computing may ultimately reign over cheap devices, which would boost the fortunes of U.S. Internet companies and make life difficult for Nokia. If the former is true, Apple's iPhone entered the rivalry best positioned. Then again, Apple's Mac also entered the PC rivalry best positioned but ultimately lost to standardized and commodified PC clones.

15. Porter, M. E., and Solvell, O. (2002), "Finland and Nokia: Creating the World's Most Competitive Economy," Harvard Business School Publishing Case, 702427, January 25, 2002.

16. Doz, Y. L., and Kosonen, M. (2008), "The Dynamics of Strategic Agility: Nokia's Rollercoaster Experience," *California Management Review,* May 1.

17. Roberts, J., and Doornik, K. (2001), "Nokia Corp.: Innovation and Efficiency in a High-Growth Global Firm," Stanford University Case, IB23, February 28.

18. Henderson, R., and Yoffie, D. (2004), "Nokia and MIT's Project Oxygen," Harvard Business School Publishing Case, 9–704–474, January 20. Now there is also a case study on the strategic options open to Nokia as it faces new competitors, particularly Microsoft. See Burgelman, R. A., and Meza, P. (2003), "Nokia Beyond 2003: A Mobile Gatekeeper?" Stanford University Case, SM113, June 25.

ACKNOWLEDGMENTS

This is the first book on Nokia's strategy, organization, and people, and the only one that is based on interviews with all of Nokia's leading senior executives in the past two decades. No other independent author has gained such privileged access. Although it is an unauthorized account of Nokia's strategy, it has benefited from the cooperation, experience, and insights of Nokia's leading executives every step of the way. I am deeply grateful for all Nokians who have contributed their time to talk about Nokia's strategy, organization, values, and people.

This project has been in the making since 2005. It has also benefited from dozens of interviews for a previous project on the rise of mobile services worldwide. I have interviewed dozens of senior executives of Nokia and Nokia Siemens Networks, including the current and former CEOs, all members of the famous group executive board, key members of the board of directors, and the chiefs of all critical functions, from the demand and supply network to branding and consumer insights, from the Nokia headquarters and the famed Nokia Research Center in Finland to the key country chiefs in large emerging economies, particularly China and India. With critical executives, I had several interviews.

In order to gain a comprehensive view, I also interviewed many of those legendary Nokia executives who contributed to the company's explosive growth in the 1990s and have now retired or serve as CEOs, policy advisors, or board directors in Finland, the European Union, or international organizations worldwide. In addition, I interviewed an estimated forty Nokia managers, partners, and suppliers whose identity will remain anonymous in this work. As visiting professor of international business in the United States, Europe, China, and many member countries of the Association of Southeast Asian Nations (ASEAN), I also met several Nokia managers and clients whose case studies and conversations have contributed to this work.

Among Nokia's current chiefs, I am particularly grateful for the executive presidents of Nokia's group executive board: Nokia's President and CEO Olli-Pekka Kallasvuo; former CEO of Nokia Siemens Networks Simon Beresford-Wylie; former CFO and current head of Nokia Mobile Phones Richard A. Simonson; and Chief Development Officer Mary T. McDowell. Nokia's functional chiefs, many of whom have been rotated in different positions, were of great assistance in outlining the drivers of Nokia's functional and business strategies. These senior executives include Anssi Vanjoki, Nokia's chief of Markets; Kai Öistämö, chief of Devices; Niklas Savander, chief of Services and Software; Hallstein Moerk, Nokia's chief of Human Resources; Robert Andersson, current head of Corporate Alliances and former chief of Devices Finance & Strategy and Sourcing; Veli Sundbäck, Nokia's former chief of Corporate Relations and Responsibility; and his successor Esko Aho, former prime minister of Finland. These discussions also gained significantly from the insights of Tero Ojanperä, chief of Entertainment and Communities, as well as Timo Ihamuotila, current CFO and former chief of sales.

In addition to Nokia's chief executives, there were dozens of other interviews that were vital to gain a deeper understanding of Nokia's strategy. The most important of all stem from several conversations with Nokia's key board members, especially Nokia's Chairman and former CEO and President Jorma Ollila, currently board director of Royal Dutch Shell, as well as Georg Ehrnrooth, a famed Finnish industrialist. In the past, I have also gained more insight into Nokia's corporate governance through Bengt Holmström, board director of Nokia and Paul A. Samuelson professor of economics at Massachusetts Institute of Technology.

I am also indebted to several former Nokia executive vice presidents, especially Matti Alahuhta, currently president and CEO of KONE, who generously gave his time in different parts of the world; Sari Baldauf, former senior vice president and manager of Nokia Networks and current board member of Hewlett-Packard; Pekka Ala-Pietilä, one of Nokia's key chiefs in the past and currently president of Blyk; Kari-Pekka "KP" Wilska, former senior vice president and general manager of Nokia Mobile

Phones, Americas; Mikko Kosonen, currently special advisor for Nokia and president of the Finnish Innovation Fund (Sitra). In the past, I have also benefited from the insights of Erkki Ormala, Nokia's vice president of technology policy. Today, Nokia's R&D and the Nokia Research Center are legendary. I am particularly grateful to Yrjö Neuvo, Nokia's former senior vice president and chief technology officer; Juhani Kuusi, former head of the Nokia Research Center; Robert Iannucci, former chief of the Nokia Research Center; Henry Tirri, current head of the Nokia Research Center; Paul Asel, partner of Nokia Growth Partners. I am also very grateful to Lauri Kivinen, head of Corporate Affairs at Nokia Siemens Networks; and Keith Pardy, former chief of Strategic Marketing.

Of the country chiefs, I owe special gratitude to discussions with Colin Giles, Nokia's global head of sales and former chief of Greater China, Japan, and Korea. David Ho, former chief of Nokia (China) Investment and Nokia Networks. In the case of Nokia's operations in India, I received great guidance by D. "Shiv" Shivakumar, managing director and vice president for Nokia India. I am also grateful to Chris Carr, vice president of sales of Nokia Southeast Asia-Pacific.

Nokia's success in mobile devices is not just about excellence in product development, manufacturing, and marketing, but also trend-setting design. I am particularly grateful for interviews with Frank Nuovo, Nokia's former design chief, and especially his successor Alastair Curtis; as well as Björn Ulfberg, chief of Nokia Customer Insights. I would also like to mention conversations with Nokia's chief of corporate strategy, Heikki Norta. Along with Moerk, Rita Vanhauwenhuyse, former director of Nokia's Talent, Performance and Competency Management, Teko Verheijen, and Rosanna Cella, director of Nokia's Management and Leadership Development, were helpful in the guidance of Nokia's management and leadership development.

For all practical purposes, my key contact at Nokia in this project has been Arja Suominen, Nokia's chief of corporate communications, whom I got to know almost a decade ago. We initiated the project several years ago at the Helsinki airport café, when she was returning from New York City and I was heading to Shanghai. It's been quite a rollercoaster ride ever since, and this project certainly could not have been completed without her infinite support and patience. I also owe particular gratitude to Thomas Jönsson, Nokia's vice president of Markets and Regional Communications. In addition, there were many communications specialists who played a vital role in facilitating and supporting the interviews, including senior communications manager Eija-Riitta Huovinen, communications directors of the functions, including Mark Durrant (CDO Communications), Douglas Dawson (Devices), Leslie Nakajima (Services), Anna Svensson (Europe), Laurie Armstrong (United States), Poonam Kaul (India), Ai Fong (Southeast Pacific and Japan/Korea), as well as Louise Ingram in Beijing, Victoria Eremina in Moscow, Vian Kobeh de Palacio in Miami, and Marianne Holmlund in Dubai.

Last but certainly not least, I owe special thanks to a group of Nokians who patiently organized, facilitated, and rescheduled conversations with senior executives across the world, particularly Ingrid Peura, senior manager of Nokia Communications, and Tapani Kaskinen, spokesman for Nokia, whose assistance was invaluable in the course of the last mile. In the past, other Nokians have also been helpful in illustrating various aspects of its operations, including Juha Putkiranta, Ilkka Raiskinen, and Tapio Hedman.

There are also many other Nokians who, in one way or another, supported or assisted in the execution of this project, as well as with the interviews. Thanks to all of them: Outi Anttila, Anna-Stina Backlund, Enore Cirulli, Deborah Ducharme, Cherry Gong, Jane Hsu, Irma Huotinen, Eija-Riitta Huovinen, Louise Ingram, Nina Jahi, Marika Koski, Heli Kumpulainen, Karen Lachtanski, Barbro Lax, Jessie Liu, Colin May, Irmeli Millner, Filippo Monastra, Yolanda Owens, Theresa Parenteau, Jonna Peltola, William Plummer, Marju Rouvinen, David Stoneham, Seija Suoniemi, Jaana Taskinen, Cindy Tay, Adam Travis, Tiina Uitto, Virpi Vuori, Robert Weisberg, Damien Yeo, and Brett Young.

The interview with Sean Maloney, executive vice president of Intel Corporation and chief sales and marketing officer, augmented others in the past, especially with former Intel chairman Gordon Moore and former Intel vice president Dr Albert Yu. I am grateful for conversations with Jack Welch, former CEO and chairman of GE; Martti Ahtisaari, undersecretary general of the U.N., president of Finland, and the 2008 Nobel Peace Prize winner; Paul Palmieri, Verizon Wireless's multimedia chief; Larry Shapiro, executive vice president of business development at the Walt Disney Internet Group; Mitch Lazar, vice president of the wireless properties at Turner Broadcasting System International; Pete Downton, heading wireless activities at Warner Music International; Jonathan Channon, senior vice president of EMI Music Publishing, who signed the first major ring tone deal with Nokia; Martin Cooper, the former Motorola R&D chief who developed the first cell phone.

I would also like to thank my colleagues in the India, China, and America Institute, in particular Jagdish Sheth, Suresh Sharma, and Reza Jafari; Donovan Neale-May of the Forum to Advance Mobile Experience; Professor Michael E. Porter of the Institute for Strategy and Competition (Harvard Business School).

Due to my own life and activities initially in Finland and Europe, during the past twenty years in the United States, and more recently in China and Asia-Pacific, I have followed Nokia's strategy more closely since the mid-1990s, from Helsinki to New York City and Shanghai. By the same token, hundreds of interviews that form the foundation of this book were conducted across the world.

I am indebted to and have learned a lot from the great professionals at Jossey-Bass and do want to thank Erin Moy, Byron Schneider, Ruth Mills, Mark Karmendy, Gayle Mak, Sarah Bayless, Bernadette Blanco, Adrian Morgan, Ruth Mills, and Amy Packard. And I want to extend special thanks to my wonderful and infinitely patient editor, Genoveva Llosa.

Finally, this is a book that I have developed, worked on, and written in numerous settings across the world, with assistants (thank you WS!)

and facilitators in numerous countries. Through these years, my family in Finland and my new family in Hong Kong and China have been very supportive of the project, and I could not be more grateful. Most intimately, I would like to thank my beloved wife Donna without whose patience and understanding this book would never have seen the light of day. I dedicate the book to her.

New York City–Shanghai–Helsinki
Dan Steinbock

ABOUT THE AUTHOR

Dan Steinbock divides his time between New York City, Shanghai, and Helsinki. He is research director of international business at the India China and America (ICA) Institute, a nonprofit research institute working to foster research and dissemination of knowledge on the rise of China and India and their impact on global markets, global resources, and geopolitics of the world. He focuses on issues of *international business* and *international relations,* including the long-term impact of the global crisis on the most advanced economies (United States, Western Europe, Japan) and the large emerging economies (China, India, Russia, and Brazil). Dr. Steinbock has consulted for multinationals (Intel, Nokia, Coca-Cola), international organizations (OECD, EU), national governments, and metropolitan cities. A senior Fulbright scholar, Steinbock is faculty spokesman for the Forum to Advance Mobile Experience (FAME), an initiative by the CMO Council representing over six thousand global executives across fifty-seven countries, and an affiliate of the Columbia Institute for Tele-Information. He cooperates with the Institute for Strategy and Competitiveness (Harvard Business School) and is a member of several advisory boards. Additionally, he has consulted and published extensively on Nokia and mobile communications, as well as Finnish competitiveness and innovative capacity. He is on the board of journals and advisory boards in the United States, Europe, and Asia.

INDEX